A COMPANION TO THE WORKS OF ELIZABETH STROUT

A COMPANION TO THE WORKS OF

ELIZABETH STROUT

Katherine Montwieler

SWALLOW PRESS

ATHENS, OHIO

Swallow Press
An imprint of Ohio University Press, Athens, Ohio 45701
ohioswallow.com

Printed in the United States of America
Swallow Press / Ohio University Press books are printed on acid-free
paper ∞ ™

30 29 28 27 26 25 24 23 22   5 4 3 2 1

Library of Congress Cataloging-in-Publication Data available upon request.
Names: Montwieler, Katherine, 1970– author.
Title: A companion to the works of Elizabeth Strout / Katherine
  Montwieler.
Description: Athens, Ohio : Swallow Press, [2022] | Includes bibliographi-
  cal references and index.
Identifiers: LCCN 2022018847 (print) | LCCN 2022018848 (ebook) | ISBN
  9780804012409 (hardcover) | ISBN 9780804012416 (paperback) | ISBN
  9780804041225 (pdf)
Subjects: LCSH: Strout, Elizabeth—Criticism and interpretation. |
  American fiction—Women authors—History and criticism. | American
  literature—21st century—History and criticism.
Classification: LCC PS3569.T736 Z78 2022 (print) | LCC PS3569.T736
  (ebook) | DDC 813/.609—dc23/eng/20220708
LC record available at https://lccn.loc.gov/2022018847
LC ebook record available at https://lccn.loc.gov/2022018848

for

Mom and Liz

Contents

Acknowledgments

Thank you, Elizabeth, for the work, inspiration, and generosity. Thank you, Ricky, Stephanie, Tyler, and Beth, for your support of this project. Thank you, Mom and Dad, for decades of support, guidance, and inspiration. My work is possible because of you. Thank you, Mom, for introducing me to the work of Elizabeth, and, Dad, for modeling trusting faith. Thank you, Janet, for reading the manuscript so carefully. Thank you, Barbara, for your extraordinary mentoring, generosity, and welcome to North Carolina. Dear Donna, so many thanks. Thank you, Erin, Heather, Johanna, Aimee, Amie, Rebekah, Kimberle, Gena, Anna Maria, Jennifer, Kristine, Joanna, Ryanne, Kris, Jeffrianne, Heather, Nicole, Quinn, Zach, Josh, Trisha, Emily, Dawn, Matthew, Melanie, Emily, Alicia, Joanna, Helen, and Jamie, for your patience, your challenges, your words, your willingness to wrestle and to help me at home and on the page. Thank you, Amy, Hannah, Michelle, Maia, Sarah, Kimi, Cala, Michelle, Kathleen, Sue, Lynn, Kemille, Laura, Donyell, Candace, Vibeke, Denise, Mike, Lewis, Dan, Bill, Vic, Meghan, Nick, Jennifer, Dana, Nina, Karen, and Lisa, for pointed conversations, humor, and companionship. Michelle, Kemille, Tiffany, Aswani, Don, Keith, Chris, Dana, and Kathleen, thank you for providing space, time, and support for this endeavor. Thank you, Joyce, Mike, Carolyn, and Jim, for long-distance support, so many recommendations, and inspiring families. Tricia, Roxanne, Anne, Elizabeth, Miranda, Nelson, Beth-Ann, and Lisa, thank you for catalyzing this journey too many years ago to count. Thank you, Malin, Trisha, Marianne, Ann, Susan, and Paula, for modeling mentoring across the miles and answering my calls. Jake and Thea, so much gratitude for the conversations, companionship, reading recommendations, patience, and love. Jan and Doyle, Curt and Alice, thank you for your patience, good humor, and resilience. Thank you to the anonymous readers who challenged me and supported this work. I'm so grateful. Dear, dear Katie—the walks, the spoken and unspoken conversations, the texts, and the provocations—your fingerprints are all over these pages. Thank you. Maisie and Averil, your spirit of adventure, zest for life, indomitability, humor, intelligence, and compassion inspire me every day. Thank you. Mark, words fail. Gratitude, respect, and love till the end of days.

Introduction

ELIZABETH STROUT IS ONE OF THE MOST POPULAR and critically acclaimed US writers of the twenty-first century. In the last twenty-one years, she has published eight books, including *Oh William!*, which appeared in the fall of 2021. Strout is the rare crossover writer, like Margaret Atwood, Alice Walker, or Marilynne Robinson, appreciated by critics and beloved by hundreds of thousands. Her ability to reach both commercial audiences and literary elites speaks to a particular consciousness, a sensitive, insightful, and humorous one that book buyers from all walks of life value. And it's not just readers. Strout's first novel, *Amy and Isabelle*, was made into a TV movie; her third book, *Olive Kitteridge*, was filmed as an HBO miniseries; the rights to her fourth book, *The Burgess Boys*, have been optioned by Robert Redford; and an adaptation of *My Name Is Lucy Barton* appeared on the London and Broadway stages before the pandemic shuttered them. Her sales and perennial presence on book club lists indicate a tremendous impact on the popular realm, and the growing attention to her in academia charts her importance in American letters. In the wake of the #MeToo movement and the awareness of the political and cultural clout of the White working class, two issues that Strout's fiction anticipated in many ways, this is the writer's moment.[1]

Born in 1956, Strout didn't publish her first novel until she was forty-two, sixteen years after the publication of her first short story. She had been working for decades on her fiction, however. As she told Mary Pols, "I spent years and years and years trying to find my storytelling voice and then I found it. And also, I got older, so there were more life experiences that arrived, that one can use in various ways in their work. But I was apprenticing that entire time. I was really working those first 20 years." Following the publication of *Amy and Isabelle* in 1998, several other books appeared: *Abide with Me* in 2006; *Olive Kitteridge* in 2008; *The Burgess Boys* in 2013; *My Name Is Lucy Barton* in 2016; *Anything Is Possible* in 2017; *Olive, Again* in 2019; and *Oh William!* in 2021. She has been not only prolific but also lauded, recognized as a finalist for the National Book Critics Circle Award and the PEN/Faulkner Award, longlisted for the Booker, shortlisted for the Orange Prize, awarded the Pulitzer Prize, and elected to the American Academy of Arts and Letters.

Strout's productivity at that particular time in history—the first two decades of the twenty-first century—merits a closer look. Biographically, her career took off once her only child left for college and she left her first marriage. But more broadly, that is a fascinating time for Strout to have made her mark. Those two decades saw the flowering of an immensely popular and influential literary genre, "chick lit," that remains popular (we might think, for example, of Helen Fielding's *Bridget Jones's Diary*, Lauren Weisberger's *The Devil Wears Prada*, or Sophie Kinsella's *Love Your Life*).[2] If "chick lit" often focuses on striving, young, urban women faced with comic situations related to sexuality, careers, and shopping, Strout's work offers a counterpoint, a kind of throwback to the domestic fiction of Anne Tyler, Sue Miller, and Alice Munro. Strout's work, while often focused on women, is usually set in small towns, features older figures, and humorously and poignantly addresses the challenges of aging.[3] I read her fiction as a thoughtful corrective to the frenetic lifestyle captured in so many of the novels aimed at those reveling in (or aspiring to) the thick of it.[4]

Perhaps, then, it's not surprising that Strout's first two novels could be considered historical fiction. *Amy and Isabelle* is set in the early 1970s in the small fictional town of Shirley Falls, Maine; *Abide with Me* is set in West Annett, another fictional small town in Maine, in 1959. With her third and most famous book, *Olive Kitteridge*, Strout moved, if not exactly to the present, then to the more recent past. However, in contrast to the "chick lit" phenomenon, even when Strout's work connects to our current moment, she encourages a reflective sensibility in her readers that encourages us to step back, to read more slowly, to recognize, not only in the cadence of her speech but in the images she captures, the small moments we might miss if we race through our days in the way that hustle culture promotes. Her small town–born protagonists may stay in the villages of their families or they may move, but they maintain a ruminative sensibility born from early struggles. Strout's work offers her readers an unhurried approach to living in the world and engaging with others, meditative rather than focused on getting ahead, reflective rather than brisk.[5] In this way, her work, with its attentiveness to detail and lyricism, is poetic, evoking her contemporaries Toni Morrison and Marilynne Robinson.[6] Strout is indeed a careful writer, sensitive to the auditory echoes of her prose. In her 2017 interview with Samantha Vorwald, she observes:

> I really believe in the sentence. Every sentence has to have
> some heartbeat of life to it. Every sentence that gets put
> down has to come from the sentence before it and lead
> into the sentence that's coming after. There has to be a
> "wholeness" at work, and there has to be a heartbeat in every
> sentence, if that makes sense. And it's not easy to learn to
> do. I trained myself over the years to get rid of any sentence
> that's dead weight. . . . That would be the business that carries
> it forward. . . . When I write, it's very aural. My ear is very,
> very important to me. So the sentence has to land on the ear
> the right way, and then if that is landing on the reader's ear
> the right way, they will be carried forward. But it's something
> I've learned to hear and learned to do and to get rid of every

twig—what I call twigs—every dead piece of wood. Just to get
it out of there.

It's not just Strout's voice that matters—it's what and whom she sees
as well: the objects, acts, and people that she draws our attention to.
Strout illuminates that which we don't often perceive, those details
we live with without even realizing they coincide with our existence.
In calling us to notice, for example, the fall of light, the way a woman
brushes her hair back, or the stoop of a man's posture, Strout reveals
not only her powers of observation, but also the sacredness of everyday life. Strout's fiction privileges qualities that Cecilia Konchar
Farr tells us "our scholarly codifications [often] leave out—affinity,
empathy, affect, education, and engagement—or, as avid novel readers have explained . . . : sympathetic connections, even identification,
from readers to characters; honest appeals to genuine emotion; ex-
citing stories that inspire conversation (and consumption); historical, political or geographical information subtly shared; comfortable
settings that tend toward the domestic; and social messages that call
readers to action" ("The Gendering," 209). Throughout this book, I
hope to show how Strout's fiction illuminates such a practice, a way
of reading that values connection and intimacy. Within the academy,
these values tend to be most closely aligned with feminist and affect
theory, and, not surprisingly, with women writers. Although Strout is
reluctant to label herself a woman writer, her subjects—relationships,
families, and homes—culturally still tend to be labeled as feminine.
That's not to say she's conservative. Strout is not advocating a retreat
to home, by any means—and neither are feminist critics. Rather, she
encourages her readers to reflect not only on the stories she presents
but on the stories of our individual lives as well.

Strout also pays particular attention to that most intense and
formative of relationships, the one between mothers and their children. For example, in *Amy and Isabelle*, when Isabelle notices her
daughter is suffering, she reacts acutely, mirroring her child: "Isabelle felt a flicker of dread. 'What's wrong?' It was impossible to feel
any semblance of peace if something was wrong with her daughter"
(65). The two women, like many mothers and daughters, are so close

that Amy's burden becomes Isabelle's own. Later, as she watches her child, "the sight of her pained Isabelle. It pained her terribly to see her, but why? Because she looked unhappy, her shoulders slumped like that, her neck thrust forward, walking slowly, just about dragging her feet. This was Isabelle's daughter; this was Isabelle's fault. She hadn't done it right, being a mother; and this youthful desolation walking up the driveway was exactly proof of that" (206). At a time when parent-child relationships are closer than ever, many readers will recognize Isabelle. In her daughter's very carriage, Isabelle sees her own defeat, her own failures. More recently, in *Olive, Again*, Olive, too, has a similar moment when she senses she has failed Chris, because he appears unhappy and he has chosen to marry a woman who yells at him, the way his mother yelled at his father. In her recognition of the vexed emotions mothers experience, Strout memorializes fleeting feelings rarely articulated on the page. These very moments, she shows her readers, deserve consideration.

Many of those moments emerge from women's relationships and are experienced physically. Those people historically denigrated as anti-intellectual or worthless, her work demonstrates, are valuable and perceptive. Her subjects tell her readers they and their observations matter, and that fiction may have a unique vantage point from which to offer readers that realization. Within Strout's work, both Lucy Barton and Patty Nicely reflect on how reading transformed their lives; when they read, they feel understood. That feeling of seeing oneself on the page is tied not only to the individual reader but also to the social project of Strout's work. If an individual recognizes herself in Strout's work and also sees how she differs from the characters, she may realize that other readers have similar reactions—that in fact they form, if only temporarily, a community of sorts. In telling her readers to pay attention, Strout offers what Janice Radway has termed a "counterpractice to the high culture tastes and proclivities that have been most insistently legitimated and nurtured in academic English departments for the last fifty years or so" (ix), and in her valuing of women's insights and women's experiences, Strout speaks to the feminization of our culture.[7]

Unlike so many of her peers, Strout is also funny. Her humor is earthy, bawdy, body-based. When we laugh out loud as we read, we are engaging socially and physically with a text and reminded of our bodies and the bodies of others. The realm of human experience, Strout has said, is her canvas, and that includes humans at their most vulnerable and stupid in addition to their most poignant. She lets us into people's lives, with an easy intimacy that is welcoming, humbling, and gross, providing a level of realistic detail that doesn't shy away from warts and ugliness but that celebrates the complications of people's lives and lived experiences. Yet, if Strout is funny, she is reverential, as Lucy Barton and Patty Nicely attest, when it comes to the power of fiction. Psychoanalysis and psychology are fair game for gentle ribbing, but often Strout reiterates how the expansiveness of fiction allows for an appreciation of the nuances of experiences that clinical labels do not. In dwelling on the messy details, fiction can be more honest, accurate, and thorough than particular theories or structures that people use to make sense of their lives. Fiction works, Strout tells us, when readers connect with it—intellectually, emotionally, and physically. We not only engage with the words on the page, but also approach the world and ourselves differently for having read it. In the interview in the appendix, Strout tells us, "I hope for a sense of transcendence to come through to the reader, in whatever way they need that to be, that the world becomes larger to them, that everything may not be just as it seems" (234). Good fiction doesn't just soothe us, though it might do that; it also troubles us, makes us think, stirs us from complacency, and perhaps inspires us to action.[8]

In the chapters that follow, I explore each of Strout's books. I attempt both to offer an interpretation of each work and to tease out the stylistic and thematic threads that link them together. In so doing, I offer a way to appreciate Strout as a writer, her vision, and the books that she's shared with the world. For as renowned as she is, Strout has not received as much critical attention as one would expect (though that dearth could speak to the historical and contemporary sexism and myopia of the academy, its undervaluing, as Barbara Waxman has pointed out, of the details of mature women's lives).[9] Another reason for the belated appreciation of Strout's work is the academy's historic valuation of separation or distance rather than, in Rita Felski's words, "relation" or "attachment" (viii); Strout, as I've been attempting to point out, privileges the latter. Her work is about connection,[10] and her career offers us a way to understand the position of the woman writer (though she herself shies away from this label) today.

In her fiction, Strout is a woman speaking primarily to women (the majority of book buyers and fiction readers are women), and most people who read Strout are not introduced to her around the seminar table but through a magazine or book club or Facebook recommendation.[11] That audience attests to Strout's particularly democratic consciousness—her readers do not buy, read, and discuss her books because they are told to do so, but for pleasure. They—we—read because we choose to. Hundreds of thousands of people choose to read Strout. We're return readers; we buy her books, we recommend them, we give them to our friends, because we liked one of them. Felski explains that "attachment doesn't get much respect in academia. It is often outsourced to others—naïve readers, gullible consumers, small-town patriots, too-needy lovers—and treated as a cause for concern" (2), but in that exclusion, academia misses out on a lot. "To be attached," Felski claims, "is to be affected or moved and also to be linked or tied. It denotes passion and compassion—but also an array of ethical, political, intellectual, or other bonds" (1). In other words, to move a reader—emotionally, physically, and intellectually—so much that she wants to share that which moved her with someone else is no small feat. In some ways, academics are coming late to the table where Oprah Winfrey, Reese Witherspoon, Strout, and a host of other women are already sitting. Those readers know that pleasure might come to them in the form of laughter—for example, cringing at the irascibility of Olive Kitteridge—or from reflection, when they are forced to consider the world as it's represented on the page and then the world around them. There is a certain sobriety in Strout's fiction, which generates its own pleasure. But there is also an edge that is disruptive—allusions to violence, cruelty, and meanness that trouble any benign reading experience. Encountering sadness and cruelty, in addition to humor and awe, is part and parcel of the pleasurable reading experience of Strout. She doesn't offer only a sop, but she makes her readers reflect, and because of the intimacy she's created, we are compelled rather than repulsed by those troubling moments.

Strout's appeal is important to recognize for several reasons. Five of her books are set in small towns in Maine and Illinois. Her protagonists are not the striving professional class of "chick lit" fame, but teachers, guidance counselors, and janitors. In shifting the center of gravity from the urban metropole to the periphery, Strout shows us that the United States is far vaster than the concentrated cities of the East and West Coast. Her characters are thoughtful people wrestling with how to live in the world, even if they don't share the education or address or political affiliation of many of her readers. Like one of her most famous fans, Oprah, Strout is a kind of democratizing influencer; her fiction welcomes readers of all class and education levels, not by catering to our base impulses but by calling us to our better angels.[12] She shows her readers we can find evidence for grace, hope, and despair across our nation.[13]

And fiction, she tells us, is a particularly effective way to reach other people; for, as Helen Taylor contends, "reading fiction seems to facilitate women's imaginations and engage us with others, so that we make productive connections between those stories and other people" (7). Reading and discussing fiction may serve as a conduit, a means for people to connect in a way that is not superficial, simple, or banal. What we read can inherently exclude—here we might think of fan fiction or Christian romance or traditional literary criticism as genres that assume certain audiences and exclude others—but arguably fiction can bridge divisions, show readers how others are suffering, and consequently how they can learn to appreciate their humanity and empathize with others. Suzanne Keen defines empathy as "a spontaneous sharing of feelings, including physical sensations in the body, provoked by witnessing or hearing about another's condition" (*Empathy and the Novel*, xx). That kind of empathy project is crucial to Strout's work and central to my reading of her. In my privileging of empathy, Felski warns I might sound "perilously close to adolescent infatuation or amateurish enthusiasm, to a treacly and treacherous cult of feeling" (30), but that diminishment does a disservice to the work of reading that Strout proffers—the comfort, the illumination, and the troubling of lazy identification.

If Strout reaches out to her readers, she also reaches back to a grand literary tradition. Suzanne Keen shows us that nineteenth-century novels try to model for their readers how to care for others, and in her exploration of individuals and individual families, Strout, like her predecessors, shows the ubiquity of suffering. Dickens, the Brontës, and Eliot all underscore the private suffering of individuals, the difficulties they have in communicating, and the necessity for compassion. And like Dickens in particular, Strout creates a multiverse; his sprawling novels encompass hundreds of characters and conversations; Strout's are briefer, but the same characters and settings pop up across her novels, rewarding her longtime readers. Unlike the Brontës and Eliot, Strout is funny (here of course she recalls Dickens, Austen, and Thackeray); her worldview is not solely sober but lively, acerbic, and sharp. And that humor in some ways makes the trials her characters face bearable. Of those characters, Strout says, "I suspend judgment. . . . When I go to the page, I am so free of judgment of my characters, and that's so fun. It's so liberating because I don't care how badly behaved they are—as long as they're truthfully badly behaved, I don't care. So I just love them, and they can do whatever they need to do, and I'm free from judgment" (Vorwald). This insight helps us understand not only Olive marking up Suzanne's sweater and stealing her shoe but also Lucy's troubled father. There is room in Strout's world for humor and pathos. Following Keen, I believe the "affective transaction across boundaries of time, culture, and location may indeed be one of the intrinsic powers of fiction and the novel a remarkably effective device for reminding readers of their own and others' humanity" (*Empathy and the Novel*, xxv).

But we also need to be wary of projections or the appropriation of others' experiences. In a commencement address Strout gave in May 2019 at the University of Maine Farmington, which awarded her an honorary doctorate in the humanities, she reflected pithily on a conversation with her mother, who told her "you never really know what goes on in someone else's house," or, as Strout inferred, "we will never, ever really know what goes on in someone else's mind." But what we can do, Strout explained, is listen to that person and try to understand her perspective. Writing, she continued, is an act of faith that attempts to imagine the world from others' perspectives and is, therefore, a necessarily empathic exercise that bridges the apparent distance between individuals. And, as she explains in the interview included in the appendix, "I guess I see writing as an act of faith because you just don't know. I mean you just don't know if it will land on the person who needs it, or will be received in a way that I hope it will be. So it's an act of faith—you put it out there and you hope" (233). In the pages that follow, I try to untangle how each of Strout's books is an act of faith, and explore the evolution of her voice, themes, and concerns. From classic domestic spats between a mother and daughter to hate crimes aimed at Muslim houses of workshop, from historical fiction to snapshots of contemporary life, Strout portrays humanity at its most brutal and its most intimate. My approach to this analysis of Strout is colored by the lenses of feminist theory, psychoanalysis, new historicism, and close reading practices. Time and place, or historical specificity, is of crucial import to her work—both that which is set in the past and that which is contemporary. If Strout's works are about individuals, I argue that they're also, by being situated at specific historic moments, about public events. Strout shows how both the long sweep of history and the vast shadows of current global struggles extend their reach into private kitchens, porches, and bedrooms. Fiction is necessarily, paradoxically, personal and public—an individual writer's reflections presented to an audience outside her home. In this wrestling with momentous events and their effects on individuals, Strout is not alone. Maria DiBattista and Deborah Epstein Nord explain that for "our most powerful and influential women writers, a critique of domestic life was more common than its celebration, the embracing or public debate and the social questions of the day more frequent than their avoidance" (2). Yet certainly Strout's focus on interpersonal relationships, especially familial ones, emphasizes patterns of human behavior revealed by psychoanalysis and psychiatry, including the work of Nicholas Abraham, Maria Torok, and Bessel van der Kolk. The lingering effects of trauma on generations, the desire for individuation of children from their parents, and the complex love we have for our birth and chosen families are themes that Strout situates at particular historical moments. If the complexities of familial relationships and coming of age are constants in Strout's opus, specific contexts create new stories around these themes.

My reading of Strout is as an explicitly social writer. Her books make us consider not only the wonder described on the page but also the evil in the world—evil which, particularly in our indifference to others, we may be responsible for. If anyone is criticized in her work, it's the people who fail to see and to salve the suffering of others around them. Her work shows us we bear a collective responsibility for others. The affluent New York parasitologist and socialite share a world with the family who eats beans and bread for dinner. In this acknowledgment of our shared world and responsibility, Strout is tapping into a kind of consciousness within academia most often aligned with feminist theory, and in popular culture most clearly personified in Oprah Winfrey. Like Winfrey, Strout uses her privilege to listen to and to elevate others, but she also recognizes the value of her voice and her perspective. That willingness to listen is often coded as a particularly feminine virtue; women are socialized to listen, to help others, to put others before themselves.[14] Women, in general, are not encouraged to elevate themselves, not to take themselves or their observations seriously. Strout answers this most forcefully in *My Name Is Lucy Barton*. Her voice and her perspective matter.

Academics might be better off if we did more listening, if we were more open to hearing what fiction resonates with women and middle-class readers. The humanities have been in decline for years, perhaps because academics have not effectively made their argument for relevance. But women are reading fiction. And we are reading communally—if not in universities, then at home. Nowhere is this more evident than in the prominence of Oprah's Book Club, where "readers are invited to engage in a process, to read both reflectively and empathically, in both academic and popular modes, and to talk about books" (Farr, *Reading Oprah*, 49). In other words, Winfrey is creating a community of readers that practically speaking reaches more people than university English classes do. And academics ignore that development at our peril. If the discipline of English studies is to survive, we might take a cue from Strout and Winfrey rather than speak to an increasingly smaller scholarly audience. Best-seller lists point to our culture's values and interests, and, as Farr points out, Winfrey's selections inspire people to buy (to read and to talk about) books. Winfrey does, then, what the professoriate has failed to do—encourage people to buy and to read fiction.

Strout is right there with her—literally and figuratively (*Olive, Again* was one of Winfrey's picks in fall 2020). Strout as a writer and Winfrey as her acolyte call for a reading practice that is critical, reflective, and appreciative. As Farr points out, "Winfrey leads middlebrow reading into the borderlands of these highbrow academic modes, to criticism, to delighting in poetic language and in the subtleties of narrative. Then she moves back confidently to comfortable popular modes, to identification, to embracing characters and life lessons, and to listening with her readers to what novels 'have to say'" (*Reading Oprah*, 51). Delighting in, embracing, and listening to are all practices that Strout's work encourages. In her work, through her characters and their observations, Strout calls her readers to an attentiveness that is respectful, mindful, and receptive.

Toril Moi explains that that attentiveness has "nothing to do with sentimentality and misplaced compassion. A just and loving gaze allows us to see the world as it is" (228). This perspective, I think, is crucial to how Sarah Payne would address the critics who see her as mawkish; I would extend this outward to those academics who find Strout or popular women's writing frivolous or the practice of reading that privileges connection naive. It isn't. If we are hungry for connection, as Janice Radway contends the popularity of Winfrey suggests contemporary humans are, we both want to understand others and to be understood by them. Strout's fiction and Winfrey's empire are built, I believe, on the foundation of recognizing the importance of understanding, not in a way that's idealized and perfect, but in one that recognizes that all perspectives are necessarily limited. I do attempt here to look at Strout with respectful discernment. Her work addresses specific people with particular foibles and frailties, indicative of their individual historical situating. Though she writes with extraordinary sensitivity about the effects of poverty, she, perhaps unconsciously, trucks in cultural myopia, and so, like her characters, she reveals she is engagingly and markedly human. We all are. And noting our limitations allows us to grow and to connect with others. *A Companion to the Works of Elizabeth Strout*, like Strout and Winfrey, is concerned with making connections, and I hope is part of a larger movement in which academics reach out generously, receptively, and humbly to listen to, learn from, and connect with the public. Strout explains in the appendix, "I want to write books that—as Lucy Barton says—make people feel less alone. But I also want to write books that open up things to the reader that they might not have quite known they knew, or maybe didn't know at all until they read about someone different from themselves" (235).

Strout's own humility connects to her affability; she presents herself as likable, down-to-earth; if pensive, she doesn't appear judgmental. Her website bolsters this perception, noting that she was "born in Portland, Maine, and grew up in small towns in Maine and New Hampshire" and that "from a young age" she was drawn to books, spending "hours of her youth in the local library lingering among the stacks of fiction" and in the outdoors, "writing things down, keeping notebooks that recorded the quotidian details of her days." She was close to her mother, a high school English teacher, and recalled in a profile by Ladette Randolph how she and her mother would "imagine the lives of strangers they saw around town. 'It seemed to me, . . . from an early age, that nothing was as fun as that. . . . The first ambition I remember having was that of becoming a writer. It seemed as natural as the fact that I would have another birthday. . . . It did not seem a wish, but a fact of life'" (174). Her father was a professor at the University of New Hampshire, "and the family lived in New Hampshire during the week, but Maine remained their emotional home throughout her childhood" (Randolph 176). Her family's isolation, Strout has observed, was self-imposed, and she "ended up spending hours alone with tree toads and pine needles, and turtles and creeks, and the coastline, and collecting periwinkles, so I think it is right to say that my interests when I was young were the beauties of the physical world" (Randolph 176). Socially isolated (anticipating Lucy Barton) and always writing, Strout was unhappy in high school, which she left early to enroll at Bates College.

At Bates, Strout found a mentor in James Hepburn, the chair of the English department, who in independent studies, Strout said, would "just let me write and he would comment, and I would turn in another story, and he would comment. . . . It was enormously helpful, his odd belief in me" (Randolph 177). Strout's gratitude to Hepburn speaks to the air of appreciation and the importance of generosity within her work. Over and over again, her work celebrates and troubles acts of kindness and caring relationships. While in school and on graduating, Strout worked in the secretarial pool at Bates, cleaned houses, played piano, and tended bar. Eventually, she enrolled in Syracuse's law school, where she met and married her first husband, Marty Feinman. Soon after earning her JD and beginning to work for Legal Services, she left the profession, feeling "like 'an unspeakably bad, incompetent lawyer'" (Randolph 178), and turned to teaching English at Manhattan Community College. Her only daughter, Zarina, was born in 1983, and Strout juggled caring for her with teaching and writing as well as she could. Ariel Levy explains of those days that "Strout and her family lived in a brownstone in Park Slope, which [Strout] said 'felt almost like a village,' except that it was full of people she didn't know. She joined a writing group, and took classes from the editor Gordon Lish. 'She really found what she was looking for in New York,' Zarina said. 'I remember clearly stacks of manuscripts throughout my childhood on the dining-room table. They weren't sacred—we'd kind of eat on them and live around them.'" She published the occasional short story in *New Letters, Seventeen,* and *Redbook*. Reflecting on this part of her life years later, Strout observed,

> There was one period of time back then when I'd probably been writing for about fifteen years with very little—a few stories—but very little acknowledgment. And I did think to myself, "I have to stop. It's just not making sense." So I decided to go to nursing school. . . . And the application was so confusing that I just thought, "Oh, forget it. I'm just going to stick to being a writer." . . . I just felt, "This isn't working," and then by the end of that day I thought, "No, too, bad, I'm just going to try this story one more time—try it a different time—try it a different way." . . . I'm always, always going back and trying it one more time.

We see in these assessments Strout's characteristic humility, her work ethic, and her humor, but they also reveal how seemingly insignificant quotidian details profoundly affect our decisions and lives. In the same interview, she observes, she was the

> poster child for rejections. . . . But what kept me going was that I just wanted to do it. And also what kept me going was that I understood intuitively that my work wasn't yet good enough. I *always* understood that. . . . But I also understood that it was getting better. . . . And then there was an editor at the *New Yorker* for fifteen years who kept rejecting my stories, but his rejection letters kept getting longer and longer, and he was helpful to me. But mostly I was just always trying. I just kept trying. I understood it wasn't good enough, I understood that it was within reach, and I just had to keep going. And I was surprised that it was taking me so long. I just thought, "Ugh, boy, I had no idea

you'd be this slow." But I did eventually figure out how to get those sentences down in the right way. I figured out how to make a muscular sentence that could carry all the stuff it needed to carry. (Vorwald)

Her first published novel was an immediate popular and critical success. *Amy and Isabelle* appeared in 1998 and was made into a 2001 TV movie starring Elisabeth Shue. The skills that Strout had toiled away at for years were seeing fruition. Strout continued to write and revise, crafting scenes and characters that would eventually find themselves in books of increasing popularity and critical attention, yet her writing routine remained consistent.

In an essay that appeared in *The Guardian* in 2017, Strout reflected, "These days I write first thing in the morning after having breakfast with my husband; my writing day starts as soon as he leaves the apartment, which is usually right after breakfast. Then I clear the table and sit down to work. I write mostly by hand, transcribing it on a computer when I can no longer read my writing, when I have made too many marks on the paper to be able to see the scene I am trying to write." She continued,

> Almost always I will start by writing a scene or a piece of a scene. I have learned over the years to take anything that is most pressing to me—it may be as mundane as a concern about upcoming dental work [we might recall *My Name Is Lucy Barton* and *Olive Kitteridge*], or as serious as worrying about the safety of my child—and to transpose that emotion into a character. This will give the scene life, as opposed to having it wooden. I am a very messy worker—I push these scenes around our table. It is a big table, and over time I realise which scenes are connected. I have never written anything from beginning to end, not a story or a novel. I just collect different scenes, and the ones that aren't any good to me, get slipped on to the floor and eventually into the wastebasket. (There are many of those.)

Of the nuts and bolts of writing, the process, Strout said to Joe Fassler in *The Atlantic*, My favorite time to work is first thing in the morning. There's a quietness then. The longer we spend in the real world during the day, the further away that imaginary world becomes. For me, the imaginary world is more accessible when I can get to it without having had too many interactions. In the afternoon, it's harder because you've been living in the real world longer. I try and write first thing in the morning, all the way until lunch. I'll put lunchtime off as long as I can—maybe to 1:30 or 2:00 p.m., until I start to pass out from hunger. There's something about having lunch—even if it's just a simple lunch, which it always is—that breaks up the pattern for me. I've just learned that it does, so I'll put it off as long as I can.

Revising is integral to her process as well. In her interview with Vorwald, Strout noted that before the scenes she's written are

> actually connecting or before that has solidified enough, there's a stretch of time where I feel like a washing machine where all the soap is coming out the doors. I feel like, "Oh, oh, oh dear, oh dear." I just feel like I'm out of control of it, that I'll never be able to pull it together in a structure that's needed. And that can last for months, and that's a difficult period because it makes me feel crazy with anxiety. . . . I do eventually get it sorted out, even though every single time it feels like I won't. Every time, at that particular phase of it, I think, "Ugh, this isn't going to happen." But then it does.

Thankfully, Strout is successful, and her routine works to bring clarity and joy to her readers. To Sally Campbell and Martha Greengrass, Strout observed, "I do write so that people will feel less alone. But I would go further than Lucy [Barton]: I write so that people can also see others, can understand hopefully—even briefly—what it means to be another person, and this can make them more empathic. This is my hope."[15] In the hands of Strout, such a humble hope becomes something transcendent—part calling, part salve—an act of faith.[16]

1

The Women's Work of Loving Imperfectly in *Amy and Isabelle*

SET IN FICTIONAL SHIRLEY FALLS, MAINE, IN THE early 1970s, *Amy and Isabelle* (1998) focuses on the complicated, intense relationship of a daughter and her mother, both outsiders in the small town they've called home for fifteen years. At sixteen, Amy Goodrow is chafing at her widowed mother's restrictions, yearning to make her own way in the world, unaware of dangers near and far. An ominousness pervades the town and their house—the word "unease" appears three times in the first few pages, a sickly smelling polluted river borders Shirley Falls, and the recent disappearance of twelve-year-old Debby Kay Dorne haunts the Goodrows. The gothic elements underscored here—a depressed working-class town, presumed violence against women, and fraught familial relationships—evoke the work of Joyce Carol Oates, but *Amy and Isabelle* also introduces many of the elements we'll see throughout

Strout's work: the distance between people, the importance of place, an attention to natural, ephemeral images, the small indignities of life, including a nearly scatological humor, and the endurance of the human condition. At the same time, the book's focus on a relationship between a mother and her adolescent daughter mines a trope typical for many "domestic" (usually women) novelists.[1] Isabelle's sudden and surprising betrayal of trust—violent, revolting, and deeply human—is the most sensational and memorable moment of the novel, but I will argue that it is Strout's attention to small finite details, endowing them with a rare wonder, that presages her future success and distinguishes her work from that of other contemporary novelists.

Dedicated to her daughter, Strout's first published novel appeared in the year Zarina began college and Strout left her first husband and her daughter's father to spend more time on her writing. They lived apart for nearly a decade before finalizing their divorce. Strout's mentor from her early days submitting stories to the *New Yorker*, Daniel Menaker, had recently moved on to Random House. Impressed by Strout's early forays, he had kept in contact with her, and secured the manuscript of *Amy and Isabelle*. It was a wise and profitable decision; the novel was an immediate best seller and optioned as a television film by the Oprah Winfrey Network before it was printed.

Amy and Isabelle launched Strout's career and introduced her as a major new voice in American letters, its critical and commercial success anticipating her crossover appeal. In the pages that follow, I argue that *Amy and Isabelle* uniquely exemplifies a kind of double bildungsroman, tracing a mother and daughter's parallel stories of education; engages, complicates, and critiques the sentimental novel tradition; and inaugurates Strout's style, complete with wry humor, initially disorienting flashbacks, and lyrical descriptions of nature that slow the pace of reading and underscore narrative action. My analysis of this novel works within the interstices of psychoanalytic and feminist theory, new historicism, and close reading to show how Strout explores the intergenerational legacy of trauma facing a mother and her daughter at the dawn of the second wave of feminism. With a sympathetic portrayal of a middle-aged woman and her teenage child, each navigating her own experiences and perceptions of sexual assault, Strout positions herself as a mediator between generations navigating the complexities and nuances of coming of age through seduction, violence, and reconciliation. Though the novel is set in the early 1970s, its concerns—as the #MeToo movement has shown us—remain relevant. I first explore Isabelle and how, within her story, Strout successfully reimagines the bildungsroman; I then look at the character of Amy and how her story reimagines the sentimental novel; finally, I explore Strout's literary style, her use of humor, her attention to detail, the importance of place, and her experiment with time. Braiding together what at first seem disparate elements, I offer a reading of *Amy and Isabelle* that reveals how the novel sets the stage for Strout's future work.

Ariel Levy describes Isabelle as an "uptight" single mother raising her daughter and working as secretary to a manager at the mill of Shirley Falls, who sets herself apart from her fellow female coworkers. But Isabelle's isolation does not signal discernment, and in the course of the novel she learns how little she knows about her daughter, her community, and herself, a trope we'll see throughout Strout's oeuvre. *Amy and Isabelle* is told in flashbacks, so throughout the novel, in bits and pieces, Isabelle's history, which she has kept secret, is revealed. By the conclusion, Isabelle learns—to a certain degree—how much she has injured herself and her daughter by keeping separate from a community that would have accepted them if she had trusted it.

As the book begins, in medias res, we quickly learn of Isabelle's literal and figurative myopia. Time has continued its inexorable march with the heroine unaware of it; even though the Goodrows have lived in Shirley Falls for more than a decade, Isabelle feels that it's a temporary lodging place: "They had lived here now for fourteen years. This thought could sometimes make Isabelle feel physically sick, as though she had gulped in stagnant water from a pond. Her life was moving forward the way that lives did, and yet she was no more grounded than a bird perched on a fence. And she might one day find herself without even the fence. . . . But she could not bear to buy the house, could not bear to stop thinking her real life would happen somewhere else" (21). The reader soon learns that Isabelle and Amy are spending the summer working together at the local mill, and that while they are close, their relationship is troubled. Each resents the other, and it's not until halfway through the novel that we learn why. We do know that Isabelle lives in her head, using aphorisms gleaned from *Reader's Digest* to structure her life, even though she harbors a private skepticism toward such platitudes: "What the *Reader's Digest* said was that if you kept on praying, your ability to pray would improve, but Isabelle wondered if the *Reader's Digest* might not have a tendency to make things a bit simple" (12). Indeed.

Strout renders Isabelle's interior poignantly, tenderly, and comically. The friendless woman has a profound, sad crush on her boss, and she fantasizes about him, not so much sexually as maternally, underscoring her loneliness—and her imaginative powers. For example, she imagines, "if *she* were married to Avery (rolling a sheet of paper into the typewriter and getting rid of Emma Clark with a heart attack that would carry only a few brief moments of panic and pain), Avery might say in response to someone's asking, A nasty bug, but Isabelle took wonderful care of me. Because she would take wonderful care of him, making him Jell-O and wiping his brow, arranging magazines for him on the bed" (64). Avery himself appears oblivious to Isabelle's feelings—her adoration as well as the slights she internalizes. Strout has characterized this disconnect between the way Isabelle sees the world and the way it actually is as the "tension of the inner life versus the outer life," observing, "We all live with some kind of inner life, and it is often not known to others, and so their perceptions of us are just partly real. My job as a fiction writer is to show that strange relationship between people's perceptions of others and the inner reality a person lives with daily" (Campbell and Greengrass). Isabelle is sensitive and quick to feel rejected by others, particularly the women of the Congregational

Church. Yearning for her daughter's approval, Isabelle wants to improve herself, and so she attempts to read *Hamlet* but finds *Madame Bovary* more accessible and compelling. We begin to hear how literary echoes run throughout Strout's work.

As Isabelle's reading choices attest, family relationships and frustrated longings are crucial to her identity. Early on, the resentment she holds toward her daughter is evident. Even as they share home and work space, Isabelle is angered to the point of revulsion by her child: "She couldn't help it: the sight of Amy licking ketchup from her fingers made her almost insane. Just like that, anger reared its ready head and filled Isabelle's voice with coldness. Only there might have been more than coldness, to be honest. To be really honest, you might say there had been the edge of hatred in her voice" (14–15). This moment points to the past conflict eventually described in the middle of the book. It's unsettling, and we'll see throughout Strout's work such moments that unnerve the reader. In attempting to untangle how such moments function, I turn to Rita Felski, who suggests that "glimpsing aspects of oneself in fictional beings involves a volatile mix of the familiar and the different; to recognize is to know again but also to see afresh. As I recognize myself in another, I may also see something new in myself, and I may be startled or discomfited by what I see" (101). In other words, Strout doesn't let her readers only imaginatively identify with sweet, maternal, altruistic feelings. She portrays feeling of hostility, and in so doing, she jars her readers into perhaps admitting the existence of such feelings within themselves. We see here an early instance of how Strout works to engage her audience in a way compelling and distressing.

The reason for the tension between the two women, which Amy imagines as "a black line . . . nothing bigger than something drawn with a pencil" (5–6) and culminates in a full-bodied fight (which their surname slyly alludes to), is revealed halfway through the novel. While Isabelle resents her daughter, she also loves her and cares for her deeply, and it's this ambivalence that Strout portrays so perceptively. Isabelle wants to provide for Amy financially, and so since she was young she has worked in the mill, sending her child, after her own mother died, to a questionable day care. Isabelle's ambivalence toward her daughter stems from her guilt and her physical and emotional exhaustion. But we also see her tenderness for her child when she comes home from work to find that Amy is not there. Isabelle panics; she assumes the worst—that her daughter has been kidnapped: "Now she felt hysterical. Now she felt as though cold water were pouring through her arms, her legs. . . . She is *never* not home from school, Isabelle wailed silently. I know my daughter, and something is *wrong*. She sat down in a chair and began to sob. Huge, awful sounds erupted from her throat. Amy, Amy, she cried" (77). Ironically, Isabelle is correct; something is wrong. Amy is being preyed upon by her teacher, though neither woman is yet aware of the threat Mr. Robertson poses. Isabelle—intense, emotional, and self-doubting—follows the archetypal heroine memorialized from *Jane Eyre* to *Self Care*—but we also see Strout's distance in her gentle humor. Isabelle is as concerned about imagined fantasies as any young girl, but rather than identifying with her, her creator realizes what the character fails to understand.

Tensions erupt between mother and daughter after Avery tells Isabelle he has seen Amy in a compromised position with a man. Shame, anger, and fear roil through Isabelle once she returns home to confront her daughter: "He's not a nice man. . . . He doesn't care for you. . . . He *says* he cares for you because he wants what he wants" (161), and Amy responds piteously, "He wants me . . . He likes me, he does so." Mother and child become hopelessly entrenched; their trouble is not solely about Mr. Robertson, however, who is merely the catalyst for the confrontation. It's that they both feel disrespected and hurt by the other. As their anger boils over, Isabelle reveals her own profound insecurity when she shouts, "You go right ahead and tell yourself that your mother is an illiterate moron and that she's too stupid to know anything about real life, but I'm telling *you* that *you* are the one who doesn't know anything" (163). In one of the rare moments of judgment, the narrator explains, "It had become that senseless and awful, yelling at each other about who was the most stupid."

Perhaps more important than the confrontation itself is the moment of clarity it sparks in Isabelle—her realization that the world and how she perceives it are not the same: "It was sinking in—trying to, as she watched her child's pale face, averted eyes—the sense that this girl had been living a separate life, the sense that her daughter was strikingly different from what she had thought, that the girl *hadn't even liked her*" (163). Isabelle's epiphany leads her to sadness, anger, and, finally, desperation, her emotions expressing themselves physically.

Strout doesn't reveal exactly what happens between the women, as if the scene is too traumatic to be rendered in words, but we learn that Isabelle's anger terrifies her daughter:

> What followed was something that Isabelle would speak of only once, years later, when her life had become a very different one. Amy, on the other hand, would later on in her adulthood tell a number of people, until she realized finally that it was one story in a million and ultimately didn't matter to anyone.
>
> But it mattered a great deal to them, to Amy and to Isabelle, and while over time they would forget parts and remember parts differently, both remembered and would always remember certain aspects of the scene. How, for example, Isabelle began throwing the couch pillows across the room, screaming that this Mr. Robertson creature was nothing more than a pimp. One of the pillows knocked over a lamp, smashing the bulb into little bits against the floor, and Amy began to cry out "Mama!"—a child terrified. (163–64)

At the same time that Isabelle is uncontrollably angry, she also feels sad for Amy; seeing her daughter afraid and cowering stirs anger in the mother, who leaves the house to confront Mr. Robertson. Psychiatrist Bessel van der Kolk explains that "when our emotional and rational brains are in conflict (as when we're enraged with someone we love . . .), a tug-of-war ensues. This war is largely played out in the theater of visceral experience—your gut, your heart, your lungs"

(65). So in some ways it's no surprise that Isabelle's emotional snapping is figured physically. But—and this is important—the scene is
also a little bit funny. While raging and throwing pillows, the worst
Isabelle can utter is that the man is a "pimp"—it's not funny to Amy
or to Isabelle, and the scene could be played straight—but we could
also see in Isabelle's untapped resentment a spoof of feminine repression and rage. The scene functions on multiple levels.

The confrontation between Isabelle and Mr. Robertson is terse;
he insinuates that she is hardly the front she presents—"*Is it
Mrs.* Goodrow? I'm afraid I was never quite sure"—and that Amy is
cut from the same cloth: "Mrs. Goodrow, Amy did not need a good
deal of teaching, shall we say" (167). In two sentences Mr. Robertson underscores and scorns the woman's complex feelings of shame,
desire, jealousy, and regret, again making apparent to Isabelle that
Amy has suffered because of her maternal failings. Isabelle tells him
to leave town, but her self-command does not last.

Shortly thereafter, in a surprising visceral attack, Isabelle comes
at Amy with scissors, trying to hurt her not physically but psychi-
cally. Whether consciously or not, she attempts to make her daughter ugly and childish, perhaps trying to protect her, so that men will
not find her attractive, but her action is also undoubtedly one of
violence and betrayal. Isabelle snaps and cuts off Amy's hair, in an
act of physicality that Isabelle has never allowed herself before. She
has been unable to protect her daughter from predators, from sexuality, and from growing up. Amy, as we soon learn, like her mother
before her, has gravitated toward a predator. The scene, then, in
Freudian terms, is one of condensation. Isabelle has not come to
terms with her own history, how a friend of her father's raped her
(though she sees it as seduction) when she was not much older than
her daughter is, and she feels all the hopelessness of her inability to
protect Amy and her own despair and resentment at missing out
on a healthy adult sexuality. But a tragic realization also shadows
the scene—for, by cutting her daughter's hair, Isabelle shames Amy
with a centuries-old punishment designed to humiliate women for
alleged sexual transgressions.

Following the fight, the two live quietly together, rarely speaking to each other, armed with tension. It's only after Amy discovers the body of Debby Kay Dorne and returns home to find her mother with Bev and Dottie, two coworkers, that she and Isabelle begin to heal. And it's at that point, after Amy finds the corpse and returns to her mother safely, sadder and wiser, that Isabelle can tell her daughter and her new friends the story of Amy's conception and birth. Learning of her daughter's discovery and having Amy return home to her after such a trauma allows Isabelle to realize that she, too, is a survivor and not the fallen woman she once thought herself. Strout's bildungsroman is a story of a middle-aged woman whose life does not end after she realizes her ancient and recent failings but begins again in a new, healthier way.

The novel concludes with Isabelle taking Amy to meet her father's family. He is now deceased, but his wife and children, having heard from Isabelle, welcome them both into their community. This acceptance pains Isabelle, as the Goodrow dyad will be broken, but it signals for mother and daughter a new chapter and Amy's entrance into a healthy adulthood. Recalling the book's opening, which alludes to the space race, Isabelle sees her daughter as "blasting off, . . . leaving forever, [and] that Isabelle was only there now to pilot the ship" (304). But she too is growing in ways she hadn't thought possible, particularly by letting her daughter go. As they drive, Isabelle considers the ride as marking the end of Amy's childhood. Years later she remembers it and "at different places and moments in the years to come, would sometimes be surrounded by silence and find in herself only the repeated word 'Amy.' 'Amy, *Amy*'—for this was it, her heart's call, her prayer" (304). Her daughter's name is the most sacred speech act Isabelle can utter, a prayer of home, regret, love, connection, and release.

As I mentioned earlier, Strout tells parallel stories of mother and daughter in the novel. Neither is told chronologically; instead, in fragments, we learn the story of Amy as well as of Isabelle. The golden-haired girl, like her mother, is ill at ease in Shirley Falls. Through flashbacks, we learn that at fifteen Amy hides behind her veil of curls, finding herself (as her mother will eventually) in books, particularly poetry. Her closest friend, Stacy, is earthy, irreverent, and sexually active, offering an alternative Weltanschauung to Isabelle's. Even so, Amy is painfully lonely, yearning to be noticed, but also afraid of attention—perfectly primed for the advances of a predator.

Her substitute math teacher, the short, hairy Mr. Robertson, begins his unlikely courtship of Amy through compliments, poems, and simply noticing her. Starved for attention, she comes to rely on his ministrations, missing them when he calculatedly withdraws. Amy is intuitive enough to realize that when they kiss, the action does not convey affection or respect: "It was absolutely incredible: Mr. Robertson had French-kissed her. Completely incredible. He had actually done that. So did it mean he loved her? The kiss had not seemed very loving" (118). Her adolescent perspective is painfully evident. She "could think of very little other than the open mouth of Mr. Robertson: the shock of his slippery warm tongue tumbling over hers, the light whisper of a groan that had risen from his throat as he pressed the back of her head with his hand, the cracking sound of his jaw at one point as his mouth had opened even further, thrusting his tongue against her inner cheek, a living warm thing let loose inside her mouth" (118). A first kiss, perhaps fantastically, is often rendered as an intimate, celebratory rite of passage, but this one is uncomfortable, not the meeting of a pair of people in love, but the violation of one body by another.

It's fitting, then, that just after this physical encounter Amy is violated emotionally by a crank call; the timing and accent suggest the speaker is Mr. Robertson. Home alone after he has dropped her off (his driving her throughout the novel another sign of her youth and concomitant paralysis), Amy picks up the phone to hear a man whisper "slowly, obscenely gentle. 'I want to lick vanilla ice cream off your cunt'" (122). If the image is funny to some—the ridiculousness of the childhood sweet juxtaposed with the act of cunnilingus—it terrifies Amy, her reaction underscoring her naïveté:

> Amy put the phone down as though in her hand it had
> become a snake. "Oh God," she whimpered. "Oh please, God."

> She dragged a kitchen chair up to the door, tilting its back
> beneath the doorknob as she had seen her mother do in
> February after the disappearance of Debby Kay Dorne. . . .
> . . . She was afraid. She forced herself to go upstairs, to
> look under the beds, to open the closets. . . .
> . . . Oh, she was so frightened! The awful, still, dark
> house. . . .
> . . . Crying softly, she crept into the front hall closet,
> sitting down on top of boots, behind the quilted hemline of
> her mother's winter coat. (122)

The phone call has infantilized Amy, rendering her afraid and submissive (recalling her mother's fear at not finding her daughter in
the house; their mirrored actions show how Amy has internalized
Isabelle's paranoia). Amy's response shows how close to childhood
she is. Mother and daughter are acutely emotional, and their sensitivity does not signal perceptiveness but a stunted sensibility. But
sexual acts have real-life consequences as well, as we see when Stacy
calls to say, "'So guess what,' . . . cheerfully, snapping gum. 'I'm rolling
along at seven months. Can you *believe* I'm pregnant?'" (123). Amy's
fragility and innocence—like Stacy's gum-snapping—contrast with
the biological consequences of sexuality. Amy walks the tightrope of
adolescence, as vulnerable as a young child even as her conversations
with Stacy, her own erotic longing, and her body's fertility have,
theoretically, prepared her for sexual encounters.

Paradoxically, as their physical intimacy develops, so does the
distance between Amy and Mr. Robertson, their very names emphasizing the power differential between them.[2] We see most of their
interactions from Amy's point of view, even though Mr. Robertson
is always in control. After the school year ends, alone with her in
his car, he is dictatorial, telling Amy to take off her blouse and bra.
She complies: "so that her hair would hide her face, she tilted her
head down, and saw between the roundness of her breasts, the pale
pink tips as excruciatingly exposed as something newborn, [and] a
trickle of sweat run down her stomach in the waistband of her lav-
ender skirt." Her awkwardness and uncertainty are painfully visible.

Mr. Robertson "asked her to turn one way then another. He asked her to raise her arm and hold her hair up and tilt her head." As Amy reacts physiologically and emotionally, so that "every squeeze of his mouth made her ache down there so that her hips began to move, her middle arching up and the sound of begging filling the air" (141), the distance between the two of them is emphasized. The young girl is ashamed she is responding, not realizing that her physical reaction is natural. "Blushing deeply, almost ready to cry with embarrassment," she confesses her underpants are wet (142). His indifference is revealed the next moment, when he does not comfort her, but says instead, "You're great. You're every man's dream. A horny girl. . . . You're so fucking horny. . . . I want you even hornier" (142). Strout lets Mr. Robertson's words and actions speak for themselves, without editorializing. Amy's perception of their encounter is far different from Mr. Robertson's: "it was terrible how wonderful he was—this wonderful, wonderful man" (143). The scenes that follow underscore Amy's blindness. She believes the older man will marry her, imagines him telling her mother, "I love your daughter and we want to be together" (171).

In letting the men speak for themselves, Strout shows how crass they are (even Avery Clark is coarse; when he finds Amy in the car, "he had thoughts that included vulgar language, and he knew if he were a different sort of man he would have told his men friends what he had seen. . . . 'A terrific set of knockers,' he might have said. 'A great pair of tits'" [155]). Amy believes the men see her as precious, even when their words and actions suggest their emotional indifference, yet she survives. Though in love with Mr. Robertson and baffled by his disappearance, she endures, to find herself the object of Stacy's ex-boyfriend's erotic attention. Mr. Robertson has introduced Amy to the uneasy world of adolescent 1970s sexuality, and in brief spots Strout alludes to the dangers facing young women after he leaves. Amy loses her innocence in several ways through this book. Mr. Robertson's kissing her is one loss of innocence, the crank call is a second, Stacy's ex-boyfriend's amorous attempt is another. But finding the body of Debby Kay Dorne replaces the conventional act of sexual consummation. The veiled brutality of the earlier moments is put into relief when Amy and Paul find the young girl's corpse in the trunk of a car. Mr. Robertson and Paul have touched Amy in their cars, signaling the historical context of the story—when the young experimented sexually in these particular liminal places—so it's fitting that Debby's corpse is located in a trunk. But even the finding of Debby's body does not signal the conclusion to Amy's education. If conventional sentimental narratives address young girls' romantic exploits as their learning curve, the stories of their loss of innocence ending in marriage or death, Strout challenges that narrative. For unlike Debby Kay Dorne, but like her mother, Amy will survive. Her story is more than the story of her sexual awakening. Amy endures the assaults (Mr. Robertson's final betrayal is to tell her she has the wrong number when she calls him), and after finding Debby's corpse, she returns home to her mother. Soon Bev and Dottie, who has just endured a hysterectomy and her husband's leaving her for a younger woman, arrive, and at this point Isabelle finally tells Amy the story of her conception. The two have a chance at a new kind of relationship that blossoms as the novel ends.

Finding the young girl's body, then, marks the death of childhood not only for Amy but for her mother as well. Isabelle can put her false claims of widowhood to rest. Amy and Isabelle realize that their relationships with men have been disappointing, and Bev and Dottie's companionship offers a contrast to the brief and physical heterosexual encounters. This community of women is an antidote to the violence and brutality of the world, even as it is imperfect; after all, Isabelle has knowingly and unknowingly hurt her daughter. The comfort the women offer each other may be tenuous or temporary, but in their very act of holding, of comforting each other, the women offer a kind of sympathy or care that sustains them. It's a nonjudgmental holding. And Amy and Isabelle are both welcomed into this fold.

The name of the town, Shirley Falls, then, speaks on one level to Amy (and Isabelle)'s experiences. While Amy believes she has a choice in acting on her desires, in other ways, as the older women could tell her if she were comfortable enough to ask them, in falling in love with her teacher and submitting to his wishes, she has little power and is following a literary script at least two centuries old.[3] But if Strout alludes to the sentimental tradition not only in Amy and Isabelle's stories, her endings complicate the conventions—and here is why historical specificity is so important. The conventional sentimental mores that steered so much of American morality as late as the 1950s and '60s are no longer relevant in the 1970s.[4] If Amy's coming of age is the story of a girl who surely falls because she misjudges the world, another way to read the most important lesson of her education is in her acceptance of and admission to the feminine community, that intergenerational inclusion a hallmark of second-wave feminism's consciousness-raising moment.

In creating and representing that community of women, Strout not only looks back to the 1970s but looks ahead to the twenty-first-century's #MeToo moment, when women across generations revealed virtually their own experiences of sexual assault, redefining what that is, and creating an online community of readers and survivors. Of course women have been talking intimately for eons, but Strout puts women's relationships—and their conversations with each other—front and center. As the title of the novel attests, as much as Amy thinks her development is about her sexuality, it is primarily about her relationship with her mother. This switch—from the conjugal relationship to the maternal and sororal one—as the most important marks a new turn for the domestic novel.[5]

By the book's end, we come to learn that Isabelle had separated herself from the women with whom she worked because she had internalized the narrative about herself as fallen after being raped by a friend of her father's, getting pregnant, and raising her child alone. Isabelle blames herself for Jake Cunningham's betrayal of his wife. It's not until she sees Dottie's despair after her husband leaves her that she can admit to her history, her desire, her sadness, and her shame. After Isabelle finally tells the story to Bev and Dottie (and Amy), the women set the stage for a new kind of understanding of identity, one that says the most important moment of a girl's identity is not sexual initiation, but rather her acknowledgment of her history to other women and her self-acceptance. In Janet Ellerby's words, Isabelle learns that shame's "stultifying grip can be loosened by narratives that reject the implacability of fate and embrace the optimistic project of transformation that comes with a legacy of truth" (194).

Isabelle moves from living in her head and pining after her boss to realizing that her most important relationship is with her daughter. This relationship is neither idealized nor romanticized. The threat of violence haunts the women the way it does Shirley Falls. This violence is the manifestation of a corruption that can be as subtle as the pollution that taints the local river or as brutal as the murder of a twelve-year-old girl. Strout experiments with gothic elements (which she'll do again in *Anything Is Possible*), but it's a sign of her subtlety that the work does not sensationalize by graphically describing acts of violence. The worst betrayal and most overt act is not between an innocent girl and a male stranger but between a mother and her child. Certainly Isabelle is jealous of her daughter's sexuality, freedom, and power, and that jealousy leads to Isabelle's cutting off her daughter's hair; that moment is the center of the story. Though men and sexual acts precipitate the conflict between mother and daughter, it's the relationship between the two women that the novel privileges.

And mother and daughter find themselves in a new network with a new kind of storyline at the novel's end. They're not in the fantasy of being in the arms of the men they've dreamed about, but with each other, on their own couch, in their own living room. Bev, Dottie, and Stacy are all earthy; they fully inhabit their bodies, while Amy and Isabelle have spent much of their lives hiding from theirs. But Bev in her digestive problems and bulk, Dottie in her "female problems," and Stacy in her pregnancy cannot escape their bodies—and they don't try to do so. Rather, they accept themselves with refreshing and healthy humor. Perhaps Isabelle's cutting Amy's hair can also function as a sign of her mental health; by expressing her frustration (and destroying the mask Amy uses to hide from others), she is doing something rather than hiding from the world. Bev and Dottie act for Isabelle the same way that Stacy does for Amy; that is, these women encourage their friends to not shut themselves off from each other or community.[6] Isabelle learns to accept their kindness. She sees that acceptance as a sort of grace, a gift from God—not attributing it to the women themselves but endowing their generosity with a higher significance. Isabelle comes to see grace in people's love and acceptance of each other, not in the Scriptures or platitudes she had used to structure her life until this point.

> It seemed to her (What was that sound? Only Fat Bev
> snoring) that kindness was one of God's greatest gifts: the
> fact that people, so many people, held within themselves the
> ability to be kind, really, was the work of God. How kind
> those women downstairs had been to her tonight! How kind
> the policemen had been earlier, the doctor on the telephone,
> the silent pharmacist (remembering only a large, white-
> coated bulk of a man). Yes, how kind people could be. . . . She
> would think about her friends downstairs, how at one point
> tonight they had *wept with her* as she told them of her love
> for Jake Cunningham. Isabelle could not get over this. These
> women had wept with her. They had heard her story of a life
> falsely lived, of other lives hurt by her own actions, and they
> had then with tender kindness kissed her good night. (282)

In turning to Bev and Dottie, women whom she had distanced herself from because she saw herself as different, Isabelle learns that they may in fact be alike. She learns that the Catholics whom she had disparaged are there for her in ways that the other women of her own church are not.

But though the women are included in the fold of a feminine community and there is a sense of redemption in the gathering, there is also a kind of distance—both realistic and literary—between them. Isabelle does not reveal to her new friends how she hurt Amy. Bev and Dottie stay silent about some of their own private troubles as well.

There had been and still was kindness in this room of shipwrecked women, but secrets remained nevertheless that would have to be borne alone. For Amy, of course, there was the astonishing voice of Mr. Robertson: "*I don't know who you are.*" For Isabelle, there was the private removal of Avery Clark from a position that no one, including him, ever knew he occupied. And even Dottie had not given all the details of her grief to Bev (recurring thoughts of Althea's vagina being fingered—a dark moist tunnel that led to her very insides, instead of the dry butchered thing that stopped short, sewn at the top now, in Dottie); and Fat Bev herself had private concerns she could not put into words, some heavy blanket of dread pressing down on her. (285)

The women are not open books, but they are present for each other, and in this way the novel is both feminine and feminist. The women survive and are stronger because of their caring for each other. In recognizing the suffering and the dignity of others, they practice what Carol Gilligan has termed an "ethics of care" that contrasts with the dehumanizing and dismissive interactions they have with the men of Shirley Falls. This feminine compassion—rooted in the maternal body—makes life beautiful and endurable. Isabelle considers this new perspective and knowledge: "What could you do? Only keep going. People kept going; they had been doing it for thousands of years. You took the kindness offered, letting it seep in as far as it could go, and the remaining dark crevices you carried around with you, knowing that over time they might change into something almost bearable. Dottie, Bev, Isabelle, in their own ways, knew this. But Amy was young. She didn't know yet what she could or could not bear, and silently she clung like a dazed child to all three mothers in the room" (286). Even as Isabelle and Amy are moving toward a healthier, honest relationship, they remain mysteries to each other: "Isabelle watched the girl's baffled look, the incoherence on her shiny face, and wondered again what her daughter had been doing driving around the back roads with some boy, wondered again what the different facets were to the girl's grief, and knew it would take

time to learn, that in fact she might never know" (287). This attention to familial intensity, this acknowledgment of that closeness
and distance, is one of Strout's preoccupations. Strout's perception
of emotional distance between people recalls both Eliot and James,
but Strout's distance is feminized—it's between women. So whereas,
for example, Eliot focuses on Tertius Lydgate and Rosamond Vincy
or Dorothea Brooke and Edward Casaubon and James focuses on
Isabel Archer and Gilbert Osmond, here Strout focuses on mothers
and daughters.

Isabelle is so hurt by Amy's rejection of her that she lashes out
and cuts her hair. That most nurturing and protective of relationships is vexed and complicated, intense and loving and hurtful. If as
adults, as parents, we prefer not to see ourselves as wounding our
children, Strout tells us we cannot look away from how we have
injured those people in the world whom we love most of all and are
duty bound to protect and to nurture into their best selves. Strout
forces us to see that we "love imperfectly," offering here what she
will continue to proffer throughout her work, examples of people
who are muddling through, learning to accept and forgive their own
and others' imperfections, and realizing that in this pain-riddled
earth we share we each have our own private suffering.

Motherhood is formative, but it does not save or redeem women;
and it does not complete them. Here, again, Strout rewrites domestic fiction. Strout's heroines are, we might say, the walking wounded,
those people who hurt and have been hurt not only by each other,
but by their own bodies. There are no saints in Strout's fiction, but
individuals who had dreamed they—and their lives—would be different than they are. And in portraying the peripheral characters
with such sensitivity, Strout again recalls Eliot and Dickens. For example, she gives us a peek into Bev's perspective shortly after she has
had her first child and finds out she is pregnant again:

> At a time when her house, her life, was filling up, she had ex-
> perienced an irrepressible feeling of loss. . . . She wasn't going
> to complain, she wasn't a kid anymore. But an ache stayed
> inside her. And a faint reverberating hum of something close

> to joy lived on the outer edges of her memory, some kind
> of longing that had been answered once and was simply
> not answered anymore. She didn't understand this. She was
> married to a good man, and so many women weren't; she'd
> had the babies she wanted and they were healthy and alive.
> So what was this ache? A deep red hole she threw Life Savers
> into and potatoes and hamburgers and chocolate cakes, and
> anything else. She didn't like being fat. But that dark red ache
> was there, like a swirling vacuum, a terrible hole. (41)

We recognize such existential ache in the work of Eliot and James,
but Strout grounds that loss in the feminine form, materializing it.
Her maternal body is not complete, warm, and holy; it is, in fact,
longing, wasted, and holey. And yet for all of those scars, that body
is also miraculous, enduring against tremendous odds. It's important, then, that *Amy and Isabelle* is set in the aftermath of the heyday
of *The Feminine Mystique*. Bev has not read Friedan and she suffers
from the problem that has no name, which her creator perceives.
Strout offers her readers some relief from profound sadness, however, by tempering these moments of loss and disappointment, the
depiction of lives of quiet desperation, with comic notes, a move
that also seems to humanize them.

The perceived distance between Amy and Isabelle and the
women with whom they share the workplace is one of the primary
sources of humor in the book. Unlike her mother, Amy is fascinated
by her coworkers. These women are united in their physicality; their
discussion of their bodily ailments—from farting to bleeding—is irreverent, almost ribald, an antidote to the ominousness that also
pervades the novel:

> "Three more weeks and Dottie can have sex," [Bev] said.
> The black line tightened between Amy and Isabelle. "She
> wishes it was three more months," and here the soda can
> was popped open. "But I take it Wally's getting irritable.
> Chomping at the bit."
> Amy swallowed the crust of her sandwich.

"Tell him to take care of it himself," someone said, and there was laughter. Amy's heartbeat quickened, sweat broke out above her lip.

"You get dry after a hysterectomy, you know." Arlene Tucker offered this with a meaningful nod of her head.

"I didn't."

"Because you didn't have your ovaries out." (8)

This conversation anticipates the humor and wisdom we will see more fully realized in Olive Kitteridge herself. Some of Strout's women are empowered by their experience, not shamed by it. If overlooked by the arbiters of popular culture, these irreverent elders speak out, sharing their humorous insights with anyone wise enough to listen (and we might remember that Strout too spent time working in the secretarial pool of Bates College and at the local mill). Bev, Dottie, Arlene, and Lenora are experienced, wise, and funny.[7]

For most of the novel, Amy and Isabelle take themselves more seriously than other characters take themselves. That very seriousness becomes funny, but it also deprives them of physical and emotional nourishment. Strout does not think—as Isabelle does—that people are noble beings chasing after their better angels. Here she recalls her medieval and eighteenth-century forebears: her humans are firmly animal. We see such a realization when the Goodrow house, "lacking an attic or basement, . . . was insufferably hot in the summer, and this summer was the worst of all. There was no escaping the heat or each other. . . . Tonight Amy, lying in a T-shirt and underpants, a bare leg draped over the edge of her bed, heard her mother fart—a short dry sound, as though some attempt had been made at being polite" (21). Simply put, the scene is funny.

Poor Isabelle. If she is pathetic in her isolation, Strout gently teases her middle-aged protagonist when she attempts to pray. "This was tricky business. You didn't want to ask for the wrong thing, go barking up the wrong tree. You didn't want God to think you were selfish by asking for *things*, the way Catholics did" (14). There is a tender poignancy to this scene; after all, Isabelle is so lonely that she resorts to praying to improve her situation, not realizing that she could reach out to people to ask for help, to assuage her loneliness. But Strout also tempers that melancholy with humor:

> If Isabelle was going to get specific she wouldn't be so vulgar as to ask for a car—she would pray for a husband, or a better daughter. Except she wouldn't of course. (*Please* God, send me a husband, or at least a daughter I can stand.) No, instead she would lie there on her bedspread and pray only for God's love and guidance, and try to let Him know she was available for these things if He cared to give her a sign. But she felt nothing, only the drops of sweat arriving once more above her lip and beneath her arms in the heat of this small bedroom. She was tired. God was probably tired as well. (14)

Strout's bifurcated narrative style—sympathetic to but distanced from her characters—gives her a voice both intimate and ironic (recalling Austen's *Emma*). Isabelle clings to some very childish ideas: believing that prayers may change things (what Freud calls magical thinking) or thinking that other people are judging her negatively (a kind of narcissism—most people in her proximity simply don't consider her). But Strout does not make her creation the butt of jokes; she is also sympathetic to Isabelle, and in this gentle teasing married to sympathy, Strout recalls Dickens, reimagining that kind, knowing narrator in the last days of the twentieth century. Strout bears witness to Isabelle's consciousness, her mindset, and in this way, Strout is profoundly empathetic. But she also elicits an understanding in her readers, an ability to see others as human. She considers catalyzing that empathy to be one of the primary movers of her writing—fiction offers us the chance to become more understanding, more tolerant of each other, or, more irreverently, "fiction can help people have a great appreciation for how big and complicated experience is. I just want to have respect for the enormous amount of mess that everyone is living with and living through" (*Atlantic*). By nonjudgmentally bearing witness to Isabelle's experience, Strout lets her readers see Isabelle's pain and also the hopeful, desperate lens through which Isabelle views the world. But, and this is important, some of Isabelle's beliefs are really funny, and so her creator gives us a break from the intense sadness that a different writer might not. That is, if we just look at the plot of *Amy and Isabelle*—a mother gets angry over her daughter's growing up and hurts her—then the story could be tragic, but by punctuating the slow, sad inevitable arc of loss with funny moments, Strout evokes Austen as well as novels of sympathy. If Isabelle's pining after Avery is pathetic and her life appears depressing, the fact that she is in a tizzy over whether to serve Jell-O offers the reader relief from potentially overwhelming sadness.

Strout's perspective yokes the specific and the timeless, the daily and the long-term. I see this style as linked to her writing process. As she tells us in the appendix, Strout writes in scenes that she later revises and then stitches together to form a narrative. She doesn't begin with a story plotted out, and perhaps because of this, her final works also appear multifaceted, their seams showing. Time within her works is never linear or chronological. She might zero in on one moment, then go back in history, or explain how that moment evokes other years or the season generally. In this novel, she begins with a sense of corrupted innocence. Rather than starting with pastoral nostalgia, the first sentence reads, "It was terribly hot that summer Mr. Robertson left town, and for a long while the river seemed dead" (3). *Amy and Isabelle* starts with a sense of loss; someone has already left; something bad has already happened. "Terribly hot and dead" recalls not a prelapsarian innocence but a place already poisoned. This river does not convey life, movement, or spiritual cleansing, but is contaminated, a "dead brown snake of a thing lying flat through the center of town, dirty yellow foam collecting at its edge" (3). This image incarnates a key stylistic feature of *Amy and Isabelle* and Strout's other works—making materially present the effects of a corrupted history. We don't know what has polluted the river—we only see its effects. We will see again and again throughout Strout's oeuvre that the characters are living with the consequences of an often unknown event. The river serves as a way into Strout's universe.

At the same time that the river evokes a general sense of innocence lost, Strout's images ground the reader in a specific time and place. Setting the novel in the early 1970s is crucial. Just after she describes the river, Strout alludes to the space race—so while many in the United States are looking up, hopeful about the future and man's potential, Shirley Falls is rooted to its polluted ground: "Some thought the world might be coming to an end, and even those women not inclined to go that far had to admit it might not have been a good idea sending men into space, that we had no business, really, walking around up there on the moon" (5). The allusion juxtaposes the pedestrian humdrum life of small-town America with the celestial dreams of many citizens. If science has finally caught up to man's dream to explore the stars, the community of Shirley Falls is firmly terrestrial, aware of how their fellow countrymen are reaching heights never possible before, but this awareness only brings their own limitations into greater relief. The women of Shirley Falls are hot and sweaty, working boring jobs, tethered to their desks and their frail, fat bodies: "the heat was relentless and the fans rattling in the windows seemed to be doing nothing at all, and eventually the women ran out of steam, sitting at their big wooden desks with their legs slightly apart, lifting the hair from the back of their necks" (4). In the days before the air conditioning became common, the ennui and mental exhaustion facing the women workers mirror their physical condition.

This narrative style plays a central role in this novel, where much of the action is revealed in flashbacks and the reader is nearly two-thirds of the way through the book when she learns how Isabelle hurt Amy. Strout will rely on flashbacks throughout her work—moments of epiphany reveal prior histories. For Strout, the most important events do not occur at the moment of action itself, but in realizing the effects of that action years later. We see this here in a relatively compressed way with Amy—her affair has ended and her mother has attacked her by the time the novel begins—and with Isabelle, when we finally learn not only of Amy's conception but how Isabelle raised her alone. If the flashbacks can be disorienting, Strout further breaks up linear narrative with her poetic descriptions of natural beauty. Within the novel Isabelle endows the lovely transience of nature with spiritual significance. As in all of her works, here Strout takes certain moments and unspools them, lingering on their beauty, particularly if they occur outside, where sunsets, breezes, clouds, and leaves serve as exquisite frames for and breaks from meditations on the characters' inner conflicts. Such a moment occurs when Isabelle steps "out to sweep her porch steps [and] felt absolutely certain that some wonderful change was arriving in her life. The strength of this belief was puzzling; what she was feeling, she decided, was really the presence of God. God was here on her back steps, in the final patch of sunlight on her tulip bed, in the steady husky chirping from the marsh, in the fragrant damp earth surrounding right now the delicate roots of hepaticas and starflowers" (107). Looking for ways to understand her immediate surroundings and to make sense of her life, Isabelle evokes both platitudes and, more surprisingly, a quiet lyrical mysticism. But the novel itself underscores an important part of Strout's vision—that which is most sacred is the connection we have with other people.

Her poetic attention to detail in these beautiful images, like the humorous comments, serves to give the reader relief from the tragedies and tension of the women's daily lives. Here Strout sets the stage for her future work with her lyricism, humor, and compassion, and these interests—like her playing with time and deferred revelations—return again and again in the fiction that follows. Domestic drama—the travails of family set against a natural stage, revealed through relationships—will appear in her next book, *Abide with Me*, when Strout stays in Maine and goes further back in history, to the late fifties, to tell the story of a widowed minister, his faith, and his family.

2

Enduring Faith in *Abide with Me*

STROUT'S SECOND NOVEL, *ABIDE WITH ME* (2006), is another work of historical fiction that seeks to cultivate reader empathy. Set in the fictional small town of West Annett, Maine, in 1959, the novel focuses on Tyler Caskey, a Congregational minister wrestling with his faith in the wake of his wife's death. His names etymologically and phonetically evoke "a man who tells," a roof builder, a doorkeeper, a barrel, and a casket—each a clue to this young man's temperament and ethical dilemmas. But the historic and international stages affect Tyler as well—here it's not the space race but the devastation of World War II and the work and life of the theologian and anti-Nazi dissident Dietrich Bonhoeffer, to which the novel alludes over and over again. As she did in her first book, Strout begins *Abide with Me* in medias res. Something bad has happened (in this case the death of Tyler's wife Lauren), and the Caskey home is now in disarray: five-year-old Katherine is acting out at school; toddler Jeannie is living with Tyler's mother; and, in spite of having a housekeeper (the mysterious and laconic Connie Hatch), Tyler seems unable to keep his child, home, and himself together. The family is in a state of chaos—individuals and the collective are broken—and *Abide with Me* is not only a fragmented account that elliptically reveals what has led Tyler to this place, it's also a description of how one mourner moves forward after a shattering loss, reinforcing the themes of love, forgiveness, and survival of *Amy and Isabelle.*

The novel, then, is both like and different from Strout's first. The geographical setting and the fragmented chronology are similar, but the protagonist, a young man, and the time period distinguish it. These differences signal Strout's staking out new terrain: she is not merely a writer of women's fiction. Though Tyler is clearly preoccupied with the domestic, as a veteran and a leader in his community, he's also profoundly masculine. That said, for most of the novel's duration Tyler primarily interacts with female characters: his wife (in flashbacks), Connie Hatch, Katherine, her teachers, his mother, and the women of his congregation. As a minister, he is in a complicated position, feminized, as much of his work involves the practice of care, but masculinized by virtue of his role as a public figure and church leader. In many ways, the novel belies the idea of separate gender spheres, even as the decade in which it's set is often caricatured as having rigidly codified them.

In addition to debunking notions about gender, the novel unsettles conventional conceptions of time. Once again, Strout's narrative style—the fragmented chronology—undercuts the universalizing "objective" understanding of the world around us, as does her voice, which she establishes in the first paragraph. Here Strout shows she is thoroughly modern, stylistically owing as much to Faulkner as to nineteenth-century novelists. Beginning conversationally, the novel emphasizes the humanity of the speaker, and in so doing, subjectivity and the impossibility of a completely unbiased account. An anonymous, avuncular voice—a person claiming a kind of intimacy with the reader, "at one time a minister up north of here"—begins to spin a yarn. He (or she—we don't learn the speaker's identity) is remembering a story the same way that Lucy Barton and the anonymous narrator of *The Burgess Boys* do in Strout's later works. *Abide with Me* is also about truth-telling (Tyler's names underscoring the two competing impulses he has—to confess and to bury), about the ways we talk to ourselves and others to make sense of our lives, and how our recollections are necessarily always imperfect.

In *Abide with Me,* the historical backdrop includes the concentration camps of World War II and the Pacific Theater, and beyond the confines of West Annett, the Civil Rights Movement and the Cold War are more clearly affecting the United States. Here, Strout lays the foundation for what will be a larger theme in her work. In her allusions, she contextualizes the struggles faced by Tyler and his flock, yet the easy intimacy of her voice emphasizes the incomplete understanding of events, whether personal or historic—that is, our own partial perspectives always limit that which we can see and that which we can know.

Their experiences in World War II weigh heavily on the characters, particularly Tyler and Charlie Austin, a fellow veteran. This is a sober book; it's quiet and literary, in conversation with spiritual readings. If the WASP characters are not direct victims of the Holocaust or segregation, they're aware of these tragedies. Their individual lives, Strout shows, unfold in a specific, broader context. As Strout has said repeatedly, geographic and historic circumstances shape the action of stories—they wouldn't happen without these particular contingencies. And we can't understand the greater tragedies or events without understanding the personal ones. Jane Thrailkill offers a useful way to see this juxtaposition: it carries "with it a philosophical premise. It is only from a particular position—from within an embodied self, which feels, acts, and thinks from an attitude of agency—that one pilots oneself through the world, casting objects and happenings and other people into unfolding stories that provide a means of feeling one's way through the day" ("Ian McEwan," 191–92). In other words, the individual matters. We hold our stories with us always. Here one can't help but see a comparison to Faulkner's *The Sound and the Fury* or, better yet, *Absalom, Absalom,* in which the fragmented layers of narration—between Quentin and his roommate, and the members of the Compson and Sutpen families—tell the story of the devastation of the Civil War and of the South itself. Our indifference and cruelty to others, our lack of compassion, can presage acts harmful not only to individuals but to nations as well, laying the seed, preparing the excuse for violence of historic and international proportions.[1]

Strout couches such generalization in the context of the domestic, the familial, suggesting that one path to understanding world events—whether historic or contemporary—is through an open stance of listening to and sharing our individual stories. At the beginning of the novel, Tyler is called into his daughter's school. The threat of the conversation makes him uneasy: "Nobody, of course, wants to start a morning this way, but it was especially true for Reverend Caskey, who had suffered his share of recent sorrows, and while people were aware of this, the man was really far more worn down than anyone knew" (7). Tragedy, doom, mystery, daily life, and intimacy with the reader are established in this single sentence. Mired in his own depression, Tyler is unaware of how Katherine has stopped speaking and how her silence reflects her suffering. If Isabelle lives in her head, Tyler does so as well, only his perception of the people and the world around him is through the muffle of a depression so dense he doesn't realize he's living within a fog. Flashbacks reveal how Tyler has been in contrast to how he is now, and how he learns to accept the limitations of his previous perceptions of the world, which he once thought clear, transparent, and true. In the course of the novel, Tyler's previous surety is undermined and replaced with a new, mature faith based on personal interactions with individuals. In this way, Strout offers us a primer in how spirit triumphs over letter and how empathy outweighs voiced commitment to abstract faith. The failings that Tyler must learn to accept in himself will help him to understand world events as necessarily imperfect actions enacted by equally fallible humans.

We learn that early in his career as a minister, Tyler had been in his element, believing "he was living and loving as God had chosen

him to do. And there were times, as he walked down the steps of a
classroom building, and felt the sharp, cold winter air stab into his
nostrils, that The Feeling would come to him. Life, he would think.
How mysterious and magnificent! Such abundance! With all his
heart he praised God. His own specific history was unfolding" (159).
He trusts wholeheartedly in God's providence and his own vocation,
but he will eventually come to terms with his inability to save his
wife and to alleviate her suffering. A likable bear of a man, Tyler
had been an innocent in spite of his service in World War II, a man
who saw people (including himself) as inherently good. His faith in
God is evident in his sermons; when he preaches, for example, "a
light seemed to flicker across his features [as he proclaimed] 'Let us
adore the snow-covered trees on the hills, the stone walls built by
strong men, the chickadees who brave the winters, and the robins
who return in spring. Let us give thanks. Let us adore him, Christ
our Lord'" (56–57). The young minister's aphorisms are more erudite
than Isabelle's, but they serve the same purpose: to offer structure
to his life and reassurance in his perception of events. Even when
his young wife falls ill, "Tyler prayed. Always he ended, 'Thy will
be done'" (92), trusting in God. After learning Lauren has cancer,
Tyler still believes "in the power of prayer . . . because his prayers felt
strong and right, like a swimmer who has trained for years and feels
safe in the water that buoys him up. Tyler loved God very much, and
God would naturally know that. Tyler loved Lauren, and God would
know that, too" (92).

Tyler had been an excellent student of the ministry, believing he
had been called to and belonged in the pulpit, but when the novel
starts, he feels divorced from God, adrift, not knowing how to re-
gain his faith. To survive, he tells himself, "keep moving":

And keep an eye out for God. Who was, if you cared for
the Psalms, as Tyler did, looking right now from heaven,
beholding all the sons of men, considering all their works.
But what Tyler longed for was to have The Feeling arrive;
when every flicker of light that touched the dipping branches
of a weeping willow, every breath of breeze that bent the

grass toward the row of apple trees, every shower of yellow ginkgo leaves dropping to the ground with such direct and tender sweetness, would fill the minister with profound and irreducible knowledge that God was right there. (15)

This despair frightens Tyler. Strout's lyrical language evokes prayer, but Tyler's inability to see the beauty in front of him shows to what lengths he has fallen. His depression manifests itself in a laconic disentanglement from the world around him that contradicts his onetime fully embodied lived experience, as he fails to see the beauty of a sunset: "what a shame for [him], who, in different circumstances, taking a moment to glance at the sky, might have thought, *Yes, the heavens declare the glory of God, and the firmament sheweth his handywork*" (29). As a minister who takes his calling seriously, Tyler wants to tend to his flock, but he finds himself unequipped to meet the emotional needs of many of his congregants, particularly the more energy-sapping ones. Doris Austin, the church's organist, is a prime example. His indifference to her plight astonishes her. He is, simply, oblivious, in no small part because "he felt debilitated by weariness" (38). Tyler is unaware of how depressed and angry he is—and so, out of touch with his own feelings, he grows increasingly frustrated and lost. We see confusion in the momentary lapse Strout allows him when considering his daughter. After the school's call, he thinks fleetingly that Katie is his "*cross to bear*—words that shot through his mind now, and made him grimace, for she was not his cross to bear. She was his gift from God" (10). Of course, Katherine is both and neither for Tyler, who uses these concepts to understand his complex feelings for his daughter. If Tyler has a hard time acknowledging this ambivalence, Strout does not.

Tyler's early life complemented his spiritual training. At home, he learned to be compassionate, to "think of the other man first" from his father, and his lessons in Scripture cemented this perspective. Tyler's spiritual study confirmed his sense of reverence for the world. But at the novel's start, he is lost in what St. John of the Cross calls the dark night of the soul, trying vainly to rely on the teachings of Catholic mystics to help him see grace: "There was a fear the man lived with, a dark cave inside him: that he might not feel The Feeling again. That the exhilarating moments of transcendence had merely been the product of a youthful—and perhaps not even manly—form of hysteria, the kind that, taken to an extreme, could arguably produce the Catholic Saint Thérèse of Lisieux, who had died while still a young girl, and whose innocence surpassed him by the length and width of heaven" (15). If his early experiences had confirmed Tyler's belief in the goodness of the world, God's presence, and his own trajectory, the crisis of Lauren's death has left him lost, wandering literally and metaphorically the roads of Maine and his own life.

Tyler's deceased wife haunts their farmhouse and his memory. Lauren Slatin Caskey, her maiden name slyly evoking her promiscuous past and dubious fidelity, is revealed in flashbacks. A beautiful, lively extrovert from a wealthy Massachusetts family, she was never fully accepted by Tyler's mother or his congregation. When Tyler interviewed for the position of minister and the West Annett congregation met Lauren, they were uncomfortable with her: she "had seemed too aware of her looks, in a manner unbecoming to a minister's wife" (52). They didn't know quite what to do with Lauren, who was "lovely, her bright hair visible above the fur collar of her beige woolen coat, lovely as she stood beside her husband on the church steps, her cheeks glowing in the winter sunlight. Even if some of this loveliness was the result of carefully applied makeup and expensive, well-fitting clothes" (59). If they allowed Lauren her beauty (perhaps because they could not deny it), they did so with the meanness of the jealous, or, perhaps, more generously, the misunderstanding. The Caskeys settled into life in West Annett, yet Lauren remained an enigmatic sore spot in the community: she, "it was said, must have been spending a great deal of time in front of the mirror, because she certainly didn't seem to be spending a great deal of time anywhere else" (59). Beautiful Lauren was not interested in these women; she (correctly) felt judged by them. But she was extremely lonely until she befriended the young mother Carol Meadows. Striking and vivacious Lauren revealed to her friend as best she could that she was bored, lonely, sad, and suffering from what Betty Friedan would come to call "the problem that has no name."

Motherhood did not reconcile Lauren to the community: "There was something—you couldn't put your finger on it exactly, but they continued to provoke a reaction, this mother and her little girl. The mother wasn't friendly enough, that was part of it. As much as Lauren Caskey would beam and smile and shake hands in the vestibule after the service, she had a certain carelessness about her, as though she had no interest in how other people lived, here in their small town" (60). The parishioners were quick to feel slighted by Lauren, when what they perceived as indifference might simply have been depression or introversion. The same distance and discomfort was transferred onto Tyler and Katherine after Lauren died.[2] Neither West Annett nor any of Strout's small-town communities is particularly welcoming.

Charlie Austin, Doris's husband and deacon in the church, claimed he saw in Lauren a "tart," the kind of woman who "could look you right in your eyes and [convey] she liked to get laid" (203). We never learn exactly what plagued Lauren, though she told her friend Carol that before she married, she had multiple sexual partners. And after she died, Tyler found the attic filled with clothes, some with price tags still on them. The wardrobe, out of place in West Annett, underscores how little Tyler understood his wife. The couple's arguments over money suggest she might have bought the clothes, but Strout also raises the possibility that Lauren might have stolen them. Though we don't witness Lauren stealing (and we are never in her head the way we are in other characters'), Carol noticed that small objects disappeared after Lauren visited, including a container of blush and a scarf. Presumably Lauren stole these symbols of femininity because it was her sex appeal that distinguished her; she derived a particular power from her sexuality and from being seen.[3] When Carol offered her a child's ring, Lauren at first refused the gift (for Katherine) and then stashed it away secretly, not giving it to her daughter, as if it was the private acts of taking and hoarding that gave her pleasure, not the objects themselves.

Tyler adored his wife: "Lauren was all light. [He] had never met anyone from whom such light shone" (153), while others, like the women of the Ladies' Aid, were put off by her charisma, or associated it with promiscuity, as her sister and Charlie did. If Tyler saw only light, Carol recognized a sadness beneath Lauren's shiny surface. Unsettling moments arise in flashbacks that make Tyler vaguely uneasy but don't detract from Lauren's magnetism. For example, when he met her family, he was distressed by Mr. Slatin's using "his fingers to eat the lamb chops" (154) and the cursing that came to all of them so easily. At one point before they married, Tyler turned "to see Mr. Slatin's eyes following [his daughter's] hips as she walked with her mother across the room" (157). Perhaps Tyler did not observe Mr. Slatin's gaze accurately, but Lauren hinted at sexual abuse; she told her husband that a family friend was the "first to complain about [him and say] that our house wasn't a nice one for girls to come to. . . . Because Daddy would give us baths" (161). When Tyler asked her to clarify, she fell into silence, unwilling or perhaps unable to continue.

She was more forthcoming with Carol. Though the reader is privy to these moments and can piece them together to try to understand Lauren more coherently, Tyler was not. Lauren told her friend, "My father gives me the creeps and my sister hates me. And my mother is a little bit of an idiot" (176). We do know that Lauren and her family were troubled. In spite of the advantages of wealth, education, and class, they were hostile and cruel to one another. And with the allusions to global tragedies—segregation, concentration camps, and genocides—Strout deftly shows how the personal and the political are related. That is, the private cruelties inflicted at home can lead to problems later in life and to cruelties on a larger scale.[4]

Tyler was dismayed by Lauren's compulsive shopping, not realizing that she did so not only because she was bored and lonely, but also because she was deeply depressed, by current circumstances and perhaps by a history that she could not articulate. While we know now that compulsive behavior often signals unresolved trauma,[5] that kleptomania can function to empower someone from whom something has been stolen and can serve to manifest a taboo act long repressed, or function as a sad cry for help, Tyler did not recognize Lauren's melancholia; he saw only its effects: how Lauren complained and how "they seemed always low on gas . . . and that she bought things more and more" (178). Yet the young minister sensed that "something was gone," and so "uneasiness sat at the table with them, got into bed with them (she no longer wanted him to touch her breasts during lovemaking), uneasiness was there in the morning, when he stood in the bathroom and shaved" (179). Later, Carol felt a similar sensation when she couldn't find a scarf after Lauren had visited her, "a real uneasiness coming over her" (183).

The unease is a metaphor for Lauren's cancer, but that corruption may be metaphorical as well as literal. Tyler's faith led him to believe that his wife would live and left him ill-prepared for the emotional ravages of the disease: "Lauren turned away at the sight of him, saying things he would never forget. Her parents came and she told them to go away. She told his mother to stay out of the room. He sat by her bed, and when she rested, his gratitude was immense, but when she woke and started picking at the bedclothes, it was agony. She seemed to get better; she could sit up again, and speak. Her fierce words to him: *You're such a coward, you know*" (187). They kept secret the pain Lauren suffered and the verbal abuse she unleashed on her husband. The people of West Annett had no idea how difficult the daily lives of the Caskeys were, how their beloved minister was being tested by the pain of his wife's suffering.

From the safe distance of their own homes, the women of the Ladies' Aid began to feel sorry for this woman they once spurned: "Soon, women in West Annett who had not wept in years stood in their kitchens weeping. That Lauren Caskey was a person who had held herself apart was forgotten or forgiven. Her fate seemed to provide a luxury of emotion that had been held in check for some time" (91). This outpouring of grief was different than compassion, though, because it didn't comfort the ostensible object but only the women's own egos. Unlike Tyler's sympathy for his flock, the

women's pity was self-indulgent. The selfishness of their feelings became clear when they didn't try to help Tyler or Katherine after
Lauren's death. To be kind to them, perhaps their reserve stemmed
from their not knowing how to approach the widower.

Katherine has become nearly mute since her mother died, and
in this way she literalizes the silence in *Amy and Isabelle*. Unaware
of the sadness her mutism signals, the minister feels close to his
daughter, although he finds her behavior puzzling. After he hears
she has said, "I hate God" in her Sunday school class, Tyler asks
himself, "What did people know about their children? When he
thought of the quiet, obedient Katherine at home, and then pic-
tured her screaming at school, saying, 'I hate God,' in kinderkirk,
this discrepancy—his own knowledge of the child, and the way
others might see her—frightened him, as though when Katherine
left the house she fell through the ice into some dark water where
he could barely see her" (110). That inability of parents to know
and to save their children is Isabelle's struggle as well as Tyler's.
Later we see Olive Kitteridge and Lucy Barton face similar situations. Katherine is an enigma, but unlike Lauren, she is physically
present for Tyler. In some ways Tyler must learn that his wife, too,
although he thought he knew her, is and will always remain a mystery to him—but that the mother and daughter's very mysteries do
not preclude him from loving them. The novel suggests, then, that
mature love can occur when one recognizes that that imperfect,
authentic love is more valuable than idealized love (for another
person or for God).

Strout offers the reader a more multifaceted look at Katie than
Tyler can have by including scenes in which he is not present. Her
characterization there is touching and unusual. When her mother is
ill, the little girl's vulnerability is rendered poignantly and perceptively: "'I want to see Mommy,' Katherine said. Oh, she was trying
not to cry, but her chin wobbled. 'Mommy's sick right now.' 'But
she'll wonder where I am,' the child pleaded, crying now" (95). Katherine's fragility manifests itself physically. Though she stops speaking, her shaking shows her feelings when words fail her. Tyler offers

the prickly child the love and compassion she needs, but her teachers do not. Her acting out—contentious or crying in class, silent at home—is a sign of distress paralleling her mother's kleptomania. And so her father and her teachers are both somewhat correct: Katie has suffered a trauma—but while her teachers attempt to understand the child clinically, Tyler (eventually) comes to realize she is as grief-stricken as he is, and that treating her gently will be crucial to helping her move forward. She is a child who has lost her mother, after all, and so, like her father, she must find a way to survive in a world where most people cannot empathize with her suffering. When she and her Sunday school classmates have to "say the Lord's Prayer with their heads bowed and their eyes closed . . . Katherine did not close her eyes. She looked at her red rubber boots and, in the middle of the prayer, Katherine said calmly and quietly, 'I hate God'" (58–59). The child's quiet utterance is funny, and if it's a cry for attention—debatable—the women's histrionic reaction is out of all proportion to the incident (as is Tyler's imaginative rendering of the scene).

But even so, Katherine does feel angry and guilty. Her simple, succinct declaration is a sign of frustration and sadness. She lacks her father's faith because she has not had her father's experience. She is a little girl who has lost her mother (and effectively her sister, since Jeannie now lives with their grandmother). And she does feel guilty, but she doesn't believe she murdered her mother, the way psychologist Rhonda Skillings claims, because she doesn't understand that her mother has died. Each time she returns home, Katherine thinks she'll see her mother again. With such daily disappointments, it's no wonder the child is shattered. And when she overhears fragments of adult conversations, Katherine fears her father will be literally pilloried. Conflating her Sunday school lessons about early Christian martyrs with Connie Hatch's childhood stories of being locked in the outhouse and early colonial punishment, she runs to her father sobbing, "I did it. . . . I did it, Daddy. It was me, it was me. I didn't mean to" (265), referring not to her mother's death but to telling a story about him. The exchange between father and daughter stays private but sets the stage for Tyler's breakdown in front of the congregation.[6] Katherine has shown him vulnerability, unconsciously modeling how he, too, can be vulnerable, be forgiven, and still be loved.

Connie Hatch does the same. Like Tyler's wife and daughter, the woman is a mystery to the minister. Hired by the congregation to help tend the Caskey family during and after Lauren's illness, Connie is an outsider, and, again, like Lauren and Katie, ostracized by the women of West Annett. But unlike his parishioners, who Tyler suspects do not genuinely care for him or his family, Connie appears to offer a kindred sympathy to the Caskeys. After returning home from the meeting with Katherine's teacher, he encounters Connie, and

> had one of those surprising moments that occur sometimes, when there's a fleeting sense of recognition, when, in less than half a second, there's the sense of having glimpsed the other's soul, some shred of real agreement being shared. This is what happened to the minister on that autumn evening, the walls of the living room now a dull, flat pink. *It's a sad world,* the housekeeper's eyes seemed to say. *And I'm sorry.*
>
> The minister's eyes said, *It is a sad world, isn't it. I'm sorry, too.* (30)

If Tyler believes they share an unspoken bond, Connie does as well. She thinks he sees her in ways no one ever has before.[7] When Tyler says to her, "Tell me about yourself" (78), she is befuddled because she "couldn't recall anybody ever saying, 'Tell me about yourself.' She didn't know what to tell. In her mind, she was a faint pencil line on a piece of paper; everyone else was drawn in ink, some—like the minister—with a firm Magic Marker" (78). Both Tyler and Connie believe they share a bond, and in spite of occupying similar positions in West Annett, they project onto each other a magical, mutual sympathy.

Like so many of Strout's characters, Connie lives much of her life in her head. When Tyler offers her more hours of work, she imagines taking care of his girls, Katherine liking her, and speaking to her dead brother of this possible future. Connie's interiority is not just pleasant daydreams, however; she is also haunted by her brother, remembering their troubled childhood, imagining his experiences in the Pacific, and recalling her own time working at "The Farm," a nursing home. After she tells Tyler how her sister had an affair and an abortion, she worries, "I come from a family of sinners," and his sympathetic response is "Oh, Connie. . . . We all do" (132). If his response is a blanket pastoral aphorism, Connie takes it more personally, for she carries a heavier burden than just her family legacy.

While she worked at "The Farm," she tells Tyler, she was terribly distressed by the paralyzed and lonely elderly. And so, speaking of one of her charges, Connie is moved to end her suffering:

> Couldn't stand to think of her going on that way. No one ever came to see her; she couldn't talk or complain—that's how it was with the feeders. And Dorothy Aldercott had two daughters. I looked in her folder. Never came to see her. So that was a pathetic woman. . . .
>
> . . . One of the cooks said one day—he'd been there for years—he said they could be put out of their misery in two seconds just by overfeeding them. . . . So I kept spooning it into her mouth one day, and she kept looking at me with those eyes, and I touched her face nicely, and said, "It's okay, Dorothy," because I loved her right then, Tyler. . . . It's intimate . . . And then—she was gone. The second one, Madge Lubeneaux, she struggled a bit, and that made me feel funny, so I never did it again. (214)

Connie does not regret what she did; she believes she was ending the women's pain. But Tyler is horrified by her actions and by the thought he might be like her. For when Lauren was so sick and angry, shouting and cursing in pain, he left a bottle of pills by her bedside, believing that she would take them. When he hears Connie's revelation, he is forced to see that his act was more cowardly than the housekeeper's. Unlike Connie, he did not end Lauren's suffering, even though he sees his leaving the bottle of pills for Lauren, assuming she will take them, as "their last act of intimacy" (285).[8] Tyler is not forced to confront his actions until he hears Connie's confession. Strout is understated in her description, leaving it for the reader to determine Tyler's guilt or responsibility for Lauren's suffering and death. Tyler's letting Lauren die alone may have been an act of mercy or an act of selfishness.

He is baffled by Connie's admission, and rather than comforting her, he is lost in his own musings, more concerned about what their friendship reveals about himself than about the woman in front of him:

> When he remembered the comfort he had received from
> her presence in this house—why, it made his soul shrink in
> a kind of sickness. When he remembered that first autumn
> afternoon, returning home after the conference about
> Katherine at school, he wondered now what it was he had
> seen when he'd looked into Connie's green eyes. What was
> that look of recognition?
>
> Tyler sat partway up, his elbows pressed into the couch.
> Could it have been some dark camaraderie? As though they
> were joined by a private, deliberate, acquaintanceship with
> death? Was *that* what had been seen in their glance that
> day? (225)

At the moment of her confession, Tyler retreats into himself. He has not yet seen that Connie needs his help, that Lauren needed it, and that Katherine will need it as she grows up. He has yet to learn to genuinely assuage the suffering of someone else—not in a way that is convenient for him but in the way the sufferer needs. After Connie confesses to Tyler, at his suggestion she turns herself in to the police. Though Tyler visits her in jail, Connie is more isolated than ever. Indeed, when the women of West Annett find out why Connie is in prison, they fail to understand her motivations. Connie says she loves her patients when she overfeeds them, but Rhonda, Jane, and Allison are led by schadenfreude. In spite of her doctorate in psychology, Rhonda concludes the act is "absolutely gruesome. And so angry! An angry thing to do." Jane and Allison concur; their heartlessness is revealed in their derisive gossip: "'Do you need a doctorate in psychology to know that killing someone is an angry thing to do?' The two women laughed until tears came to their eyes" (254). They could not be any further away from Connie. And yet. And yet, while Connie may be motivated by love, she might also be motivated by a profound unarticulated cry for help and against the injustices and suffering of the world. Unlike Rhonda, Allison, and Jane, Tyler and Connie are not cruel and indifferent; they do not traffic in the suffering or pain of others.

The Dickensian echoes of the names Allison Chase and Rhonda Skillings hint at the troubles these women will present to Tyler and Connie. Gathering for morning coffee "gave the women something to look forward to, especially now that the days were shorter and darker, and the boredom of changing sheets or cleaning a bathroom could sometimes mushroom into a private despair before noontime even arrived" (85). Their proximity to melancholy does not inspire compassion; they are eager to explore "the details of Katherine . . . with some relish" (85). The acerbic Ora Kendall, the predecessor to Strout's most famous creation and a member of the guild, refers to the Ladies' Aid as "that little coven of witches," warning Tyler that the group "is having a fight, a revolution to match Cuba's" (131). The Ladies' Aid indeed.

If the women are without compassion for Connie, Lauren, or Katherine, Strout is not without compassion for her creations. As Katherine's young teacher prepares to meet Tyler, she admires her "red knit dress because of the way it showed off her figure" and rehearses "in front of the mirror, trying on expressions of kind-hearted, authoritative patience. She'd remembered to wear the little silver cross around her neck, so the man could see she was religious" (31). Such asides recall Austen. Yet these women, too, Strout reveals, are deeply unhappy. Though self-satisfied with her progress on life's trajectory, still "sometimes, like this morning, [Allison] had a momentary shiver of some irretrievable loss, and even as the principal,

Mr. Waterbury, raised a cheerful hand and she waved back, she longed, in some deep part of her, to bury herself in a grown-up's lap" (133). This longing for comfort, particularly the comfort of a parent, runs throughout the book. A moment later, Allison fails to see that Katie's scorn is a sign of her attempt to ward off sadness. Teacher and student, like so many of Strout's characters, long to be comforted. If Allison seems petty and cruel, she is wounded as well.

In spite of occupying typically feminine spheres—homemaking and teaching—Rhonda, Jane, Mary, and Allison lack compassion. However, when Tyler breaks down in front of the congregation and they bear witness to his suffering, they do—to a certain extent—learn what they have denied him, his family, and themselves. Not until then do they understand how much pain he is in. After Tyler stumbles, unable to continue the service, Mary realizes, "He was a man grieving, and she was ashamed at the kind of pleasure she had experienced in excoriating him to her friends and husband" (278).

Tyler's unhappiness culminates when he attempts to give a sermon and is so enraged by his congregation's lack of compassion and charity that he simply cannot speak. "A tear filled his right eye. He felt it grow, slip down his face. From both eyes now, tears came over his cheeks as he stood there. He wept, and wept, his shoulders shaking slightly. He did not hide his face; it did not occur to him to do so. He felt only the wet splash from his eyes, blurring the faces before him. Every few moments, he held his hands forward, as though trying to say something" (272). At this moment of crisis, Tyler's body speaks in a way that he cannot (and in a similar way to how his daughter's did earlier). Finally, it is Doris, previously so angry at him, and her husband Charlie, who had shown such hostility to Tyler, who offer him compassion and grace, in the wordless acts of playing "Abide with Me" and "taking his arm, helping him through the chancel's door, helping him down the few steps" (272). Charlie and Doris suffer and sin, but here they are kind. Arguably, Charlie Austin is the saddest character in the novel, the most damaged man in town. Though he loves his children, he is also disgusted by his son: "That he had reproduced any part of himself seemed to

Charlie a mistake of almost biblical proportions. That this repro-
duction should present itself in such big-eared, pale-skinned innocence brought a searing pain to Charlie's troubled stomach. . . .
He closed his eyes, and an image came to mind: walking up behind
his boy, wrapping an arm around his skinny body, pressing his own
cheek against the boy's, saying quietly, 'You are good, and you are
loved. And for your own sad sake I wish you hadn't been born'" (67).
His self-loathing is manifest in his hostility toward his child. That
it's Charlie, lost, damaged, and hateful, who becomes the vehicle
for love, forgiveness, and healing is important. That forgiveness is
crucial to Strout's project and to Tyler Caskey's as well. Mercy does
not come at the hands of an idealized feminine figure, but at the
hands of an angry and embittered, possibly abusive man. Tyler will
learn to realize that life is neither simple nor Manichaean—there
is a complexity to the world, to the community, that speaks to the
beautiful imperfections of the human comedy. Accepting Charlie's
offer expresses Tyler's humility. He is as vulnerable as he has ever
been. But from a position of devastation, a position of uncertainty,
he can grow. Tyler must allow himself to feel, to be hurt, and then
to forgive those who hurt him. That position of forgiveness is where
his spiritual authority will eventually come from.

His public breakdown forces Tyler to look at himself and his
history with Lauren, to step out of the fog that has surrounded him.
He admits to himself that his own experiences cannot be reconciled.
"The complexities of this, and of Connie and what she said she'd
done, seemed more than he could understand, and he suspected he
would never understand, and that he would have to accept this"
(285). Tyler's acceptance of the limitations of knowing is important
here. He realizes finally he can only know certain versions of an
experience that transcends human understanding. We could build
on Jane Thrailkill's insights and say that in Tyler's experience, his
coming to terms with his limitations, *Abide with Me* "makes the case
for a constructionist making-up, for the necessary creation of stories, and the equally necessary methods of reflection, calibration,
and revision. It also offers a critique of a dogmatic account of truth,

one that is immune to the insights provided by narrative wisdom, scientific integrity, and collective oversight" ("Ian McEwan," 197). Tyler must give up his previously untested religiosity and step into the maturity of taking a leap of faith—of not knowing and yet moving ahead—with his congregation and what remains of his family. When Tyler wrestles with his own actions and approaches his mentor in the ministry, George utters a phrase we see in many of Strout's works: "We love imperfectly, Tyler. We all do. Even Jesus wrestled with that. But I think—I think the ability to receive love is as important as the ability to give it. It's one and the same, really" (285). George then advises Tyler, "I suspect the most we can hope for, and it's no small hope, is that we never give up, that we never stop giving ourselves permission to try to love and receive love" (285). Strout offers us nothing less than a radical reconceptualizing of love, which, in Rita Felski's words, is "about allowing oneself to be reoriented by others" (149). Ron Charles agrees, noting that "dark as much of this beautiful novel is, there's finally healing here, and as Tyler should have known, it comes not from strength and self-sufficiency, but from accepting the inexplicable love of others."

George's approach to love and community is magnanimous; it's expansive, not limited by one set of beliefs or structures. But we can use tenets of certain structures to help us understand the world. After all, psychologist Rhonda is partially right: both Tyler and Katherine feel guilty, just not for the reasons she identifies. It is not Tyler's unconscious hostility toward his mother that he regrets, but his leaving his wife alone at her death. He loves as imperfectly as any of us do. Tyler moves from the prelapsarian innocence of his early marriage to an awareness of his own failings. Some might turn to Freud; others might turn to Scripture; but Strout suggests that compassion, human conversation, an openness to others that accesses our own vulnerability, is what will help us the most. She leaves unanswered whether Connie Hatch's killings were an act of mercy or an act of evil. And, that, Strout says in her afterword, is part of her job as a writer: "We are often at sea with questions of right and wrong. At sea seems to me an honest place to be. My job as a storyteller is not to supply any answers, but to raise the questions in a way the reader may not have seen before" (298). She witnesses and tells; she does not cast judgment. This, like the rendering of the actions of Isabelle or Amy, allows readers room to empathize and to relate. Strout wants to discomfit us; she doesn't let her reader sit comforted in an easy narrative but allows a kind of reckoning, a puzzling out. If we are lost, we are not alone in our confusion.

Tyler, Allison, Doris, and Charlie learn to feel in the novel, and in some ways they have to unlearn the rugged individualism they had internalized. They must learn to soften, to take cues not from the harsh landscape or taciturn people around them but from their own need. They are of small-town Maine, and, as we saw in *Amy and Isabelle*, and as we'll see in Strout's next two books, that locale shapes characters both physically and emotionally. After showing how children "were not allowed Novocain when having their cavities drilled" because "life was a struggle [and] character [could be] honed every step of the way" (56), Strout goes on to describe how setting shapes her characters' lives.

> Life *was* a struggle. There was, up in West Annett, thick ice
> that needed to be chipped away all winter long from door-
> steps and windshields, chains to be put on tires so the cars
> could crawl slowly over snow-packed roads just to get to the
> grocery store. Often families heated only one or two rooms
> during the winter months; furnaces broke, wood-burning
> stoves needed logs brought in from the barn, or up through
> a cellar door. Most homes were not within easy walking
> distance of one another, and the isolation was hard on the old
> folks, mothers with small children—hard on everyone, really.
> People went to church not so much because they believed
> they should but because it gave them a chance to get out of
> the house, dress nicely, pick up a bit of local news. (56)

Strout depicts the isolation again years later in "Snow-Blind" in *Anything Is Possible*. That isolation can lead either to compassion or to indifference. But it's never irrelevant.

After Tyler's breakdown on the chancel, perhaps because of that psychic and physical isolation, "uneasiness took hold of many" (277). The congregation is vaguely aware of how they have contributed to Tyler's suffering: "It was as though a death had occurred that could not be absorbed, and a New England reticence took hold, a sense of respectful silence—mixed with some level of guilt—regarding what had been witnessed" (277). The reckoning has come not just for Tyler but for his parish as well, and they are rattled, thrown by it, forced to see their meanness, and, then, eventually, that the way to endure in the community is through mercy and compassion. Tyler must learn to forgive them, and they must learn to forgive Tyler, in some ways to live with more warmth than the landscape would suggest. Loving is not only romantic or filial; here it's *agape*, the love a minister must learn for his congregants and what they must learn as well, a mature acceptance and a deliberate decision to move forward together, aware of each other's weaknesses and vulnerabilities.

Tyler eventually comes to realize that "what he had experienced the day he stood weeping before his congregation . . . was The Feeling. This surprised him. It was very different from the times before, but that's what it had been, The Feeling" (293). And so Tyler realizes that God is manifest in ways he hadn't realized before, that epiphanies might not always be wondrous and joyous, but that God's grace may occur in the acts of kindness between fallen individuals.

It is in Tyler's compassion, his concern for his parishioners even as he faces his own grave struggles, that we see one of Strout's enduring legacies—that through the sharing of stories (as Strout puts it in her note to the novel) "we have a chance to see something about ourselves and others that maybe we knew, but didn't know we knew. We can wonder for a moment if, for all our separate histories, we are not more alike than different."[9] Tyler and Charlie perform the kind of ethics of care described by Carol Gilligan, and in Strout's portrayal of this work, caring for those who have been traumatized by intimate and global violence, she shows her readers not only the limitations of a 1950s postwar American exclusionary sensibility but ironically also a way toward a more inclusive compassion, even if—given the time it occurs—it's in a context of masculinity and communal responsibility. As Bessel van der Kolk tells us, "denial of the consequences of trauma can wreak havoc with the social fabric of society. The refusal to face the damage caused by the war and the intolerance of 'weakness' played an important role in the rise of fascism in the 1930s. . . . This cascade of humiliation of the powerless set the stage for the ultimate debasement of human rights under the Nazi regime: the moral justification for the strong to vanquish the inferior" (187). We ignore individual trauma and suffering at our communal peril.

At the novel's very end, Tyler and Katherine leave their home to start a new one in West Annett. This movement is an embrace of the possible, a willingness to risk and to love. Tyler will endure after he has done that which he couldn't imagine. His faith is no longer simply about a chosen path but embraces the shadows as well. And his most important relationship will be with this young girl who needs her father, who will remain mysterious, but who nevertheless will be walking with him in a new world not solely of their making or their imagining.

Taken on its own, *Abide with Me* seems a departure from *Amy and Isabelle* in terms of content, character, gender, and focus, and it is clear Strout is experimenting here, testing her limits and shifting her subject. When we look at the novel in relation to her other books, though, we can see it in terms of an expansion, of her bringing her consideration of empathy to new muses, as an attempt to include men more fully in her consideration, and her attempt to forge bridges to people in other times.

3 Finding Her Voice in *Olive Kitteridge*

IN *OLIVE KITTERIDGE* (2008), STROUT EXPLORES various psychological responses to a range of frailties. The entire short story cycle describes the effects of myriad personal, often unspoken traumas afflicting the characters, allowing readers to assume a greater empathy for all of them.[1] This, then—in terms of the development of reader empathy—builds on the project begun in her first two books. Nearly all of the thirteen stories take place in the small town of Crosby, Maine, and feature the eponymous abrasive, direct, and suffering heroine. Given the geographic specificity, Helena Kadmos tells us the book "could be read within the longstanding tradition of what Sandra Zabarell calls 'narrative of community'" (41). Crosby's dramas—the quotidian familial tragedies that affect contemporary Americans who desire a meaningful existence—are on a small scale. The most serious dilemmas facing the characters are not grand epic battles (though there are passing references to contemporary events, including 9/11 and the Abu Ghraib horror), but once again the painful cruelties inflicted on and by those we love. Hurt and loss affect each of the characters. Moments highlighting natural beauty are still evident, as is Strout's characteristic understated humor. In *Olive Kitteridge*, Strout homes in on the foibles and indignities of growing old gently and tenderly, as she moves from the historic to the contemporary and from the conventional novel form to a short story cycle, her Crosby a reinvention in style and structure of Sherwood Anderson's *Winesburg, Ohio*, and Sarah Orne Jewett's Dunnet Landing.[2] The fragmentation of *Olive Kitteridge* emphasizes the inability to objectively understand one's own history, what Donna Haraway terms "the privilege of partial perspective," a stylistic and narrative concern Strout explores at greater length in her later works.[3]

A best seller, Pulitzer Prize winner, and inspiration for an HBO miniseries starring Frances McDormand, *Olive Kitteridge* has sold more than one million copies and has also had its share of critics. Craig Morgan Teicher astutely observes, "As Strout shows us Crosby bit by bit, Olive ultimately becomes a testament to the risks and rewards of old-fashioned self-reliance—her rigid personality allows her to withstand immeasurable losses, but leaves her lonelier than most" (32). Other readers have been put off by Olive's directness. Perhaps mixed reactions are not surprising given the sometimes frustrating eponymous heroine whose first uttered words describing her husband's new assistant, "Mousy.... Looks just like a mouse.... No one's cute who can't stand up straight" (5), reveal as much about the speaker as the ostensible subject. Rarely shy about offering her own opinion, Olive calls out the world, her neighbors, and her family on what she perceives as their shortcomings. If this bluntness endears her to some readers, it alienates others. Strout has said that as she was writing the stories, she realized that "[Olive's] an awful lot to take. I need to hold her back and then I remember thinking . . . no, let her go; let her be Olive, and that was an enormous moment for me because I realized, 'Okay, sorry, readers, we're going to have to go with her'" (Book Passages). That act of alienation is one that Strout explores repeatedly and in different ways throughout this book. Like the small town where most of the stories take place, Strout offers her readers an uneasy intimacy that paradoxically encourages and undermines security, particularly one's security in her knowledge of the world.

In this chapter, which builds on an earlier article that appeared in *Short Story*, I explore how Strout disorients her characters and her reader, the effects of this disorientation, its implications, and the faith acts that can arise from these unsettling moments. I see an act of faith as requiring an initial instability, for it's only from the position of not knowing the ground under one's feet that one can step forward into the unknown, with trust rather than with certainty. Faith is about risk-taking, about moving ahead without a guaranteed outcome. Here, as in *Amy and Isabelle* and *Abide with Me*, Strout's characters reckon with their past, recognize the hurts that afflicted them when they were young and that they inflicted on others, and then choose to live blindly (as they unknowingly did previously), to succumb to despair, or to forgive and to accept their own and others' limitations and forge ahead. To varying degrees her characters recognize the importance of this self-aware act of faith, though Strout's vision is directed not at them but at the reader.

As Lauren Slatin Caskey's death haunts *Abide with Me*, the shadows of past violence and suicide loom in *Olive Kitteridge* as well. Coming face to face with this recognition of how brutality and loss permeate our lives is crucial to this book and is played out directly in "A Different Road." But usually the characters address the threat of violence and the depression that ensues more elliptically. If "resilience" has received a great deal of attention recently, "endurance" seems better suited to characterize the emotional state of these Mainers.[4] They have survived difficult childhoods, bitter disappointments, devastating betrayals, and emotional and physical violence. For most of their lives, the characters live with these experiences buried just under the surface, but within the stories presented they are forced to confront them. In the pages that follow, I argue that this book is about confronting one's memory or history. Rather than confirming one's position in the world, the articulation of memories disrupts one's perception of events: over and over again, what a character thought she knew is called into question. Throughout the short story cycle, characters misremember, misunderstand, and misconstrue events; drawing on Svetlana Boym's *The Future of Nostalgia* and Nicolas Abraham and Maria Torok's *The Shell and the Kernel*, I examine how the process of remembering disorients the characters within and the reader of *Olive Kitteridge*. And yet such a disruption is not necessarily negative; when the ground under one's feet is unsteady, one can recognize one's vulnerabilities and step into the unknown in an act of courage. I also contend that the genre of this book, the short story cycle, in its destabilizing of narrative convention, requires another leap of faith.[5]

In moving away from conventional narrative, Strout frees herself further. Letting go of traditional narrative arcs and trusting her own writing and intuition, Strout produces a remarkable tour de force. Within her short story cycle, Strout refines her nonlinear style, moving in between the characters' present and their past. The stories are set at different times and not arranged chronologically, so the reader remains perpetually off-balance, attempting to understand how the tales fit together under the unifying bridge that is Olive Kitteridge. Her married name itself is a portmanteau, the auditory echoes recalling "skitter" and "edge." Though Olive herself is large, solid, and ambling, often moving slowly and deliberately through the world, the very edges between depression and contentment, life and death, past and present, or present and future are ones that most of the characters find themselves negotiating in the course of the collection. To "skitter" also means to skim lightly along boundaries, and we can interpret this metaphorically as well as literally in this book. Olive herself figures in some of the stories prominently, and in others she's on the periphery. The title gives a lie that the book will be unified and/or consistently told from one point of view.[6] But Olive plays different roles in different stories—for example, she is the wife of the subject of one, the former teacher of the

subject of another, a neighbor in one, a client in another—and all of
the characters see Olive differently. We might use the metaphor of
a prism; whoever Olive is is seen through the various facets of the
individuals whom the story centers on. Kadmos tells us that seeing
Olive in connection to others is very important, for the "interconnected stories open new ways of understanding women's relational
autonomy, and the importance of continuing relationships of independence and care" (39). And thus, this book too is an expansion
of Strout's exploration of relationships and self. Here the character
contains multiplicities, all brought forth by different relationships.
The very title of the book, which might suggest a unifying consciousness, ironically addresses the multiple and necessarily limited, fragmented perspectives through which each character sees the world.[7]

   Olive Kitteridge is unique in at least two ways that mutually in-
form and influence each other: its genre and its chronology. Though
the title suggests a linear trajectory, the book is composed of stories
that, like the unconscious, are not presented chronologically, but in
fragments. Even as the title points to a unifying personality, within
the work itself Strout consistently discomfits her characters' and
readers' sense of security, particularly their sense of personal history. Gently, Strout encourages her reader to untangle how the various stories and characters who populate them fit together in much
the same way that her characters try to comprehend their own lives,
and how their past has led them to their present. As the characters
realize the tenuity of their memories, so they realize the fragility of
their present. We see the awareness of the frailty if not downright
deceptiveness of recollection when Olive hears of her son's hostility
toward her; in Kevin Coulson when he returns home to kill himself
as his mother had decades earlier; and, most clearly, in the story "A
Different Road," as Olive attempts to comprehend her terrifying
encounter with gunmen. Rather than offering a seamless narrative,
the stories of *Olive Kitteridge* jar the characters (and the reader)
into the uncomfortable realization that the past does not offer the
secure foundation they thought, and so the present, and the future,
are also unstable.

I'm relying on the work of Svetlana Boym to understand the role of memory here. In *The Future of Nostalgia*, Boym explores ways we relate to and understand the past, both personally and collectively. Nostalgia, she contends, "is a longing for a home that no longer exists or has never existed" (xiii), "a yearning for a different time—the time of our childhood, the slower rhythm of our dreams" (xv). More subtly, she discriminates between "restorative nostalgia," which "attempts a transhistorical reconstruction of the lost home" (xviii), and "reflective nostalgia," which thrives in "the longing itself, and delays the homecoming—wistfully, ironically, desperately. . . . [It] dwells on the ambivalences of human longing and belonging" (xviii). If some of Strout's characters initially appear naive and sentimental, believing in a mythic restorative nostalgia, by the end of each story they are brought to a new, difficult, and unsettling understanding of their lives. Strout's telling itself—using multiple narrators, times, and settings—also works to disarm the reader. Like the characters, the reader, too, is engaged in a humbling process, becoming aware of her own desire for the narrative closure of restorative nostalgia and the impossibility of its fulfillment. Within the short story cycle, we learn that, "far from being reassuring, the retrieval of the past into the present is profoundly dislocating, disorienting. Bringing forth beginnings results in the loss of bearings" (Probyn 114). Throughout *Olive Kitteridge*, the community of Crosby, Maine, becomes aware of the tenuousness of our collective grasp on the past and the impossibility of predicting the future.

Strout's Maine, as we have seen in her other books, is no pastoral utopia, but is cold, brutal, and unforgiving. Its rocky cliffs are beautiful from a distance, and treacherous up close. Here we have a metaphor for the past's intrusion on the present. If we look at the past from a distance, thinking we remember accurately the tastes and smells of our childhood, Strout's characters who begin to consider their past more closely find themselves unhinged, realizing the past is not what they thought—and that they themselves are distanced from the people they once were.[8]

Thematically, many of the stories address coming to terms with the past, as survivors attempt to understand their complicated family legacies. Many feature epiphanies in which characters tragically learn the world around them and the relationships they thought they had are not how they perceived them. For example, marital infidelities haunt the collection as characters realize what they thought were solid marriages were facades. Only then do they come to find their marriages were different than they had previously considered, and their spouses, too, are not the individuals they assumed. In Boym's terms, the characters—and subsequently the reader—move from a "restorative nostalgia" that confirms one's sense of self to a "reflective nostalgia" that is "ironic, inconclusive, and fragmentary" (50). For example, in "Winter Concert," when Bob Houlton confesses an affair, his wife moves from a complacent contentedness, assuming all is right within her marriage, to feeling "her bowels ache and an age-old sliver of anguish . . . deep within her—how tired it made her, that particular, familiar pain; a weight that seemed to her to be like a thick, tarnished silver spreading through her, and then it rolled over everything, extinguishing Christmas lights, street lamps, fresh snow, the loveliness of all things—all gone" (136). While Bob both dismisses and apologizes for his behavior, Janie still feels "that her heart was broken again. Only now she was old, so it was different" (138).

Janie's emotional pain is so intense it manifests itself physically, a transition we will see again and again throughout Strout's work, as she emphasizes the embodied experience of living. Even though she suffers sharp despair and regret, Janie moves from dwelling on her grief to taking "a deep, quiet breath and [thinking] how she did not envy those young girls in the ice cream shop. Behind the bored eyes of the waitresses handing out sundaes there loomed, she knew, great earnestness, great desires, and great disappointments; such confusion lay ahead for them, and (more wearisome) anger" (139). If her husband's revelation destroys her sense of peace, her sense of her marriage, and her sense of self, it also makes her more compassionate to others, knowing they will face currently unimagined struggles. Perhaps, then, it's not surprising that at the end of the story, she calms her husband after he has had a nightmare, tenderly "putting her palm to the side of his face. Because what did they have now, except for each other, and what could you do if it was not even quite that?" (139).[9] If the distance between two people is seemingly vast and unknowable, Strout shows how embodied acts of tenderness work to bridge this emotional void, if only and necessarily temporarily.[10]

Janie is not the only person in the book who struggles to create a coherent narrative about her life. The first story, "Pharmacy," focuses on Olive's husband, the generally gentle and well-meaning pharmacist (we'll see a few of them through Strout's oeuvre) Henry Kitteridge, who has recently retired. The bookends of the story are set in the early 2000s, when Henry is remembering working at the drugstore in the late 1960s and particularly the young woman Denise who worked there with him. The single-word title, "Pharmacy," refers to Henry Kitteridge's place of employment and his line of work, but it also looks back to the original definition of the word, a medicine, and indeed many of the stories in the collection are about restoring characters to some kind of health. The title also evokes Anderson's "Paper Pills" in *Winesburg, Ohio.* What ails Henry, and what is the medicine that he requires? In the story he is afflicted with middle-age depression, and his cure comes in the form of his new assistant, a young woman whom Olive cannot abide but who Henry trusts represents a positive future for the United States. It's a time of turmoil in the nation, with "hippies" and "marijuana" (11) frequenting the streets and news, and Henry sees Denise Thibodeau as a kind of palliative, a sign perhaps that the nation is not heading in the wrong direction but can be healed. Henry's own marriage at the time is rocky (though, caught up in his own midlife melancholia, he is unaware of it), with Olive pining after a fellow teacher with whom she works and their adolescent son Christopher profoundly unhappy.

The representation of time within "Pharmacy" is similar to what we have seen before in Strout's work; it's simultaneously historical, cyclical, specific, and general. Strout's writing allows us to understand the passing of time as fluid, then, not in any kind of unidimensional or linear sense but as a multidimensional way to trace our existence in the world: "For many years Henry Kitteridge was a pharmacist in the next town over, driving every morning on snowy roads, or rainy roads, or summertime roads, when the wild raspberries shot their new growth in brambles," but "retired now, he still wakes early and remembers how mornings used to be his favorite, as though the world were his secret" (3). Strout offers an elision between past and present, and the natural world, rather than cementing the difference, shows their connection. Now, years later, Henry is remembering the early days of working in the pharmacy. While there's a sweetness in remembering these days, Strout soon troubles all vestiges of lingering pastoral sentimentality, letting us know that "any unpleasantness that may have occurred back in his home, any uneasiness at the way his wife often left their bed to wander through their home in the night's dark hours—all this receded like a shoreline as he walked through the safety of his pharmacy" (4). We learn that it's not just the recent past that shakes the younger Henry, for "inwardly, he suffered the quiet trepidations of a man who had witnessed twice in childhood the nervous breakdowns of a mother who had otherwise cared for him with stridency" (4). But his wife's severity ruffles Henry, so he watches to see that she "did not bear down too hard on Christopher over a homework assignment or a chore left undone" (4). Olive hovers in the background, an angry, obscured unknown whose volatility threatens to erupt at any minute. Tenderhearted Henry seeks sanctuary in his work, a space away from Olive and their son's mood swings, as unpredictable as they are loud and divorced from the quiet that mild-mannered Henry craves. Shortly after the equally quiet Denise begins working for Henry, he imagines their relationship developing, longing "to be in the presence of [Denise and her husband]" (5), picturing "their trailer, cozy and picked up—for Denise was neat in her habits" (6), or dreaming of her hands that touch "her husband lovingly . . . [and] with the quiet authority of a woman, [would] someday pin a baby's diaper, smooth a fevered forehead, tuck a gift from the tooth fairy under a pillow" (11).

The first year Denise works for him is one of the happiest in Henry's life, and then tragedy strikes when Denise's husband dies at the hands of his oldest friend in a hunting accident. Her loss allows Henry to care for his young employee more, to tend to her paternally, though he also wistfully imagines "moving far upstate, living in a small house with Denise. . . . She could have a child. A little girl who would adore him; girls adored their fathers" (24). Denise, however, does not pair off with Henry, but rather, with his grudging approval, with a young delivery man whom they have encouraged to return to school. The new couple moves away, Denise writing to Henry yearly. The story's present is the moment when Henry realizes that Denise did not write to him this year, and he wonders what her silence means. This moment allows Henry to reflect on his past and his present, to consider what his life might have been, and to realize the fantasy work of those dreams. In other words, Henry is at a moment of reckoning—a realization because he did not hear from a now older woman whom he once loved—that he perhaps didn't know her and consequently he didn't know his own emotional state or himself either. We begin with a moment of absence, a moment of loss and grief.

Eventually, in what we will come to recognize as Olive's characteristic abruptness, she brings Henry a card she forgot to give him in which Denise relays that she "had a scare late in the summer. Pericardial effusion, which . . . 'put all my priorities straight, and I have lived every day since then with the deepest gratitude for my family. Nothing matters except family and friends. . . . And I have been blessed with both'" (28). This condition—extra fluid around the heart—exerts pressure on the muscle, leading it to work less efficiently, and is of course metaphorical as well as physical. Learning this old acquaintance, this once young woman whom he loved, is alive, well, happy in her marriage and in her feelings of tenderness for him (for she signs her note "love" for the first time), Henry feels not just relief, but also "suddenly, queerly, . . . an odd sense of loss, as if something significant has been taken from him." News of her happiness and in some ways of her indifference to him undoes Henry. Denise has thrived without him, and Henry has never admitted to himself how her moving away let him fantasize about her and stay removed from his wife all the more. At this time, Henry realizes he's suffering what Leslie Jamison calls *saudade,* not a "longing for any particular object, but longing for that very state of yearning" (169). Loving Denise from afar shaped his existence. His apparent irrelevance to her is humiliating. Henry finds himself horrified after reading her card and recognizing that "all these years of feeling guilty about Denise have carried with them the kernel of still having her. . . . He cannot bear this thought, and in a moment it will be gone, dismissed as not true. For who could bear to think of himself this way, as a man deflated by the good fortune of others?" (29). This moment of epiphany is one Strout will return to throughout the collection—a moment when individuals realize they are not who they thought they were, that they are neither perfect nor, consistently, their best selves. If most of the story focuses on Henry's feelings for Denise, however, its subject for Henry is not just this loss, but the loss of his wife as well. In dreaming about Denise, he has forgotten to see the woman next to him. This awareness of how much he has lost marks the dawning of consciousness for Henry. We see this in his plaintive cry, "Olive. . . . You're not going to leave me, are you?" (29). The fear he has—that he has already lost Olive through his own neglect—is pitiful and poignant.

That look back at the past, the recognition that his history is not what he thought it was and that he is not who he thought he was—a kind of counter to nostalgia—is one of the governing themes of *Olive Kitteridge.* Henry may not realize that he might have lost Olive at the same time he was imagining Denise, but Olive in a subsequent story realizes her son does not share her memory of the past—and so he does not see her the way she sees herself. The realization is devastating.

The short story cycle is a particularly rich genre for exploring these themes. We're allowed multiple perspectives, which underscore the limitations of any singular point of view. If Olive hovers at the margins of the first two stories in the book, in the third she is front and center, wrestling with her reaction to her son's wedding and his new wife.[11] Olive, like Henry in "Pharmacy," is ashamed of her feelings; in particular, she is ashamed of her jealousy, and she wishes she had been a more magnanimous, kinder person in the past and were today as well. The regrets Strout's characters have are not for wrong decisions they've made so much as for the way they've thoughtlessly hurt people they care about and love. They usually regret they did not act with more patience and compassion.

More often the realization of the unreliability of our perceptions saddens individuals. We see this movement in "The Piano Player," when an old lover returns to see the elderly Angela O'Meara, whose makeup and look of expectancy are "no longer appropriate" for a woman her age, to cruelly tell her that her mother had an affair with him years earlier; in "A Little Burst," when Olive finds out her son resents his childhood (and his mother particularly); in "A Winter Concert," when Janie learns her husband of decades had an affair with a woman years earlier; and in "Basket of Trips," when Marlene discovers her recently deceased husband had had an affair with her cousin. Again and again in these stories we see a person becoming disillusioned with a relationship. The short story cycle explores the lives of couples after they have been married for years, and so it is a portrayal of life after the wedding, when individuals, usually—but not always—older women, find themselves on the other side of the fairy tale. If in her first book Strout rewrote the sentimental novel, and in her second the modernist novel, here she rewrites domestic fiction, suggesting that a wedding does not signal the end of a drama but the beginning of one where a couple does not live the same dream, though occasionally their dreams intersect.

It's ironic, then, that in the last story of the book, "River," Olive finds herself taking a risk, or, if you will, a leap of faith, a risk on love with the widower Jack Kennison. Here Strout offers a tender parody of the trajectory of the young romance; Olive and Jack fall into their relationship with all of the doubts and insecurities and experiences of decades of living in this world, and of knowing their own—and others'—fallibilities. And yet they try, and in having them take a chance on each other, Strout offers a hope for connection, a suggestion that one can take a chance on love, can try, can risk.

Lovemaking does not always imply a sentimental connection; sometimes it can manifest betrayal. In "The Piano Player," Angela O'Meara's former boyfriend from years ago returns unexpectedly to tell her that "[your mother] once came to Boston to see me. . . . She took the Greyhound bus. . . . And then took a taxi to my apartment. When I let her in, she asked for a drink and started taking off her clothes. Unbuttoned that button slowly at the top of her neck" (58). The cruelty cuts three ways: the first and second, the twin acts of betrayal of her mother and lover; the third, the unnecessary revelation years later.[12] The confession blindsides Angela, and moments later her current lover of twenty-two years berates her for calling him at home earlier that evening. These brutal speech acts are compounded by her realization that her nursing home–bound mother has been abused. The story ends in a Jamesian moment as Angela leans against a wall in the house where she rents a room, and "fingering her black skirt, [she] felt she had figured something out too late, and that must be the way of life, to get something figured out when it was too late" (60). What "that" is remains elusive: The cruelty of her mother? The cruelty of men? The physical abuse of elders? Our indifference to others' suffering? Like James, Strout leaves the realization for the readers to untangle, and, like Angie, we remain somewhat unmoored, flailing for our bearings.

The revelations of betrayal are not limited to sexual infidelities. The afternoon of her son's wedding, Olive lies down alone in his bedroom, listening to the sounds of the reception. She's shocked when she overhears her son's bride speaking of her new mother-in-law and her relationship with Chris.

> For Olive it is as if these women are sitting in a rowboat above her while she sinks into the murky water. "He's had a hard time, you know. And being an only child—that really sucked for him."

Seaweed murmurs, and Suzanne's oar slices through the
water again. "The expectations, you know."

Olive turns and gazes slowly around the room. Her son's
bedroom. She built it, and there are familiar things in here,
too, like the bureau, and the rug she braided a long time ago.
But something stunned and fat and black moves through her.
He's had a hard time, you know.

. . . What had Christopher said? What had he remembered? A person can only move forward, she thinks. A person
should only move forward. . . .

Oh, it hurts—actually makes Olive groan as she sits on
the bed. What does Suzanne know about a heart that aches so
badly at times that a few months ago it almost gave out, gave
up altogether? It is true she doesn't exercise, her cholesterol
is sky-high. But all that is only a good excuse, hiding how it's
her soul, really, that is wearing out. (70–71; italics Strout's)

The revelation causes Olive a palpable discomfort, a literal heart-
sickness that the world, her past, and particularly her child-rearing
are not what she thought they were.[13] Her disorientation is so complete that even objects she spent hours making become unfamiliar.
Most significantly, she finds out that her son does not see their past
or her the way she thought he did. That he perceives their shared
family history differently, ambivalently, puts into question Olive's
own Weltanschauung. Chris's repression and disclosure bother
Olive, but not nearly as much as the realization that he thinks that
in his childhood she did not give him what he needed. Though blaming Suzanne, Olive is undone by her own sense of inadequacy. If she
cannot be certain of her mothering, what can she know?

Perhaps the most obvious image of disorientation within the
collection is the physical setting.[14] The town of Crosby sits perched
on rocky cliffs overlooking the ocean, and more than one character
finds himself unwittingly swimming in its dangerous currents. The
rocky crags, like the character of Olive herself, are hardened, rugged,
difficult, and so the very landscape mirrors the titular heroine: "A
sky as gray as November hangs over the bay, and against the dark

rocks the water slaps ceaselessly, swirling seaweed around, leaving it bumpily combed out along the higher rocks. Right down to the point the rocky coast looks barren, almost wintry, only the skinny spruce and pines show dark green" (176). Rather than confirming our smooth understanding of the world and ourselves, others' recollections of the past, like Crosby's rocks, are slippery and treacherous. The reader, too, must attempt to navigate the tricky terrain of chronology, the book's very disorientation demanding an active, engaged, and careful reader, attentive to losing her footing or her sense of direction. Characters who leave for New York, California, and Texas are haunted by the landscape they left behind, unable to let it go, aware of its seemingly magnetic pull on them.

That Kevin Coulson returns to Crosby to die is significant. Years earlier his mother killed herself in the family kitchen, and Kevin, lost ever since, now hopes for a kind of closure, believing that ending his life where his mother took her own will give him a sense of order that science, psychoanalysis, and art have been unable to provide. Kevin wants "to see his childhood house—a house he believed, even as he sat in his car now, that he had never been happy in. And yet, oddly, the fact of its unhappiness seemed to have a hold on him with the sweetness of a remembered love affair. For Kevin had some memories of sweet, brief love affairs . . . and none measured up to the inner desire, the *longing* he felt for that place" (44; emphasis Strout's). Kevin hopes for restorative nostalgia—but Strout will not allow him such an easy solution to his persistent questioning. For once he returns to Crosby, he is met by the caustic Olive, who waylays his plans. Perhaps Olive's interference comes from her own experiences with suicide, but, seemingly intuitively, she recognizes Kevin's intentions, and by engaging in desultory, even annoying conversation, she refuses to let him—at least temporarily—act on them. Olive's apparently meaningless banter prevents Kevin from taking his own life, and leads him to saving another's. The poignancy of this event—Kevin's saving of Patty Howe, who has fallen into the sea—is a stroke of ironic serendipity. If Dickensian in terms of good fortune, the event also disrupts Kevin's circular trajectory, knocks him off of his intended course. Strout does not give him the annihilation of memory he craves, but instead forces him to live, survive, save others—and this very act of survival will carry with it the burden of the past.

In Crosby, history weighs heavily on survivors. A staggering number of characters bear the legacy of depression, living with its effects and the memories and consequences of their parents' actions, whether this is genetic or the internalization of their parents' neuroses as psychoanalysts Abraham and Torok suggest. Though Kevin doesn't know his mother's motivation for suicide, he realizes "her need to devour her life had been so huge and urgent as to spray remnants of corporeality across the kitchen cupboards" (33). Abraham and Torok contend that even if the child does not know the originary trauma that precipitated parents' neuroses, the child still mimics their reaction to the trauma, enacting the neuroses without realizing the cause. Abraham and Torok claim the trauma "is the more unknown for not being derived from the child's own desires or drives but from another place: the father's or the mother's unconscious, in which are inscribed the parents' unspoken fears, their apprehensions, the reasons for their enslavement, their hidden faults. Inscribed there is also the fact that parents are not at all the gods of coherence and consistency, courage, and power that their young offspring would wish" (180).

In other words, the prime mover that affects the child is inaccessible, locked within a sort of mental crypt, but sending forth a ghost that haunts the child nevertheless. The child's despair and drive to suicide may be the effect of having "no way of directly evoking the contents of [his] crypt. . . . The only resolution available to [him] is to *use [his] own body in a quasi-hysterical fashion, thereby avoiding the fantasy of endocryptic identification*" (italics theirs; 163).

But to revisit the past does not always portend tragedy. Kevin's disastrous plans result in salvation. And it is Olive, his middle school math teacher, who is responsible. She sees young Patty Howe struggling in the ocean and, not being able to swim herself, motions to Kevin to go to her rescue. Kevin does, and in this act of saving Patty, he also—at least temporarily—saves himself as well. He has returned to Maine, having lived in Texas, Chicago, and New York, studied psychiatry, and been involved with various women, to return to the "scene of the crime," as it were, where his mother, a pediatrician, shot herself. Though Kevin doesn't look at the past as a time of sanctuary and sweetness, he returns with the idea of closure—that he will finish what his mother began thirty-odd years ago. Rebecca Cross suggests that the reader of *Olive Kitteridge* also looks for closure. The stories, she observes, "present characters who experience a void in life, and . . . describe the characters' respective searches to fill those voids. . . . These absences create the affective experiences of yearning, frustration, and fulfillment for the reader. The absences construct these emotional reactions, which become affective reactions to the text" (67–68). But whether Olive intuits Kevin's wishes or their conversation is a serendipitous occurrence, she interrupts him in the process, forces him to talk with her, and then urges him to save Patty. Kevin's original desire is thwarted; he finds himself instead swimming desperately, reaching Patty, strengthening "his grip on her arm to let her know: He would not let her go. Even though, staring into her open eyes in the swirling salt-filled water, with sun flashing through each wave, he thought he would like this moment to be forever: the dark-haired woman on shore calling for their safety, the girl who had once jumped rope like a queen, now holding him with a fierceness that matched the power of the ocean—oh, insane, ludicrous, unknowable world! Look how she wanted to live, look how she wanted to hold on" (46–47). It's not, then, just the past that is elusive for Kevin. It's the present—and the future, too. That which he wants to do, that which he expects he will do, he does not do. Instead, circumstances thrust themselves before him, and he finds himself in another world, where the past is not what he thought, he is not who he thought, and he is not ending his own life but saving someone else's.

While we briefly see Kevin's memories, we cannot access his mother's, or the reasons for her actions. Olive does not know why her father killed himself either, but she and her son bear the scars of this wounding in their own bodies, hearts, and minds. According to Abraham and Torok, "unbeknown to themselves, [such people] carry the concealed shame of their families. These people are prey to strange and incongruous words or acts, transferred from events unknown to them, events whose initiator was *an other*" (188). Thus, although Chris Kitteridge might blame his depression on his childhood, it might also be the effect of a traumatic event that predates both him and his mother, an event that neither of them can access, but that still tugs at their collective unconscious. Kevin knows his mother took her life, and he plans on enacting the same conclusion to his, but he does not know her originary trauma. Rather, he has lived with its encryption, until another fall (Patty Howe's) leads him down a different path. Perhaps this trauma, the trauma of watching and interrupting a possibly suicidal accident, will jar him from the repetition compulsion of his mother's legacy. Strout does not allow him the nostalgic narrative coherence he desires, but propels him into a brave new world haunted by the past: "Again the water rose, they both took a breath; again they were submerged and his leg hooked over something, an old pipe, unmoving. The next time, they both reached their heads high as the water rushed back, another breath taken. He heard Mrs. Kitteridge yelling from above. He couldn't hear the words, but he understood that help was coming. He had only to keep Patty from falling away, and as they went again beneath the swirling, sucking water, he strengthened his grip on her arm to let her know: He would not let her go" (46–47). Like the rocks underneath them, the past rears up at Kevin and Patty, damaging, dangerous, and also paradoxically sustaining. The waves of the present battle around them as they try to endure, and a woman stands on the shore, calling out to them to hold on. Whether they will survive is as unknown as their family mysteries. But what is clear is that, as in Strout's other work, while her characters are united in the fear of falling, they inevitably are presented with a choice—to fall or to take a leap of faith toward redemption.

Perhaps the clearest manifestation of the impossibility of restorative nostalgia in this book comes in "A Different Road," when

Olive and Henry make the unfortunate decision to take a bathroom break shortly before the bungled robbery of drugs at a small hospital.[15] The story is told in fragments, as Olive attempts to understand the events of that night and their effects; as Bessel van der Kolk tells us, "The imprints of traumatic experiences are organized not as coherent logical narratives but in fragmented sensory and emotional traces: images, sounds, and physical sensations" (176). Olive believes she accurately remembers the night up to a point, but once she tries to access the robbery itself, her memories break down: "After that, it was like painting with a sponge, like someone had pressed a paint-wet sponge to the inside of her mind, and only what it painted, those splotches there, held what she remembered of the rest of that night" (113). Arguably the worst trauma Olive suffers is not the event of being held hostage but her reactive cruelty toward her husband. At the moment of crisis, she speaks hatefully to him, and though Henry says that he forgives her, she cannot accept her own meanness. According to Olive, "they would never get over that night because they had said things that altered how they saw each other" (124). But here Olive sells herself short, for ultimately, within all of the stories, there is a reaching out, an attempt at connection across distances physical and metaphorical, a compassion, and an acceptance of others' failings. That acceptance of the cruelty of others and of ourselves, of the parts that we would like to gloss over or ignore, is crucial to the differences between restorative and reflective nostalgia. Olive must realize that just as she will never remember the night clearly, neither has she been an ideal, flawless mother or wife; this unsatisfying lack of affirmation is in fact all she has.

If Olive's betrayal is her own cruelty, Henry's is his stroke. Both incidents are beyond their control, the complicated legacy of historic circumstances. In one fell swoop, the trajectory of Olive's life is changed. Just as her son's marriage and move to California had done, her husband's fall into a vegetative state shakes her very foundation. Though she still talks to Henry, he no longer communicates with her. His catatonia strikes them both, making him unknowable to Olive and the reader. And yet, Olive still feels a deep tenderness for Henry. Though outwardly abrasive, she visits her husband twice a day, desperately misses Chris, and longs to touch others.

The final story, and indeed the final scene of the book, echoes this need, when Olive and Jack Kennison go to bed together. If Olive, the other characters, and the reader are disoriented through much of their time in Crosby, Strout allows us a sense of hope and intimacy at the book's end. It's not idealized, youthful intimacy but an alternative connection the more poignant for its very lack of wistful idealizing. Olive initially dislikes Jack because of "the kind of arrogant furtiveness in the way he held his head thrust forward and didn't look at people" (251) and his reputation as someone who went to Harvard, may have taught at Princeton, and, like many in his class, retired to "the coast to live out their last days in a setting of slanting light. They were apt to have money, and, often, a grating sense of entitlement" (252). But if there are aspects of Jack that Olive doesn't like, including his politics, his pedigree, and his past, eventually she doesn't let those stop her from attempting an uneasy intimacy with him, an intimacy only possible perhaps in advanced age, with the wisdom and kindness that come from making, admitting, and forgiving mistakes. As Jack waits in bed for her, Olive acknowledges, "I . . . hit my son. . . . Sometimes when he was little. Not just spanked. Hit" (269). Olive does not ask Chris for forgiveness, but she asks Jack to see her as a flawed adult, someone sometimes cruel to those she loved. Her admission allows Olive to accept Jack's overture, "to sit down beside him [and] to close her eyes to the gaping loneliness of this sunlit world" (269). In Jack's eyes, Olive sees "the vulnerability, the invitation, the fear, as she sat down quietly, placed her open hand on his chest, felt the thump, thump of his heart, which would someday stop, as all hearts do. But there was no someday now, there was only the silence of this sunny room" (269).

What's particularly striking about concluding the book with this story is that it occurs after we have seen Olive at moments of disgrace, disgruntlement, and meanness—at her most awful, and consequently at her most vulnerable. She is not an ideal person; she is impatient with and possibly abusive to her son (who resents

her), neglectful of his children (powerless toddlers who could potentially harm themselves), horrid to her husband at moments of
crisis—which do not encourage her to feats of heroism, but rather
reveal her limitations, and yet Strout gives her a moment of love, of
hope after all. Strout ends the book with a moment of faith that is
not insipid; the difficulties that Olive has gone through make this
chance at happiness, both silly and poignant, all the more touching.
Olive thinks to herself:

> What young people didn't know, . . . lying down beside this
> man, his hand on her shoulder, her arm; oh, what young peo-
> ple did not know. They did not know that lumpy, aged, and
> wrinkled bodies were as needy as their own young, firm ones,
> that love was not to be tossed away carelessly, as if it were a
> tart on a platter with others that got passed around again.
> No, if love was available, one chose it, or didn't choose it.
> And if her platter had been full with the goodness of Henry
> and she had found it burdensome, had flicked it off crumbs
> at a time, it was because she had not known what one should
> know; that day after day was unconsciously squandered.
>
> And so, if this man next to her now was not a man she
> would have chosen before this time, what did it matter? He
> most likely would not have chosen her either. But here they
> were, and Olive pictured two slices of Swiss cheese pressed
> together, such holes they brought to this union—what pieces
> life took out of you. (270)

The lead-in to their lovemaking shows Strout at the height of her
powers. Olive and Jack's bodies exemplify their mortality, their
limitations, and their neediness.[16] Olive's appreciation of the risk
they are taking and allowing each other is touching, yes, but also
funny in a way that only Strout can be, with references to the appe-
tizers that get passed around or the comparison of Jack and Olive
to cheese. Susan Gubar confirms that "sexuality in old age requires
a sense of humor as well as patience" (113). The holes not only point
to what they have lost, but also indicate their survival, how their

losses have shaped them to become the people they are today. It is the spaces those holes have shaped that Strout explores so beautifully, painfully, and poignantly. Strout never allows her characters to lapse into sentimentalism, claiming to be whole or perfect for long, but, as Boym suggests, she allows them a more profound intimacy than a false collective past or imagined future. And the act of reading the stories creates a reader necessarily aware of the limitations of her perspective.

It's crucial, then, that the book takes the form it does. For in its very mixing of narrators, time, and perspective, the stories reveal that there isn't one single entity that is Olive Kitteridge. Rather, the genre of the short story cycle underscores the lack of a coherent trajectory. Perhaps, then, as we see the entity that is Olive Kitteridge through refracted prisms, the genre offers an alternative to the tyranny of novel conventions; or, as Kadmos puts it, "the placing of each story within the collected whole enables the cycle to achieve a deeper and richer meaning than the singular story on its own. The stories achieve their full potential . . . when read in the context of the stories with which they are connected; in the same way that individual subjects can be better understood within the web of relations they are situated in" (40). Rather than coherence and a clear history of causes and effects, Strout offers us scenes, unforeseeable shifts, contingencies, adaptations, and characters who are forced to survive and accept or at least live with a shifting reality. Perhaps our lives do not follow the long arc of a century but instead are composed of what Olive calls "little bursts," small moments that stand out, that may or may not follow each other logically, and that necessarily rely on the "holes," the unspoken, invisible connections between them. How lovely, then, that the "Reader's Guide" at the end of the book includes three voices: Strout's, Kitteridge's, and the Random House Reader's Circle. This coda underscores the multiplicity of voices and perspectives at work in the short story cycle—and by so doing, it showcases the necessity for and Strout's command of this complex, illuminating, and complicated genre.

4 The Burgess Boys
Literary Leave-Takings and Homecomings

IF STROUT BRIEFLY VENTURES OUT OF MAINE IN *Olive Kitteridge,* she does so overtly, and at greater length, in her next book, *The Burgess Boys* (2013). The novel begins in New York, and many of the scenes are set there, though they are accompanied by forays into Maine. The protagonists of *The Burgess Boys,* Bob and Jim Burgess, have left their birthplace for the city, but are pulled home by family obligations. The Burgess brothers have an uneasy relationship with Maine, which incarnates for them their troubled past, particularly the death of their father. The Burgess family (and the town of Shirley Falls) has accepted that Bob at four years old caused the car accident that killed their father decades earlier, though eventually we learn that older brother Jim believes he was at fault for the accident (but never spoke of his responsibility to anyone). But the Maine the Burgess boys left years ago has changed

in the interim, as their sister, who never strayed far from home, realizes. The changes in Maine allow Strout to take risks in this novel
that she hadn't in her earlier fiction. The Whitest state in the union
(even today), Maine, and particularly the fictional town of Shirley
Falls (once home to Amy and Isabelle), now houses a growing Somali immigrant community. Strout again addresses issues of memory, family, and loss, yet she also takes on different characters, issues,
and settings, and in doing so, moves from what Suzanne Keen terms
"bounded empathy," "on behalf of members of one's own group," to
"ambassadorial empathy," which "attempts to move more distant
others on behalf of those represented empathetically" ("Empathetic
Hardy," 365). If Strout's earlier characters considered themselves
outsiders, they still found themselves, if uncomfortably, in familiar
surroundings; they knew the landscape, and they knew the people
and the history around them. Venturing into New York for much of
the novel and creating Somali characters, who are minor but play
important roles within the novel and the White Burgess brothers'
lives, Strout extends her reach.[1] With this endeavor, she can no longer be classed as a regional writer—a label she rejects—or a writer of
domestic fiction, as she tackles a broad landscape and contemporary
political issues without the patina of the past to separate the reader
from American racism.

We still, however, see details that we have come to recognize as
essential to Strout's style and concerns. Her images are heartbreak-
ingly beautiful, though they're not confined to the natural world
the way they were in her previous fiction—here, New York is also
the focus of her attention. True to form, family complications and the
ways the ones closest to us hurt us continue to be major concerns for
the novelist. As the title suggests, the crucial relationship is between
Bob and Jim Burgess, and this exploration of fraternal—rather than
filial or conjugal—relationships seems to mark a turning point for
Strout as well. In spite of *Abide with Me*'s portrayal of Tyler Caskey,
it would be easy before the appearance of *The Burgess Boys* to classify
Strout as a "women's novelist," preoccupied with feminine domes-
ticity (even Tyler is concerned primarily with his relationships with

girls and women). But here for most of the novel she inhabits the consciousness of Bob Burgess, a divorced and childless man alone, stricken by guilt, and bound to his birth family in ways that are perhaps rare for many people today.

That fraternal relationship is important not only literally but metaphorically as Strout addresses race and racism. Bob and Jim's return to Maine is precipitated by their nephew's throwing a pig's head into the Shirley Falls mosque at the beginning of Ramadan.[2] The older men, who have lived in New York for decades, are stunned by Zach's crime; because they have so rarely visited Maine, they haven't seen how threatened the longtime White residents of Shirley Falls have felt by their new immigrant neighbors. On a certain level, then, Bob and Jim's perspectives resemble those of Strout and her husband, Jim Tierney (to whom the book is dedicated and whom she married in 2011). Raised in Maine, her husband lived there for much of his adult life, eventually becoming the state's attorney general before moving to New York. At the time she wrote the novel, Strout and Tierney lived in New York and had a complex, complicated relationship with their first home. In *The Burgess Boys*, Strout attempts to explore this relationship—the one she and Jim, and to a certain extent many of us, have to the places where we were raised. If sentimental toward the geography and understanding of certain cultural peculiarities, she does not allow her characters a nostalgic warm fuzziness for "home," but forces them and her readers to see the place with a sense of discomfort. The Burgess brothers have changed since they moved to New York; they are, to a certain extent, like the Somali émigrés Abdikarim and his family, unhomed, exiles of Maine and not fully inhabiting New York. In this chapter, I explore how Strout establishes a narrative frame that she then disrupts, and the effects and implications of this movement, which complicates and builds on her previous work. I then turn to the characters and the settings, knitting these threads together to show how the novel encourages us to further recognize the limitations of our perspectives and to recognize our shared humanity. Finally, I address how *The Burgess Boys* further situates Strout within the tradition of American letters.

In her fourth book, Strout experiments with narrative even as the novel formally recalls *Amy and Isabelle* and *Abide with Me*. *The Burgess Boys* follows one character as he comes to terms with understanding his past and present. In this novel's prologue, Strout hints at the novel to come, *My Name Is Lucy Barton*. *The Burgess Boys* begins with a conversation between an anonymous woman, a New Yorker, talking with her mother in Maine about the Burgess brothers and deciding at the prologue's end she will tell their story. But by not including a coda at the novel's conclusion, Strout emphasizes narrative conventions and makes us aware of our positions as readers. Rather than ending with a neat sense of closure by returning to the narrator, she leaves her readers expectant, waiting for a resolution that never arrives. If her first two books had somewhat conventional trajectories and the third challenged linear narrative, this book, with its refusal to end, conclusively performs one of its subjects, our lack of certainty about the stories we think we know.

The "boys'" story is an object of conversation between a mother and daughter. With this opening, Strout underscores how personal, intimate domestic relationships structure our lives. As we saw in her three previous books, great political and social issues—racism, classism, and hate crimes—do not occur in a world divorced from families, but are connected to the personal. In beginning this way, we see how political issues, including abstract ideas of justice and citizenship, are part and parcel of our human connection; neither is divorced from the other. This realization is one that the characters in the novel will come to as well. The world and its historic and contemporary institutions and problems are first mediated through familial relationships. Learning who our family is and tending to our larger human family become part of the novel's broader lessons.

The tone between mother and daughter is conversational, again recalling *Abide with Me*: "My mother and I talked a lot about the Burgess family," the novel begins.[3] Yet at the same time, the narrator tells us, "I lived in New York and she lived in Maine"—emphasizing both their attempt to communicate with each other and the geographic distance that literalizes emotional space. The mother's matter-of-factness looks back to Olive Kitteridge as she says to her daughter, "Kids are awful. Honest to God" (5), and ahead to Lydia Barton. We learn the narrator and her mother have both been widowed in the past year, and that the narrator's children have gone to college. They are women who are alone but who are trying to connect. In spite of its placement, the prologue takes place after the novel ends, again manifesting the experiment with our understanding of time that we see throughout Strout's fiction. We learn in the prologue that the women are happy "that Bob Burgess had found a good wife in the end. The wife, Bob's second and we hoped his last, was a Unitarian minister" (4), displaying the women's familiarity and comfort with the subjects of the book.[4]

The narrator continues, "And so it began. Like a cat's cradle connecting my mother to me, and me to Shirley Falls, bits of gossip and news and memories about the lives of the Burgess kids supported us. We reported and repeated" (7). The phrasing and image emphasize the fragmented and complicated quality of the story, that it is pieced together, the gaps filled in with speculation. But when the narrative of Bob and Jim Burgess begins on the next page, though there's Strout's customary fluidity between past and present, there isn't a sense of "gossip and news and memories" constructing the narrative until the very end. Most of the novel is told from Bob's perspective, and we perhaps might naïvely trust that events happened the way he has always assumed—that he accidentally killed his father when he was a young child. The narrator sets the stage in the prologue when she recalls, "The grown-ups were strict in setting us straight, so if a child on the playground was overheard saying that Bobby Burgess 'was the one who killed his father' or 'had to see a doctor for mentals,' the offender was sent to the principal's office, the parents were called, and snacks were withheld at snack time" (6). But Strout also sets out breadcrumbs, letting the astute reader know that what the characters think happened may not be accurate—and this confusion is one of the themes of the novel. After the narrator tells her mother that she's "going to write the story of the Burgess kids" even though "people will say it's not nice to write about people I know," her mother responds, "Well, you don't know them. . . . Nobody ever knows anyone" (8), recalling a refrain that runs through much of Strout's work.[5] The novel, though, offers an imaginative sympathetic identification, perhaps an antidote to not knowing anyone completely—that is, the hopeful recognition that even if we don't ever really know anyone, we can sympathize with them nonetheless (literature and imagined identification offer a way to understand people whose lives are vastly different from our own).

This sympathetic identification, this recognition we are like others, has everything to do with this novel's greater purpose; pithily, to proclaim the world's people are one family. The protagonists' very name underscores this theme. A "burgess" etymologically refers to a citizen or legal representative, underscoring how this novel is about citizenship and legal representation. We'll see these issues play out in the lives of the Somali migrants who come to the United States and the working-class citizens of Shirley Falls, who seem to have been left behind even as the Burgess brothers have thrived as New York professionals. Jim and Bob are both lawyers, their careers based on addressing justice, ethics, and responsibility (and we might remember that Strout worked briefly for Legal Aid after she earned her JD). Their nephew's action is uncontested—he threw a pig's head into a holy site. But his action raises a host of other questions: Was it a hate crime? Why would he do it? What responsibility does the country have to its new and long-term citizens? How does brotherhood—literal and figurative—factor into our understanding of ourselves and our responsibility for our genetic and metaphorical family members?

Strout leaves many of these questions unanswered. At the end of *Abide with Me*, she says her job as a writer is not to answer questions, but to raise them. And Zach is the shadowy unknown center of the novel. Strout portrays him through his uncles' and mother's eyes—and these middle-aged adults are profoundly worried about this troubled young man. That she doesn't let us into Zach's mind is an interesting narrative choice. The reader, then, is left like Jim, Bob, or Susan, trying to understand issues in some ways beyond our ken. Violence haunts the new and longtime residents of Shirley Falls, who wrestle with how to live near and with each other. Strout suggests novels may play a part in community building, for by portraying individuals with grace and sensitivity, fiction may help obliterate ignorance by showing the humanity of individuals; seeing compassionate portrayals, readers may become more open-minded and consequently more ethical. The novel seems to promote this idea at the same it acknowledges its Pollyannish quality, for the pig's head conjures the looming violence of *Lord of the Flies*, and "Burgess" also brings to mind the author of *A Clockwork Orange*. If we find ourselves sympathizing with victims, we might also find ourselves sympathizing with bad actors, which might lead to an uncomfortable realization for some readers. Strout highlights the goodwill that humans may share, and she also shows us how selfishness, self-preservation, intolerance, and sadism shadow our existence.[6]

After the prologue, the narrator begins the novel by describing Jim's wife, Helen Burgess, as she pauses while packing for a vacation to the Caribbean. Immediately, Strout sets a scene of wealth and luxury, and subtly points out Helen's indifference to others' suffering. As we saw in Strout's first three books, much of the suffering she sees is caused by people living too much in their own heads, failing to see the world around them. Helen is one such type. Her husband's brother, Bob, has just called her, distraught about an argument he has witnessed. Shortly after she hangs up, Helen falls into a fantasy about talking with a woman about the Burgess family history, imagining she would say, "'Bob's an interesting fellow.' She might even mention the accident—how it was Bob, four years old, who'd been playing with the gears that caused the car to roll over their father and kill him" (12–13). This moment reveals Helen's self-absorption and her cavalier attitude toward her brother-in-law's and husband's suffering. Helen dreams of revealing these family secrets, so loaded that they haven't been talked about for thirty years, to an acquaintance she doesn't even like.

Helen does not grow any more likable as the novel continues. She is sometimes generous to Bob (when she doesn't imagine using him as social capital), sharing the coziness of home and children with him, thinking of him as Jim's younger, damaged brother. And yet her generosity is questionable. Helen is primarily interested in her own image, so consumed with her looks that she can't be genuinely kind to others. Strout doesn't let us into this character in the way she lets us into others—and in this way Helen is like the elusive Lauren in *Abide with Me*, another wealthy beautiful stranger just out of reach of the reader's understanding.[7]

Bob comes over at Helen's invitation; he is clearly upset and even so she interrupts him to say, "I have to tell you what I saw on the news last night. This segment called 'Real Men Like Small Dogs.' They interviewed these different, sort of—sorry—faggy-looking guys who were holding these tiny dogs that were dressed in plaid raincoats and rubber boots, and I thought: This is news? We've got a war going on Iraq for almost four years now, and this is what they call news? It's because they don't have children. People who dress their dogs like that" (15). Helen is dismissive about gay men and people without children, thoughtlessly indifferent to Bob, even as she claims the moral high ground by decrying the war in Iraq. Her thoughtlessness reveals that she doesn't see the suffering man in front of her because she is so taken up with her own outrage. While Bob is present, Susan calls horribly upset because Zach has told her he threw a pig's head into a mosque and that the police are looking for him. Hardly concerned about her nephew, Helen is worried that Jim will cancel their vacation to St. Kitt's to look after his sister and nephew. As Jim talks with Susan, Helen asks Bob, "Why would *anyone* go to Shirley Falls except in shackles?" (17), not only slighting the Burgesses' hometown, but also displaying her disinterest in descendants of enslaved peoples. If Helen is compassionate to some people, it's on her own terms, and her kindness is nothing if not limited.

And even when she travels further afield, to St. Kitts, and her travel companion attempts to educate her on the plight of Somali refugees with a magazine, Helen, although she begins to read the recommended article, is not moved to sympathy but apathy. Here perhaps is Helen's cardinal sin. She has a chance to learn of another person's suffering, and yet instead of looking outward, she once again retreats into herself. If this is a human reaction, Strout does not cut Helen any slack. After starting to read the article, Helen decides she won't continue because she does not want to feel "like a bad person" (45). She rejects the choice to be educated. Suzanne Keen tells us that the time is ripe to consider reading experiences that "clearly have negative emotional valences. . . . In the psychological literature, personal distress is regarded as an empathetic reaction, but a form of empathy oriented primarily toward the self (though it is stimulated by reaction to another). It causes aversion from the source: people experiencing personal distress seek to avoid or discontinue contact with the cause of their feeling. Unlike other-oriented empathy, which could lead to mature sympathy or even prosocial action on behalf of others, personal distress shows when the people feeling it push away, tune out, or refuse to engage" ("Narrative and the Embodied Reader," 44). While her traveling companion appears to judge Helen, Strout does not, portraying a self-absorbed woman who (without knowing it) is at loose ends, lost in some ways after her youngest child has left and not knowing what to do with herself.

The closest that Helen comes to being a sympathetic figure is early on in the novel when she reflects on missing her children. Yet, and this is an important distinction, Helen misses what she thinks she had, perhaps more so than the people themselves, recalling Boym's distinction between restorative and reflective nostalgia. Helen remembers her kids "splashing in the play pool in their yard in West Hartford, the moist skin of their little limbs pure as they crawled in and out; saw them as teenagers moving down the sidewalk in Park Slope with their friends; felt them curled up next to her on the couch on the nights when the family gathered to watch their favorite TV shows" (46). But even this feeling of loss is somewhat self-serving for Helen; Strout suggests she doesn't miss them for who they are now so much as for who Helen remembers them being. At the same time, even if the past didn't happen exactly as Helen remembers, what she remembers is more important in shaping her

sense of self than any facts. When Helen has the chance to learn of
others' suffering, she turns instead to her own possibly manufac-
tured memories, which show her to advantage.

Helen reflects on the early days of their marriage, when Jim
successfully represented a singer accused of killing his girlfriend, but
the memory does not lead her to a reflection on guilt or justice or
American politics. Rather, thinking about those days, she remembers what she "had never told anyone . . . that those months had
taught her what it must feel like to be the First Lady. One had to be
ready for a camera click at any moment. One was building an image
always. Helen had understood this. She had been excellent at the
job. . . . Any photo taken of her—she and Jim at a restaurant, at the
airport, stepping from a cab—had, she felt, hit the right note each
time" (70). Helen remembers how she dressed; how she looks and
how others perceive her are what she values above all else.

She is not alone in being at sea without her children. Jim, too,
is confused, though it's not until the end of the novel that we realize
the extent of his suffering. He shows his unhappiness through temper
tantrums, which Helen hates. She tries to calm him, but after finding his outbursts so "*unappealing*," she doesn't stop to wonder what
could be wrong with her husband, instead turning to "worry—to
believe—he found her unappealing as well. Both aspects made her
feel terrible. Old, she felt. And snappish" (113). She's frustrated, too,
but true to form, she turns her anger inward after their interrupted
vacation, when she "suddenly flung a black ballet flat across the bedroom. 'Damn you!' she said. She picked up a white linen blouse and
could have ripped it in half. Then she sat on the bed and wept because she did not want to be a person who threw shoes or swore at
people even when they weren't around" (112). Often Strout is at her
best when she describes the fleeting moments of self-hatred faced
by her characters. Upset with herself for not being as generous as
she would wish, upset with her husband, and unable to express her
own frustration, "So it seemed to begin: the business of Helen hating
the sound of her own voice, its undercurrent of unpleasantness, and
trying to get back to what she thought of as herself. Each time, like

tonight, she hoped it was merely one incident, related to nothing else" (116). These moments of characters' introspective self-loathing recall Eliot. Helen and Jim, so consumed with their appearances, fail to recognize that they need to give each other and themselves comfort and compassion. Their life together is racing toward a collision that they fail to see. Helen is not alone in being adrift, but she lacks the ability to see that others are also lost. These include Jim, her husband, whose boisterousness masks a pain he has never come to terms with; Bob, who wears his suffering visibly; his ex-wife, Pam, who wonders throughout the novel whether she is living the right life; Susan Burgess Olson, lost when her husband left her and baffled by her son; and Zach Olson, whose inexplicable acts set the surface plot of the story into motion.

Most of the novel follows Bob, whom his brother and sister see as an incompetent mess. Bob recognizes that he is lost; throughout the novel, he recalls his deceased therapist, his childhood, and his former wife. And yet he doesn't realize he is depressed—that his disengagement with the world and his drinking are signs of an unease with his current life. When we first meet him, we learn that "he was a likeable fellow. To be with Bob made people feel as if they were inside a small circle of us-ness. If Bob had known this about himself his life might have been different. But he didn't know it, and his heart was often touched by an undefined fear. Also, he wasn't consistent. Friends agreed that you could have a great time with him and then you'd see him again and he'd be vacant. This part Bob knew, because his former wife had told him. Pam said he went away in his head" (13).

We could call Bob a depressed alcoholic, but such a label is oversimplified and reductive. Strout's portrayals of survivors of tragedy offer a more complex, complete portrait of how trauma affects people than pigeonholing allows. She offers us glimpses into the events that have affected her characters, but she doesn't describe those events in detail; instead, she sketches nuanced pictures of the effects of these events on their lives in the aftermath. As we've seen in her other books, Strout is not concerned with rendering a climactic tragedy; rather, her focus is on the effects of that tragedy on those who survive, and her work shows how art offers a more sympathetic and capacious look at people's lives than clinical labels do. For example, early in the novel, after Bob has visited Helen and Jim and sits alone in his apartment looking at the people in the building across from his, Strout does not spell out that Bob is damaged; instead, his actions speak for themselves:

> Bob poured more wine, settled himself at the window again. What*ever*, as people said these days.
>
> Be a chef, be a beggar, be divorced a zillion times, no one in this city cared. Smoke yourself to death out the window. Scare your wife and go to jail. It was heaven to live here. Susie never got that. Poor Susie.
>
> Bob was getting drunk.
>
> He heard the door open in the apartment below him, heard footsteps down the stairs. He peered out the window. Adriana stood beneath a streetlamp, holding a leash, her shoulders hunched and shivering, and the tiny dog was just standing there shivering too. "Ah, you poor things," Bob said quietly. Nobody, it seemed to him in his drunken expansiveness, nobody—anywhere—had a clue. (25)

When Bob is drinking and alone, he feels compassionate toward his fellow sufferers, even though he doesn't know them. In this way, then, he is different from Helen, whose judgment of others and concern with her own appearance are her hallmark qualities. Bob is indifferent to how he appears, and feels only sympathy for those who seem lost around him. He is, in some ways, though, also out of touch with himself and with others—his drinking is a sign of his self-protectiveness, an attempt to isolate himself from further suffering.

We see his vulnerability more poignantly when Jim and Helen leave for their Caribbean vacation and Bob is transported back to the day Jim leaves for college. At the current moment, Bob is self-aware enough to recall how his therapist would have said to him at times like this, "Bob, stay in the present," but he is unable to do so. And then he recalls the accident: "Bob, who was four years old when his father died, remembered only the sun on the hood of the car that day, and that his father had been covered by a blanket, also—always—Susan's little-girl accusing voice: 'It's all your fault, you stupid-head'" (30). The moment of Jim and Helen's leaving is compounded by Bob's earlier sense of abandonment and guilt. His is a fragile, broken life. Bob accepts, just as everyone else (including the narrator) does, that he is responsible for his father's death, even though he doesn't remember the accident consciously. He has gone through life knowing his own guilt, and his gentleness, compassion, or big-heartedness comes from how he has lived with and perceived this formative experience.

When Bob returns to Maine to tend to Susan and Zach, his depression sharpens and he regresses to a kind of childlike ineptitude. We see how he struggles at the moments when time collapses for him at his sister's house: "He felt the sickness of an early breaking of drugged sleep, and with this came the thought that his sister, in her fury yesterday, had sounded remarkably like their mother, who, when the kids were young, would have spells of loud fury herself (never directed at Bob, but aimed at the dog, or a jar of peanut butter that rolled off the counter and broke, or—mostly, usually—at Susan, who did not stand up straight, had not ironed a shirt properly, had not cleaned up her room)" (65). Though Bob goes to Maine to help his sister and nephew, the pull of the past is too strong for him to live in the present in a healthy way. It's not surprising, then, that lost in a moment of reverie, he almost accidentally hits a woman with his car. The near-accident unnerves him, and he rushes back to New York, reluctant to stay in a place where he feels as lost as he did when he was a child.

It doesn't help Bob that his sister and brother are as thoughtless and cruel to him as adults as they were when they were children. The Burgess siblings have been unable to become healthy, confident adults. The brothers' dynamic was established early in their lives. Bob's future wife Pam realizes this when, as his girlfriend, she visits their house and the brothers' responses on seeing each other are "Slob-dog, how are you" and "Harvard man, you're home" (106). Jim's diminishment of his brother, and Bob's idolatry of his, continue for most of their adult life as well. Yet, probably because he felt responsible for his father's death and he entered therapy when he was young, Bob has achieved some kind of gentleness of spirit. At the same time, he has internalized the way his brother and sister see him. For example, shortly after Jim criticizes his brother's recent actions (and his job and his life), Bob silently concurs, thinking "he was a knucklehead, even Helen was mad at him. He had gone up to Maine and done nothing except respond like an idiot, panic, and leave their car up there. He thought of the gracious big-boned Elaine, sitting in her office with the fig tree, explaining so patiently the replication of the response to traumatic events, the masochistic tendencies he had because he felt he needed to be punished for a childhood act of innocence" (103).

When Bob returns to Maine a second time with Jim, he is alternately comforted and discomfited by his surroundings. For some, that discomfort can lead to compassion. In Maine, when he reflects on his life in New York, it appears sad to Bob: "And he wondered fleetingly what it was like for the Somalis, if they lived constantly with the sense of bewilderment he felt at this moment, wondering which life was real" (150). This moment is crucial for Bob; eventually Jim and Susan face similar realizations. That is, when they are discomfited, they do not retreat inward (the way that Helen does), but they realize that other people may be similarly lost and therefore needing their compassion.

Jim is cruel to his brother; Bob is healthy enough not to take his brother's jabs seriously, except when Jim tells him his ex-wife came on to him years ago. Here we see Bob's vulnerability; he believes his brother rather than trusting Pam. Bob doesn't know not to trust Jim. At the same time, he realizes "he was being ridiculous, and conjured up the image of his long ago and ever lovely therapist Elaine. What is it that's bothering you most about this, Bob? The fact that she's not who I thought she was. And who is it you think she was?

Bob didn't know" (181). This initial confession of Jim's disorients Bob, but a further confession unsettles him even further. Months later, Jim tells him,

> I killed him. . . .
>
> . . . You were in the backseat. So was Susie. You were four years old, Bob, you don't remember a thing. I was eight. Almost nine. By then you remember some things. . . . The seats were blue. You and I had a fight about sitting in the front seat, and before he walked down the driveway he said, Okay, Jimmy in the front seat this time, twins in the back. And I moved over behind the wheel. Even though we'd been told a million times we couldn't ever sit behind the wheel. I pretended I was driving. I pushed in the clutch. . . . And the car went down the driveway. . . .
>
> I pushed you into the front seat before Mom even came out of the house. Way before the police came, I'd climbed in the back. Eight years old. Almost nine years old, and I was able to be that sneaky. (225)

Bob can't believe Jim is remembering the accident accurately because he has built his life around another version of events. Spiraling into confusion, Bob again relapses. Just after Jim tells Bob about the accident, they learn Zach has traveled to Sweden to see his dad and begin to repair their relationship. While one person is on the path to health, another's world begins to unravel.

Bob has built his life around his assumed guilt. Though it's a terrible burden he carries, he doesn't know how to live without this narrative to structure it. After Jim's confession, Bob is completely discombobulated: "His incredulousness at discovering that his past might not be his past seemed to affect his ability to understand what lay ahead, and he spent a great deal of time walking the streets of New York" (232). Given Jim's earlier confession—and then retraction—that Pam came on to him, Bob is confused about how to make sense of this newest development. If that which he has built his life around is not true, then what ground does he have to stand on? He is not sure: "To have Jim raise [the accident] after all these years (to claim it as his own!) was disorienting in its awkwardness, impossible to comprehend. Walking through the park, he felt he'd been asleep for years, and had now wakened to a different place and time" (233). He cannot believe this new version of events, and so, understandably, he feels both ambivalent and hostile toward his brother as he tries to make sense of this new version of his history: "As those first days went by, anguish came to meet him. His mind, jumpy and distracted, told him, It's not true, and if it is, it doesn't matter. But this gave him no relief because the constant repetition of these thoughts told him otherwise. . . . In his state of drunken clarity, Bob saw his brother as someone unconscionable enough to be almost evil" (234).

Jim's confession devastates Bob. For a while he drinks heavily, and he loses touch with his brother and sister-in-law. Then he realizes he no longer needs to play sideman to his brother or therapist for his ex-wife; he can be the protagonist of his own life, and so he stops drinking and seeing Pam. On a later trip to Maine, he comes across Margaret Estaver, the Unitarian minister, and intuitively knows he will marry her. When he finds out that Abdikarim has led the Somali community in forgiving Zach, he realizes the gentleness and grace of forgiveness and that he can act this way too. Finally he reaches out to Jim, only to learn that Helen has kicked him out of their house and he has lost his job.

If Bob is the protagonist, the title tells us the book is Jim's as well. The mean-spirited golden boy is full of self-loathing because he thinks he killed his father and has never admitted it. The reader doesn't learn the secret at the heart of Jim's performance until Bob does. Instead, we see Jim through others' eyes. Unlike his brother, he is not likable. When we meet Jim, he derisively greets his younger brother, "Out of my chair, knucklehead. . . . Glad to see you. It's been what, four days? . . . Trouble in the graduate dorm?" (16–17). In the space of four sentences, Jim denigrates his brother three times. Bob does not respond negatively, but sees his brother as heroic, capable of great feats; after their father's death, Jim took on the role of man of the house, and never walked away from it. If Bob is resentful of his brother's successes, he never says so out loud, but privately muses to himself watching him speak, his heart unfolding "with love. Look at him, his big brother! It was like watching a great athlete, someone born with grace, someone who walked two inches above the surface of the earth" (151).

That drive is accompanied by personal demons. In addition to the hostility he directs toward Bob, Jim is generally quick to get frustrated. His anger is often directed at his brother; for example, when he and Helen are in St. Kitts, he swears over the phone, "You're a fucking mental case, Bob! . . . You're a fucking mental case! An incompetent fucking mental case!" (71). Later, when we learn that Jim thinks *he* is responsible for killing their father, his anger begins to make sense. If it is apparently directed outward at Bob, it is because Jim has not confronted his own guilt and shame.

But the rest of Jim's family take his surface performance at face value. They see him as extraordinarily capable—it doesn't occur to them that he is lost or roiling. While both Bob's and Susan's marriages end in divorce, Jim's union with Helen seems ideal. Bob believes that "two-thirds of the family had not escaped. . . . He and Susan—which included her kid—were doomed from the day their father died. They had tried, and their mother had tried for them. But only Jim had managed" (179). What Bob fails to realize is that Jim has not survived unscathed; each member of the family carries the legacy of that day within them; only Jim's trauma is expressed in sublimating that guilt into a work ethic and professional determination. Jim has been successful because he has channeled his guilt into his career, but his standing rests on his defense of a man who in all likelihood killed his girlfriend. His career, like his life, is based on a guilt he has not articulated.

After Zach's actions bring the Burgess brothers back to Shirley Falls, Jim's life begins to unravel quickly. Does the return home precipitate Jim's breakdown? Or had he begun to flail about earlier—when his youngest child left for college? At some point, he begins an extramarital affair with a paralegal who eventually accuses him of

sexual harassment, leading to his being fired and Helen throwing
him out of their house. Only then is Jim forced to reckon with the
consequences of his actions. But Jim's complete loss, his desperation
and vulnerability, allow him to turn outward, to become less selfish,
more human, kinder, humbler.

Trapped in her own head, Helen cannot see Jim's suffering.
When she talks to Bob about Jim's betrayal, she is still angry. He
tells her Jim has carried the weight of their father's accident his
whole life, and her response is not one of compassion, but indig-
nation. "'Don't you get it?' she asked, tears glistening in her eyes.
'He is not. The person. I thought. He was'" (297). As we saw in her
first three books, the revelation is one Strout returns to throughout
her fiction. Some marriages survive these epiphanies, but others do
not. This novel ends at a moment of ambiguity, rather than with
a sense of closure, mirroring the open-endedness of the beginning
discussed earlier. In this way, then, the novel anticipates *My Name Is
Lucy Barton*, where Strout more explicitly experiments with closure
and objectivity. If we have learned what causes Jim's severity in the
world—why he is so cruel to his brother and to himself—we haven't
learned what causes Helen's.

The woundedness has affected Susan as well, more obviously
than Jim and Bob, who have run from Maine and their histories. She
has stayed in their hometown, even after her mother died and her
husband left her. We meet Susan first through other characters, and
their perceptions of her are not generous. Bob tells Helen that in a
recent conversation, Susan had complained to him that "the Somalis
were invading the town. . . . Arriving in droves. She said three years
ago just a few families were there and now there's two thousand,
that every time she turns around a Greyhound bus unloads forty
more. I said she was being hysterical, and she said women were always accused of being hysterical and regarding the Somalis I didn't
know what I was talking about since I hadn't been up there in ages"
(18). Susan is partially right; women are often accused of hysteria,
and Bob hasn't been to Shirley Falls in years. But her xenophobia is
unsettling. Susan's characterization is deliberate on Strout's part. If

the portrayal of Susan's racism may let Strout's cosmopolitan read-
ership feel smugly superior to her, she offers an example of Bob's
racism as well when he sees a Somali man and thinks, "Cool . . .
just as long as there aren't too many of them" (53). With these instances, Strout jolts her reader into awareness, an acknowledgment
of her own position as reader and the dangers of identifying with
a character. Bob is differently racist than Susan is. Strout encourages her reader to be compassionate to but not blindly enthralled to
her characters; recalling Toril Moi, we might remember that ideal
reading may encourage both empathy and judgment, two qualities
crucial to democratic citizenship (228). When Bob visits his sister,
she begins describing the Somalis, and while she's puzzled by their
bartering and their "secretiveness," it's soon clear that she bears
more hostility toward the "liberals" of Shirley Falls than toward the
new immigrants. The do-gooders have been quick to offer generous
gifts to the immigrants, but they never offered to help Susan: "And
it hurts, Bob. That's how it was for me, back when Steve left. I was
scared to death. I didn't know if I'd be able to keep this place. Nobody offered to buy me a refrigerator. Nobody offered to buy me
a *meal*. And I was dying, frankly. I was lonelier than I'd bet these
Somalians are. They have family crawling all over them" (50). She is
unbearably lonely and forlorn. She lashes out because she has been
so hurt. Though Zach never explains why he threw the pig's head
into the mosque, it's clear that both mother and son are profoundly
hurt, alone, and suffering.

Susan works as an optometrist (classic Strout irony), so she
serves the public. When she is in the office one day, she finds herself
ruffled by a few Somali women who enter. She is confused by what
she perceives as "a deep and haunting apathy. . . . At the same time,
the absolute foreignness of these draped women gave Susan an inner
shuddering sigh. She wished they had never heard of Shirley Falls,
and it scared her to think they might never go away" (99). Dressed in
robes, holding hidden children, speaking a language Susan doesn't
understand, the women are strangers in her hometown whose presence underscores her own displacement.

It's not just the Somalis who are mysteries to Susan; it's her own child as well. The sibilance of her name audibly recalls Isabelle's, as does her position as an outsider in Shirley Falls, a single mom raising her son, but she is sadder than Isabelle. She seems more damaged, lost:

> For most of the nineteen years of Zachary's life, Susan had done what parents do when their child turns out to be so different from what they'd imagined—which is to pretend, and pretend, with the wretchedness of hope, that he would be all right. Zach would grow into himself. He'd make friends and take part in life. Grow into it, grow out of it. . . . Variations had played in Susan's mind on sleepless nights. But her mind also held the dark relentless beat of doubt. He was friendless, he was quiet, he was hesitant in all his actions, his school-work barely adequate. Tests showed an IQ above average, no discernible learning disorders—yet the package of Zachness added up to not quite right. And sometimes Susan's melody of failure crescendoed with the unbearable knowledge: It was her fault. (169)

She is bewildered by her son, saddened by the miscarriages she has suffered, and devastated by her husband's leaving her. Like Isabelle, she blames herself for her child's unhappiness. Susan's grief has corroded her; like her brothers, she is damaged, and in ways that she doesn't understand, doesn't see, and hasn't come to terms with. Psychiatrist Bessel van der Kolk tells us that parents preoccupied with their own trauma may "be too emotionally unstable and inconsistent to offer much comfort and protection [to their children]" (118). It's not until Zach begins a new life in Sweden with his father and sends her a picture, in which he looks open, handsome, and apologetic, that she realizes how she has negatively affected him:

> The flush of pleasure [at seeing him so healthy] had first produced had given way now to a sense of something unbearable—loss, and a glimpse of past behavior as mother and wife.

> . . . In glimpses of herself—shouting at Steve, at
> Zach—she recognized her own mother, and Susan's face
> burned with shame. She had never seen what she saw now,
> that her mother's fits of fury had made fury acceptable, that
> how Susan had been spoken to became the way she spoke to
> others. Her mother had never said, Susan, I'm sorry. I should
> not have spoken to you that way. And so years later, speaking
> that way herself, Susan had never apologized either.
>   And it was too late. No one want to believe something
> is too late, but it is always becoming too late, and then it is.
> (253–54)

While the moment is painful, what gives Susan hope is the fact
that Zach, in finally leaving Shirley Falls—in finally leaving
her—appears to have recovered from the slings and arrows of his
childhood. After having suffered, after having caused suffering to
others, he is now on the path to recovery. That that path isn't one
created by her is heartbreaking for Susan. But Strout allows Susan
the chance to learn to empathize with others. She will not be stuck
as bitter as her mother was.

We see her chance at redemption toward the novel's end when
she visits Bob in New York and tells him (about the accident), "I
always thought I'd done it. . . . I thought it was why Mom yelled at
me so often. She never yelled at the two of you. So maybe I did it,
I've often thought that. And since Zach left I've been having these
terrible nightmares. I can't remember them when I wake up but they
are *awful*. And they sort of, you know, feel like that" (263). Bob is
stunned by her assumption; both are learning, in Strout's words,
that "memory can be more revealing than what actually did happen.
We're all sitting on top of a slippery mess of memories, and no matter how *true* they are, they're real in the sense that there's some reason they're there. More than anything, maybe, they tell us who we
are" ("By Heart"). Bob asks Susan about all the times she said when
they were little, "It's all your fault, you stupid-head," and she replies,
"Oh, Bobby, of course I said that. I was a scared little kid" (263). She
seems finally to have forgiven herself.

While she is in New York, she feels lost (here we might recall Olive when she visits Chris), but it is not so much the city that terrifies Susan as her brothers. "Who *were* they? How they could live this way? They were not the Bob and Jim from her childhood. . . . Her brothers, even after they had moved from Shirley Falls, were still her brothers. But not now. What Susan was experiencing now, as she blew her nose on toilet paper, was some tilting of the universe. She was utterly alone, attached only to a son who no longer needed her" (264–65). This disorientation leads her to a moment of clarity and of compassion for the Somalis. For when she returns home, she observes,

> When I was in New York, it went through my mind, maybe this is how the Somalians feel. I'm sure it's not, well, maybe a little. But coming here where everything's completely confusing. I didn't know how to use a subway and everyone was rushing past, because *they* knew. All the things people take for granted, because they're used to it. I felt confused every minute. It wasn't nice, I'll tell you. . . . My brothers seemed the strangest of all. . . . Maybe when Somalian family members make it over here, the family that's been here awhile—maybe they seem strange too. (276)

Susan's insight is on point. If Strout's former subjects have been emotional outsiders, not feeling like they belong in the towns in which they live, her Somali characters are not native Mainers who feel alienated from their hometowns but immigrants, refugees who have left Mogadishu to find themselves in the northern United States. In her moment of clarity, Susan is given a chance at connection in which, in DiBattista and Nord's words, she may "move beyond national identity and division to imagine spiritual and political possibilities that transcend geographical boundaries and rigid definitions of self" (11). And Strout attempts to adopt a multiethnic, multinational consciousness here. Susan's recognition of the similarities between her and the Somali immigrants points to a new understanding, an openness, a capacity to grow.

The Somali immigrants do not look like the traditional residents of Shirley Falls, and their appearance in all senses of the word disturbs the longtime residents. They are Black. They are Muslim. They are new arrivals. They speak a different language. They keep to themselves, and their presence shows visibly just how much Maine has changed since the 1970s. Their portrayal is complicated, and Michael Tager suggests that by "not developing the Somali characters as deeply [as the White characters], Strout potentially opens herself to criticism of using the Somalis primarily as a plot device, as a problem for the Burgesses to overcome, and thus subordinating their perspective to the dominant white culture" (436). Within the novel Strout focuses on one Somali character in particular, Abdikarim, who along with his family has faced brutality and hardships unknown to most people living in the United States. Abdikarim's presence and history allow Strout to offer her readers a window into a community most likely not their own. If someone like Helen is reluctant to read an article about refugee camps, she might be more likely to read a novel in which a refugee appears peripherally. Keen tells us that counter to what we might think, "readers' perception of a narrative's fictionality enhances the likelihood of empathetic response to authorial strategic empathy, regardless of their identity" ("Empathetic Hardy," 366). Through fiction—what she terms storytelling—Strout can portray those experiences with a dignity, a reverence, and a narrative that straight reportage may not and reach a different audience. Reading about Abdikarim may allow Strout's more sheltered readers to empathize not only with people who have shared experiences—whether personal or national—but also with people who seem mysterious, different, or other. In prepping for this book, Strout followed Somali immigrant communities for several years, interviewing people and listening to their stories. The Maine of *The Burgess Boys* belongs not just to people whose families have made their homes there for centuries but also to a new population, strangers who find themselves sharing the streets.

And, as Strout has said, the people who read, who share stories, may find out that they are more alike than they first realize. But her portrayal is also potentially risky and could lead to accusations of ventriloquism. For example, Abdikarim's homesickness is similar to Bob Burgess's ache for home. Both men are exiles to a certain extent, living in an unfamiliar world, and compassionate to others who appear to struggle. That exercise in compassion, which we see in all of Strout's books, is important. Abdikarim's and Bob Burgess's compassion may be born from suffering, Abdikarim's from the loss of his son and the genocide he's experienced, Bob's from his belief in his responsibility for his father's death.

Abdikarim is displaced, alienated: "He did not know how he could ever get used to living here. There was little color anywhere, except the trees in the park in the fall. The streets were gray and plain and many stores were empty, their big windows blank. He thought of the colorfulness of the Al Barakaat open market, the brilliance of the silks and colorful *guntiino* robes, the smells of gingerroot and garlic and cumin seed" (95). Strout is carefully respectful of the Somali immigrant experience—and doesn't appropriate it. Eventually, she portrays part of his story. With Abdikarim, Strout is enacting what Keen calls "ambassadorial strategic empathy . . . calling forth the empathy of targeted others for needy strangers, or for the disenfranchised, despised, or the misunderstood among us, often with a specific end in mind" (370). That is, Strout is attempting to encourage her American readers to empathize with Somali refugees. She, like Thomas Hardy, represents in fiction "members of despised groups," bringing "attention to neglected individuals whose perspectives were unlikely to command the attention of investigative journalists" (370). But doing so is not without complications. Abdikarim's history and dream collapse in his recollection of an act of violence that recalls *Olive Kitteridge:*

> His son, tall, dark-eyed, looking at his father, terrified, and behind him the street, and the walls becoming upside down, dust and smoke and the boy falling, as though his arms had been pulled one way, his legs another—To shoot was bad enough to last this lifetime and the next, but not bad enough for the depraved men-boys, who had burst through the door,

the splintered shelves and tables, who swung their large
American-made guns. For some reason—no reason—one had
stayed behind and smashed the end of his gun down onto
Baashi repeatedly, while Abdikarim crawled to him. In the
dream he never reached him. (204)

The inclusion of this memory marks Strout's book as not just
comfort for first-world readers. With it, Strout can be situated within
DiBattista and Nord's tradition of women writers who "through
split narratives, palimpsests, and renderings through memory . . .
go beyond questions of immigration and geography to existential
questions of belonging and to an exploration of individual, rather
than national, identity. In this they echo [Willa] Cather, who de-
clared that the history of every country begins in the heart of an
individual" (221). If we carry our individual histories with us, we
also carry our nation's historical legacies. To be observant, we must
attend to both the personal and the collective. With Abdikarim's
story, Strout shows her readers how they share the world with individuals who have been harmed by atrocities that we must confront.
For Abdikarim,

> The very worst moment of his life, and his deepest longing
> was to return to that moment, to touch the wet hair, to hold
> those arms—he had loved no one as much, and even in the
> horror, or perhaps because of the horror, to hold his broken
> son had been as pure as the sky had been blue. To lie down on
> the spot his son had last been, to press his face into whatever
> dirt or rubble had been replaced a hundred times in the years
> since, was, it felt, at those moments, all he wanted. Baashi,
> my son. (204–5)

Strout describes this violence not in the dry analysis of "causes" but
by showing—to a certain extent—"what it feels like to be trapped
within it" (DiBattista and Nord 235). This longing for a return to a
moment—a wish for a moment to be different—is what Abdikarim,
Pam, Bob, Helen, Susan, and Jim share. This moment, the intense
longing of a parent for a child, recalls *Amy and Isabelle* and *Olive*

Kitteridge. But Abdikarim's loss is different than the other characters', for his child is dead. As we have seen her do in her earlier works, Strout takes international events and explores them through one family's experience.

When Abdikarim sees Zach in court, he remembers his own son and realizes, "That boy. . . . He is cutting my heart. . . . He's not what we saw in the newspaper. He's a frightened . . . child" (204). This compassion, if on one level comforting, could also be problematic and point to Strout's less successful exploration of race and racism. Abdikarim's distinguishing of what he sees from newspaper articles underscores the limitations of factual accounts and, in so doing, elevates other kinds of storytelling. As Strout explains in the appendix, "I knew if I did not take on a Somali point of view, they would remain 'the other,' and the whole point of the book was to make them not that" (236). Whether she is successful in getting her point across is indeterminate. Unlike Dorothy, who dismisses Helen's novel-reading, Strout claims novels can also teach, can enlarge our compassion not only for individuals but for larger social problems as well.

Strout is not didactic. She doesn't come out and say White people need to be educated about the Black experience in the United States, but she shows some of the limitations, the myopia of White privilege. Whether it is Jim realizing, "I don't have any idea what it's like to be black in this country" (306), Abdikarim reflecting on how the United States is "gratifying itself with the impression that all Somalis were pirates" (282), or Pam outraged by the practice of clitoridectomy, Strout shows her readers the limitations of perspective. But she may also draw on uncomfortable stereotypes. After all, Zach does not go to jail because Abdikarim "took a real interest in Zach—campaigned for him with the elders" (317). Abdikarim shows Zach compassion, and through his doing so, Bob, too, learns the power of sympathy, which Strout extends outward to the reader.

That compassion that Abdikarim, Bob, and eventually Jim and Susan also exhibit is accompanied by depression. Abdikarim's catatonia is linked to his emotional side: "He lay on the bed, and there was darkness inside him and darkness in the room," and Susan drives "to work wearing sunglasses even when the mornings were overcast" (95). But the metaphorical darkness that inhabits their bodies and the literal darkness that surrounds them point to the novel's vexed portrayal of Black-White relations. If Abdikarim's and Susan's experiences have been different, their carriage is alike, bearing the weight of their historic (and current burdens). And the novel explains that it's not just the Somali immigrants who need our compassion; we also need to be compassionate toward the Zach and Susan Olsons, the White working-class people who feel left behind by their communities. They, too, she shows her cosmopolitan liberal readers, are othered and deserving of compassion—and fiction in particular offers a way to instruct us in these lessons.

Time has not been kind to Shirley Falls:

> The days were short now, the sun never climbing very high in the sky, and when a blanket of clouds sat over the small city it seemed as though twilight began as soon as people finished their lunch, and when darkness came it was a full darkness. Most of the people who lived there had lived there all their lives, and they were used to the darkness this time of year, but that did not mean they liked it. It was spoken of when neighbors met in grocery stores, or on the steps of the post office, often with an added phrase of what was felt about the holiday season to come; some liked the holidays, many did not. Fuel prices were high, and holidays cost money.
>
> About the Somalis, a few townspeople did not speak at all: They were to be borne as one bore bad winters or the price of gasoline or a child who turned out badly. (132)

In introducing the Somalis, Strout is clearly expanding her range as a writer, but this comes with risk, even as it seeks to address the racially narrow scope of her earlier works. The argument can be made that in rendering Abdikarim as a compassionate figure she denies him justifiable outrage and makes him nonthreatening (likable) to her White readers, an observation that conjures a different

New England literary history, one traceable to Harriet Beecher Stowe. For like Tom, Abdikarim weeps over a fallen child. If Strout is clearly trying to expand her project of eliciting readers' empathy, Abdikarim's story may also raise legitimate questions of appropriation. The Somalis materialize the unease in the town, but it takes a deft hand to metaphorize them as a force of nature in a paragraph discussing the darkness that had descended on the town. The paragraph echoes Melville's "the blackness of darkness," but it doesn't carry the same ironic weight. And the inclusion of details about Wally Packer, the Black defendant of Jim's who probably murdered his White girlfriend, echoes the stereotypical literary baggage in Richard Wright and Harper Lee. Strout may inadvertently draw on racist tropes even as she clearly attempts to enter an ongoing conversation about the rise in racism and xenophobia and the plight of immigrants in the United States. These particular examples show work still needs to be done. To be fair to Strout, the stories of Abdikarim and the Somali community are left unfinished and resonate with both a sense of continued unease and the hope of reconciliation through communication.

Zach is the enigmatic center of the book. Why does he throw the pig's head into the mosque? We never learn, though Van der Kolk reminds us that "kids will go to almost any length to feel seen and connected" (115), including committing crimes, and Tager suggests Zach "seems to have absorbed the general hostility or fear of Muslim people of color present in his hometown" (438). We are never inside his head; he remains outside of the reader's consciousness even more than Jim does, and yet his body, as we saw with Abdikarim, Bob, and Susan, shows his despair. He seems lost through most of the novel. We see the heartbreaking moments in preschool when Zach "cries without stopping" or is pushed by a boy and is "so skinny [he] toppled over like a stick."

> By elementary school he was teased mercilessly. By middle school he was beaten up. By high school his father left. Before Steve left, there were loud arguments that Zach must have heard. "He doesn't ride a bicycle. He can't even swim. He's a

total weenie and you made him that way!" Red-faced, Steve was
adamant. Susan believed her husband, and thought that if Zach
had turned out differently, his father might have stayed. So that
was her fault too. These failures isolated her. Only Zach was
present in her quarantine, mother and son knit together by an
unspoken sense of bafflement and mutual apology. At times she
yelled at him (more often that she knew), and she was always,
afterward, sick with regret and sorrow. (171)

Susan does not realize how wounded her child is. She doesn't know
how to help her son, what tools or environments he needs to help
him grow. She doesn't know what she needs, let alone what he needs.
Because she doesn't accept herself, she can't accept anyone else. This
is the damage, the fallout she has faced from the childhood accident. Susan's failure to forgive herself mirrors Jim's. It never occurs
to them that they ought to forgive themselves and then that they can
forgive others. Strout's work calls for us to be kind to ourselves and
to others, to recognize that they are suffering and that even if they
commit heinous acts, they are still worthy of compassion.

But the book, in spite of the seriousness of some of its subjects,
is also funny, if more pointedly than her previous works were. Strout
reflects on novel-reading (and novel-writing) in humorous ways. If
novels can teach ethics by showing compassion, they can also be
entertaining. For example, when Helen and Dorothy are sunning
themselves in St. Kitts, Helen tells Dorothy, "Don't feel bad about
dropping out of book club." Dorothy responds that she doesn't and
continues, "A lot of women in New York are not stupid until they
get together and then they are stupid. I really hate that" (43), explaining, "women telling women to read stupid books when there's
a whole world out there. Here, read this article. It's related to your
sister-in-law's crisis that Jim was talking about last night" (44).
But while Dorothy distinguishes between silly novels (and the silly
women who read them, recalling George Eliot) and serious articles
that address human suffering, Strout does not. This book shows how
novels might offer comfort and entertainment, but they can also
unsettle readers, leading them to self-awareness, to compassion for

other people, and to ethical, political action. Strout's unsettling the reader, which she does throughout *Lucy Barton* as well, underscores the false divide between reading and action or literature and ethics. Literature—even fiction—can make us more aware of the humans with whom we share the earth, can help readers to recognize their suffering and shared indignities.

If Maine is as much a character in this novel as it is in her other works, here Strout also looks at New York. For example, when Bob goes to meet Pam for a drink, "the colors of Central Park were quietly fall-like: the grass a faded green and the red oaks bronzed, the lindens changing to gentle yellow, the sugar maples losing their orangey leaves, one floating here, another falling there, but the sky was very blue and the air warm enough that the windows of the Boathouses were still open at this late afternoon hour, the striped awnings extending over the water" (81). We get the lyrical language and attention to natural detail we've come to expect from Strout, but her reverie has a different focus. With New York as her canvas, she can no longer be legitimately called a local writer:

> In Brooklyn, Park Slope had spread its edges in every direction. Seventh Avenue was still its main street, but two blocks down Fifth Avenue was starting to open one trendy restaurant after another; boutiques sold fashionable blouses and yoga pants and jewelry and shoes with prices you might expect to find in Manhattan. Fourth Avenue, that wide mess of traffic and grit, now had, surprisingly and suddenly, large-windowed condos among the old brick dwellings; diners appeared on corners, and people walked on Saturdays up to the park. Babies were pushed in strollers as spiffy as sports cars, with fast-turning wheels and adjustable tops. If the parents held inner worries or disappointments, you didn't glimpse it in their flash of healthy teeth and toned limbs as the more enthusiastic ones made a day of walking across the Brooklyn Bridge. . . .
>
> It was April, and while the days were often chilly, there was an exuberance to the forsythia that opened in front gardens. (231)

In classic Strout fashion, she offers the natural world, as well as evidence of social change and historical events. In New York, "midtown was a crowded place at lunchtime, sidewalks overflowing with pedestrians who moved through the traffic-jammed crosswalks, some on their way to a restaurant to maybe make a deal. There was an added urgency today, because just that morning the world's largest bank had reported the first mortgage-related loss at well over ten billion dollars, and people didn't know what that meant" (201). We know the world through our senses and also through our minds, processing intellectual facts distinct from our empirical, lived experiences. In economic terms, the state of the country is about to get a whole lot worse.

Strout continues to experiment with rendering time. Here it's not just cyclical seasonal signs but also historical, personal, and national inflections that she observes. Past and present and multiple perspectives also collide at Zach's hearing, where the courtroom becomes a place that showcases multiple narratives. So it's not just literature that allows us to hear different stories, voices, or perspectives; the law does as well.

At Zach's hearing, the prosecutor speaks of how Zach's action recalls for the Somalis their experience in Africa. We learn not only some of their collective history, but also how people in the courtroom react to its recitation:

> Against the objection of Charlie, the judge allowed Mr. Hussein to speak of the camps of Dadaab, the *shifta,* bandits who came in the night to rob and rape and sometimes kill. The sight of the pig's head in their mosque had made them very afraid, as afraid as they had been in Kenya, as afraid as they had been in Somalia, when doing any daily task could mean the possibility of a surprise attack and death.
>
> Bob wanted to put both hands to his face. He wanted to say, This is awful, but *look* at this boy. He's never heard of a refugee camp. He was teased to death when he was a kid, beaten up on a little playground in Shirley Falls, no bandits around. But to him the bullies were like bandits, and—can't you see he's just a sad-sack kid.

But the Somali were sad, too. Especially the first guy.
After testifying he had taken his seat in the courtroom and
not looked around, keeping his head down, and Bob saw the
exhaustion in his profile. (186)

Both Abdikarim and Bob feel sorry for Zach. This gendering of
compassion is interesting. Men in Strout's work, from Tyler Caskey
to Henry Kitteridge, are often benevolent, kind, and gentle. Abdikarim and Bob follow suit. The men show us that just as there
isn't a limit to suffering, so there isn't a limit to compassion. When
one exercises sympathy, one's sympathy grows. There is always the
chance to learn, the chance to improve, and the courtroom, like
narrative, offers a space not just for facts but for evoking history,
personal and collective, distant and recent, emotional resonances,
and ethical responsibilities, in addition to allegedly objective observations. Toril Moi warns that "a traumatized society needs more
than just facts" to create just laws and to care for its citizens (242).
I believe Strout would argue the same. Moi tells us we cannot "reduce the difficult of reality to the flat and flattening categories on a
general questionnaire [lest we] use language to avoid responsibility"
(242). In other words, language can separate us or draw us together.
Abdikarim's leading of his community allows Zach the chance for
redemption and Shirley Falls the ability to move forward in love, to
not "proceed as if rules, benchmarks, and checklists abolish the need
for human judgment," to not "hide behind their rules and regula-
tions, and their vague, lifeless, and peculiarly impersonal language"
(242). Storytelling offers a more multifaceted look at the human experience than legalese does.

But more important to the story than the courtroom scene is
the relationship between Jim and Bob. The novel is a book about
relationships, and the primary one is between the Burgess brothers
themselves. Strout does not idealize fraternal relationships any more
than she does any other. When the men return to Shirley Falls, driving up at dusk while "the horizon line seemed cracked open to give
a peek at the heavens far beyond [and] thin clouds became pink and
stayed that way, until finally darkness emerged, almost complete,"

apparently in companionable silence, "Bob was unutterably happy. He had not expected the feeling, which intensified it. He gazed out the window at the black stretches of evergreens, the granite boulders here and there. The landscape he had forgotten—and now remembered. The world was an old friend, and the darkness was like arms around him" (140). But next to him, his brother is not filled with wonder or even appreciation, but eventually says aloud, "This is just unbelievably depressing" (140). The two men inhabit the same plane, but see it vastly differently.

Those differences in perception, however, can have devastating consequences. Susan is shocked to learn that Jim thinks he caused the accident that killed their father: "Seriously? Oh, wow. But of course he didn't. You don't think it's true, do you?" Bob replies, "I don't think we'll ever know. . . . [But] he seems to think he did" (317). That the three of them have never talked about the effects of this moment on their lives shows how isolated they have become; because they only saw things from their own perspective, they didn't realize their siblings were also carrying burdens. The past, they realize now, may not be what they thought it was, and, by implication, perhaps the present isn't either. Bob "understood they would probably never again discuss the death of their father. The facts didn't matter. Their stories mattered, and each of their stories belonged to each of them alone" (318).

This, then, is where Strout underscores the importance of stories, or, in scholarly terms, narrative. If facts are elusive, we can use narrative to understand the world around us, others, and ourselves. We must, Strout urges, use those narratives to extend our circle of understanding beyond ourselves toward others. Storytelling, she shows us, offers us a chance to inhabit the world of others, to realize the myopia of our own perspective, to listen rather than to already know.

5 Declaring *My Name Is Lucy Barton*

PUBLISHED IN 2016 AND LONG-LISTED FOR THE Man Booker Prize, Strout's fifth book, *My Name Is Lucy Barton*, differs from its predecessors in two significant ways: it's told in the first person and its settings are New York and Illinois. Employing a kind of Faulknerian stream of consciousness, this novel depicts a writer's self-reflective psychological archaeology of her childhood and time in a hospital when as a young woman she fell terribly sick. As Lucy recuperates from the unnamed disease, she talks with her mother and recalls growing up and her life to date. But, as Sarah Lyall writes, the novel "is really about a great deal more: a terribly troubled past, a present that is slowly imploding, the yawning spaces between even the closest of people, [and] our frequent inability to see what's in front of us" (1). *My Name Is Lucy Barton* marks a departure in more than style and setting for Strout; if in her first four books she expands her experiment of compassion outwards across time and space to gradually include more people, in this novel she turns her focus internally to the writing process and to a person struggling with creation and with her past. In this book more than any other to date, Strout identifies as a writer's writer; she explicitly engages with stories others (including Eliot, Austen, Charlotte Brontë, James, and Faulkner) have told. As a writer she's born into a literary world filled with traumas and tales, and *My Name Is Lucy Barton* enacts another leap of faith; Strout asserts her own place in this constellation.

If Lucy's illness recalls Esther Summerson's in Dickens's *Bleak House*, the distance between people recalls Eliot's and James's themes, and her name evokes Elizabeth Gaskell's and Charlotte Brontë's characters. *Lucy Barton* is a particularly literary, or intertextual, novel. The eponymous heroine wrestles with being a writer, her obligations to her audience and her families, and recognizing beauty in the midst of violence and indifference. Like her nineteenth-century precursors, Strout calls us back to fleeting acts of kindness between people, allowing us a sense of hope for the bitterly divided and chaotic planet we call home. If there are moments of grace, there is also always the threat of doom, its anticipation recalling the unease that haunts Strout's previous works. Here, the genocide of American Indians, World War II, the Holocaust, and the AIDS crisis hover at the margins of Lucy's narrative, their effects permeating the lives of characters. But, as if to counter these grand events, the book focuses on the mental interior of the narrator, her own personal journey.

Once again, Strout shows how political events affect our personal stories, and how great tragedies stem from individuals' private experiences. If we privilege empathy, kindness, and listening, Lucy shows, we can set the stage for a future dominated not by violence but by peaceful respect for others and ourselves. That power of sympathy is rooted in the personal, but harnessed it can change the world, for as Strout claims in an interview with Sally Campbell and Martha Greengrass, "I write so that people can also see others, can understand hopefully—even briefly—what it means to be another

person, and this can make them more empathic." *Lucy Barton,* I believe, offers a uniquely feminine perspective and, in that particular
stance, a feminist one as well. I read this novel as an experiment in
which a woman discovers her voice and, just as importantly, her
ability to act to change her life and her world.[1] Lucy breaks with a
generational cycle of abuse, refusing to pass on what Abraham and
Torok identify as intergenerational neuroses to her own children.
Though the title suggests agency, the novel's fragmented narrative
underscores the effects of trauma Lucy has suffered.[2] She does not
make sense of her existence in a linear way, but she can still claim
her name and her story rooted in her wounded feminine body at the
book's end.

Having grown up on a farm outside the tellingly named Amgash, Illinois, Lucy has made New York her home for years. And
New York through the decades (of the 1970s, '80s, and the current
moment) is one of Lucy's subjects. But the other is the growth of her
own mind, and this novel, as its title suggests, is a *Kunstlerroman,*
a coming-of-age, stream-of-consciousness narrative in which Lucy
realizes the effects of poverty and abuse on her siblings, herself, and
her development as an artist. As we have seen, Strout experiments
with form throughout her earlier work, and here she adopts the
voice of an older woman who looks back on her life.[3]

Lucy's unreliability and mysterious illness recall Dickens's Esther Summerson, and her name evokes the heroines of Charlotte
Brontë's *Villette* and Gaskell's *Mary Barton,* so Lucy seems in many
ways a nineteenth-century character, a woman who has been hurt,
wounded often, and yet endures to become an artist. Indeed, Lucy's
own realization is to a certain degree how her parents hurt her, how
history has hurt others, and what she has given up in leaving two
homes to pursue her craft. The overt references to nineteenth-century
fiction are important because in this literary novel Strout is writing
about being a writer—if her earlier fiction was about families (and to
a lesser extent about social problems), here her subject is how storytelling itself is a lifeline for writers and that which separates them from
others. The other author who silently influences the novel is James.

In some ways, *Lucy Barton* is quiet—but, as in James's work, the vagaries imply that certain actions have occurred that have not been disclosed within the book.[4]

Lucy Barton has suffered, as her namesakes have suffered, and this wounding, as Strout points to in an interview with Sally Campbell and Martha Greengrass, may lead to her artistic consciousness and her literary productivity. But suffering in and of itself is not enough for a person to become an artist; otherwise Lucy's brother and sister—also victims of her parents and social ostracization—would find themselves artists (as would a whole host of other people).[5] In addition to that early wounding, within the novel Lucy, her mentor Sarah Payne, and her friend Jeremy all suggest that artists, too, need to take time to themselves to create. While some might term this setting apart selfish, Sarah and Jeremy suggest that space and time are as crucial to doing the work as early suffering is. Without time taken to care for oneself, the art simply doesn't get made.

Once again we see the allusive symbolic resonance of names for Strout, not only in Lucy's hometown, but also in her first and last names. "Lucy" refers to light, and the lights of the Chrysler Building illuminate Lucy's consciousness, providing her as much hope as any eastern star offers others. Lucy finds her own light in the city; New York gives her the freedom if not exactly to escape her past at least to grow into her own consciousness.[6] But "Barton" resonates symbolically as well, referring to a "farmyard," like the kind where Lucy grew up, though earlier definitions also refer to "fold-yards," "backsides," and "outhouses." Within this book, Strout is shedding light on understories, those that generally remain hidden, and the secrets are disturbing, disgusting, and rooted in physicality. The "backside" is "the reverse or the wrong side of something" (*Oxford English Dictionary*, s.v. "backside"), and we might consider the Bartons, in their poverty, abuse, and cruelty, as the wrong side of the American dream, those people whom middle- and upper-class people, the wealthy and privileged residents of cities, would prefer to forget or ignore.[7] A backside refers to land not rented out but saved for the landowner's use, alluding perhaps to the character trait Lucy,

Jeremy, and Sarah all claim is necessary to create art: being posses-
sive of one's time. The auditory echoes of "barter" are important as
well; "to barter" is to trade something in exchange for something
equally valuable. But what is Lucy bartering? Her story? Her family's
story? And what does she get in exchange? Her voice, her book, and
her name. Eventually we learn that Lucy leaves her marriage because
within it, she did not feel she had the space to write. Bartering her
family homes gives her the opportunity to become a successful artist.[8] What Lucy perhaps does not realize at the time but comes to
learn later is that in walking away from her husband, she is seen by
her daughters as walking away from them, a loss that has stricken
all of them.

Leaving her birth family is crucial for Lucy's mental and physical
health. Leaving her marriage is necessary for her artistic career. Both
decisions have multiple implications for the people she leaves behind; Lucy's brother suffers, alone and distressed; her saving herself
means, to a certain extent, abandoning him. And her sister, if on the
surface appearing healthier than their brother, also struggles.[9] Lucy
sends money to Vicky, but joylessly, indicating her own ambivalence, reservations, resentment, and guilt about leaving. And Lucy's
daughters also feel abandoned, and resentful of her leaving. Finding
herself is not without complicated consequences.

The book is also a meditation on how we tell stories and how we
know ourselves, recalling the fragmentation of Charlotte Brontë's
Villette and Dickens's *Bleak House*, where the protagonists suffer unnamed unspecified illnesses, leaving the reader vaguely searching
for a diagnosis. James takes such unsettling to another level when
something lies just out of reach of telling but haunts the characters, the action, and, consequently, the reader. In some ways *Lucy
Barton* is at its least successful when Lucy reveals things—when she
remembers how her father walked through the house masturbating or publicly humiliated her brother. In an age where "trauma"
has become a buzzword, Lucy's revelations are less effective than
the moments she can't remember. It's what Lucy can't say that
seems most interesting—what Claire Messud describes as Strout's

"vibrating silences"—that seem most profound. What is it that Lucy can't remember?

If we recall *The Burgess Boys*, we might realize it's not so much the events themselves that matter. What matters is that Lucy is haunted by something that she cannot identify, cannot name—and in this way her past relates to her illness. When Strout shows the effects of something rather than the thing itself, her writing is more powerful than any label.[10] But the novel has other subjects as well: femininity, abuse, suffering, coming to voice, and surviving. Lucy's experiences are always mediated through her gender and her childhood, and she suggests that one's history may be the hardest, most difficult subject a writer faces. How does one conceive of and write about one's own history, particularly one etched by suffering at the hands of those we love? *Lucy Barton* performs hesitation, the lapses, pauses, and repetition showing the effect of her private history. In other words, while we see Bob Burgess's drinking, his sister's isolation, his brother's volatility, in *My Name Is Lucy Barton* the narrating itself is tentative, questioning, reflective, the prose style exemplifying chaos, confusion, and self-doubt, the halting effects of trauma. Lucy doesn't come out and say she has been abused, but the narrative reveals the effects of that early suffering. To Joe Fassler, Strout said, "I wanted to make [Lucy] as reliable a narrator as possible, which is why she's always qualifying her memories, as in: *I think that's what my mother said, though I'm not sure.* . . . She's an honest narrator. She's being upfront about the slipperiness of memory—the fact that all of us, sometimes, cannot be quite sure how things happened." When we speak, we often hesitate, backtrack, modify what we have said before, or underscore it—in other words, we don't speak flawlessly, perfectly; but when reading a novel, we often expect polished prose, which theoretically is uncensored but is consistent in its delivery. In *Lucy Barton*, however, the narrator often second-guesses herself, saying things like, "That's what I saw. Or I think it's what I saw." This is refreshing, direct—if our writing, when it appears perfectly polished, often does not show our insecurities, our fallibilities, Strout offers a corrective. She forces us to see how the damage inflicted on

Lucy has affected her very iterations (as well as specific moments of her adult life).

When she tells us the events she remembers, the tenor of her voice begins to make sense. She begins, "There was a time, and it was many years ago now, when I had to stay in a hospital for almost nine weeks" (3). Her hospital stay, a hiatus in her life, in some ways is the physical manifestation, years later, of her childhood trauma. Bessel van der Kolk explains that alexithymia is "the technical term for not being able to identify what is going on inside oneself. People who suffer from alexithymia tend to feel physically uncomfortable but cannot describe exactly what the problem is. As a result they often have multiple vague and distressing physical complaints that doctors can't diagnose" (272), and alexithymia usually points to underlying conditions. A young mother who falls ill, Lucy finds herself in the hospital; soon her own mother visits her, and much of the novel takes place during the conversation between the two women. But the beginning underscores that Lucy has since recovered, and if her sickness is what precipitates her mother's coming to visit her, it is Lucy's recovery—not just from her unidentified illness but also from her childhood—that resonates. Strout plays with frames here as well. Not only does present-day Lucy recall her time in the hospital, she also recalls her childhood and her young adulthood in bits and pieces. Instead of the frame within a frame, say of conventional nineteenth-century narratives or of *The Burgess Boys*, here the framing is interrupted, as Lucy skates in between the present, the past, and the very distant past. Strout's very fragmentation packs a punch different from books that offer a traditional sense of closure.

Lucy reflects on her own childhood and how, lost at home and at school, she found herself in the pages of fiction, as so many introspective, introverted children do, leading her to become a writer as an adult: she wants to comfort others the way she has been comforted.[11] Lucy explains that her own journey to become a writer was neither straight nor linear, but jagged. The novel begins in medias res, but goes backwards and forwards in chronology—pointing out that fiction consistently gave Lucy a pleasure, a sanctuary that she couldn't find at home (though we never learn, I believe, the extent to which the Bartons injure their children) or at school when the other children ostracize her. In books, she is safe, liked, and capable.

Lucy's motivation to create art comes from an explicitly social place. She wants to heal people, to salve their suffering, and in this way she serves as an emblem for Strout herself. This desire may appear to counter the selfishness that Sarah and Jeremy say is necessary for an artistic career, or how her daughters feel she treats them; and this tension between these two desires—to comfort and to create—runs throughout Lucy's life and her career.[12] If Lucy wants to comfort her readers, she does not offer balm to her families. For in writing honestly about her life, she betrays the Bartons.

To save herself, Lucy leaves home: in going to school, in marrying her husband, in leaving her husband, and in writing her memoirs. Lucy must un-home herself; she must be lost to write. And though she does not offer comfort to her families—her parents, her husbands, her children—her story may offer comfort to others, may let readers who have suffered abuse know that they are not alone and that they can survive and even thrive.[13] Lucy's feelings for her own children are complex; we see her tenderness toward her daughters, both when they are young and when they are older, and yet she leaves them to write. Her leave-takings are necessarily related because she must leave her home to write her story—and telling her story is how she endures, owning her name and her artistic identity. It is how she is able to say, "My name is Lucy Barton." Once again Strout does not shy away from articulating the ambivalence of parenting. Lucy feels great affection for both her daughters and her mother—and these intergenerational ties are important—but she needs to sever them to become the artist she wants to be.

Her neighbor Jeremy tells her that to write she must be ruthless. Sarah Payne's advice is somewhat different. Sarah tells Lucy that she must be honest, and speak the truth no matter how "painful"— here Sarah is talking about Lucy's relationship with her mother and her father. In both cases, these mentors express to Lucy that she must put her work before the feelings of others. But—and this is important—Lucy doesn't overtly confront her mom about her child-hood, perhaps because she can't speak directly about everything that has happened to her. There are some things that she cannot narrate, perhaps because she cannot see them. Van der Kolk explains that "many traumatized children and adults simply cannot describe what they are feeling because they cannot identify what their physical sensations mean. . . . Not being able to discern what is going on inside their bodies causes them to be out of touch with their needs, and they have trouble taking care of themselves, whether it involves eating the right amount at the right time or getting the sleep they need" (98). But Strout is different from James in that she addresses poverty and classism through a particularly feminized lens. This book, like Strout's first, is very much a book about women.

Though Strout is reluctant to call her writing "women's fiction," the principal concerns—shame, family, art, and voice—are nothing if not gendered, even though the novel's trajectory does not follow the conventional coming-of-age storyline. Nevertheless, Lucy's ex-periences and the way she inhabits the world are necessarily feminine. For example, the abuse that she describes in the most vivid detail is at one remove—when her father humiliates her brother by march-ing him down the street wearing women's undergarments over his clothes. The sight devastates Lucy and her sister, who try to leave the scene behind them; yet the memory stays with the future writer, who remembers how her father—an adult who is supposed to protect and love his children—hurts his son. That betrayal of trust cannot be undone or forgotten. Psychoanalysis tells us the child who witnesses a sibling being beaten feels despair at witnessing the event, relief that she was not hurt, sympathy and schadenfreude for the victim, and guilt at not intervening—in other words, ambivalence. We see a similar ambivalence play out in Lucy's adult life when she talks with her mother in the hospital, yearning for her companionship, even though her mother hurt her when she was a young girl. Socialized to be submissive, to be quiet even in the face of abuse—whether their own or others—girls, Alice Miller explains, have a particularly am-bivalent relationship to their abusers.

Lucy's experience with her father's humiliation of her brother shames her in various ways; she is ashamed of her brother's appearing in drag, of her father's verbal and physical abuse of him as he parades him along the street, and by her reaction—that she does nothing to stop it. She's also ashamed of her father's chronic masturbation and her family's poverty. As a child, Lucy is mocked and derided for her poverty, and as she grows up, she feels ill at ease in middle- and upper-class America as cultural references pass her by.[14] Such experiences with shame speak to a particularly feminine way of engaging with the world. Rather than calling out others on their bad behavior, Lucy feels bad about herself, her shame turned inward, again recalling nineteenth-century heroines who suffer from melancholia. Shame is one way that women process the bad things that have happened to them, rather than anger at the social and structural circumstances that allow such events to take place (here we might also think of Isabelle Goodrow and Susan Burgess). But Lucy, unlike Isabelle or Susan, writes, perhaps modeling for her readers a healthy way to deal with the horrors of their lives. In recording what has happened to her—and perhaps particularly in her halting and self-deprecating style—Lucy both asserts her own voice and articulates these experiences; she will not be silent about these tragedies, small and large, that she and others have faced.

The abuse that Lucy experiences and the shame she suffers as a result have everything to do with her gender, her first family, and her complex, complicated feelings toward her parents, her siblings, her husbands, and her children. She adores her parents, in spite of how they hurt her. Lucy wants to please them; she loves them, in spite of their thoughtlessness and cruelty. In *The Drama of the Gifted Child*, Alice Miller explains that many daughters find themselves looking to assuage their parents' suffering, considering themselves responsible for their parents' emotional problems, not realizing they stem from early, deep-seated issues. Lucy is no exception. When Lucy finds herself in the hospital, small, helpless, and sick—in other words, feminine—she cries out to be held. A young mother herself, Lucy wants to be babied, but her mother is not equipped to offer such emotional support. Although she attempts to leave the Bartons, first by going to college and then by moving to New York, Lucy is unable to make a clean break, to feel irresponsible for her parents, brother, and sister. Again, this seems a particularly feminine response. In the United States, women traditionally do most of the heavy emotional work of child-rearing and caring for older parents. Her surprisingly unfeminine choice is leaving her first husband.[15]

Lucy becomes more prolific, more productive after she leaves her husband; that leaving enables her to create art, but she is torn about it, particularly about being perceived as abandoning her daughters. She becomes an artist, but in pursuing that path, she hurts them. Again, Lucy's perception of her struggle strikes me as particularly feminine. That is, women are encouraged to judge themselves harshly for decisions they make, and that distress is often coded as a kind of feminine anxiety. But Lucy channels that anxiety into this memoir, which, we will learn in the next book by Strout, offers a lifeline to its readers. This book, as its title underscores, is about feminine agency—Lucy names herself; she owns her name and her history, telling it the way she chooses. She writes her story the way she wants to, with compassion toward her parents but also a veiled look at the pain and suffering they caused her. Her narrative is not linear and it lacks closure, and with those choices Lucy rejects a phallogocentric concrete narrative style. She may not know everything—indeed, she says as much over and over again—but she knows her "name is Lucy Barton" and that behind that statement there is a valuable story.

Her tentative style is also a performance of femininity. Throughout the book, the tone is intimate—a quality we've come to expect in Strout's work—but in addition, it is self-effacing, unsure. Unlike an "objective" masculine tone, this one luxuriates in not knowing. Lucy stresses that she is not a reliable narrator, but Strout tells us that in doing so, Lucy is more believable than she would be if she claimed she knew exactly what happened. Lucy's relationship to language, to artistry, to her families (birth and chosen), and to literature are all inextricably linked to her femininity. In some ways, what it is that

Lucy can't remember (sexual abuse and beatings are the obvious examples that come to mind) is less important than the fact that she can't remember. Something haunts her—for example, she thinks she remembers being locked in her father's truck with a snake—but she can't tell exactly what that is.

The novel begins in some ways with Strout's customary easy intimacy. "There was a time, and it was many years ago now, when I had to stay in a hospital for almost nine weeks" (3), recalling *Abide with Me* and *The Burgess Boys*. While Lucy emphasizes a closeness to the reader, a sense that this will be a story about relationships, she also stresses chronology—"time," "years," and "almost nine weeks" appear in the first sentence. This novel is about history. We learn that Lucy has survived, that she is older, and that she will tell us a story. As Lucy continues, "May," "June," and "young women—my age" all appear in short order. But even while Strout emphasizes chronology, she also evokes an almost mystical quality not apparent in her earlier works. "This was in New York City," she continues, "and at night a view of the Chrysler Building, with its geometric brilliance of lights, was directly visible from my bed. During the day, the building's beauty receded, and gradually it became simply one more large structure against a blue sky, and all the city's buildings seemed remote, silent, far away" (3). Strout offers a specificity with proper names, only to wash them in a kind of lyrical glow, a soft, slow Didionesque quality. Lucy's New York is unknown and mysterious. In this way, then, the city is also a metaphor for Lucy's relationship to her past and indeed Lucy herself. If the book is a psychological excavation, it's one that reveals that at its center is not a simple answer but a kind of vagueness. Just as Lucy doesn't know, neither do we what exactly—in terms of concrete details—happened to her and shaped her to become the person she is today.

When Lucy claims, "To begin with, it was a simple story," perhaps alarm bells should go off. In some ways, her story is anything but "simple"; she continues, "I had gone into the hospital to have my appendix out. After two days they gave me food, but I couldn't keep it down. And then a fever arrived. No one could isolate any bacteria or figure out what had gone wrong. No one ever did" (4). With the repetition of negatives, Strout emphasizes what we do not know rather than what we do—and indeed, the working title of the book, Strout observes in the appendix, was "*Idiopathic*, meaning no known cause" (244).

Lucy's world is one where awful things happen; she refers to the existential horrors of the American Indian genocide, the concentration camps, the AIDS pandemic, family abuse, and indifference to children's physical and psychic pain. Suffering is not limited to great social events; we also see her zoom in on the quotidian moments of tragedy that wreak havoc on sensitive children. For example, when her young daughters visit Lucy in the hospital, "They were really frightened. They sat with me on the bed while I dried their hair with a towel, and then they drew pictures, but with apprehension, meaning they did not interrupt themselves every minute by saying, 'Mommy, Mommy, do you like this? Mommy, look at the dress of my fairy princess!' They said very little, the younger one especially seemed unable to speak, and when I put my arms around her, I saw her lower lip thrust out and her chin tremble; she was a tiny thing, trying so hard to be brave" (5). This distillation of a child's pain rendered in her body, transient, emotional, and physical, is wrenching (and recalls Katherine Caskey in *Abide with Me*). These moments of specificity—not everything is vague or hard to follow—create lucid images poetic in their intensity. Strout does not give us the same clarity about other moments in Lucy's life. When her little girl is scared, she is quiet, wordless, like her mother. How does one speak when one is frightened? We see in the course of the book that Lucy has spent much of her life afraid, but finally she finds herself capable of telling her story.[16]

Her daughter's vulnerabilities mirror Lucy's own. Both are terrified, confused, desperate for attention, and afraid to ask for it: "Had anyone known the extent of my loneliness I would have been embarrassed. Whenever a nurse came to take my temperature, I tried to get her to stay for a few minutes, but the nurses were busy, they could not just hang around talking" (6). Lucy is as fragile as

her daughter, as desperate for attention. Shame and loneliness connect Lucy to her childhood—and so her husband, reluctant to visit
the hospital himself, arranges for her mother to come. That action
shows both his tenderness and his own emotional paralysis—he
thinks he doesn't have the wherewithal to care for his wife, but does
what he thinks he can to bring her comfort. Lucy is overcome by her
husband's and mother's gestures—Lydia has never been on a plane
and never visited her daughter.[17]

Lucy wants to hear about her father, but her mother talks to
her instead of other people, including her brother, who at thirty-six
still lives with his parents and doesn't work, but "spends the night
with any animal that will be killed the next day. . . . He goes into the
Pedersons' barn, and he sleeps next to the pigs that will be taken
to slaughter" (9). This aside is all that Lucy's mother tells her about
Pete, who hovers just outside of Lucy's consciousness. Lydia then
tells Lucy stories of other families, as if stories of their own home
life, past and present, are too painful to express.[18]

Lucy vacillates between remembering her time in the hospital and
the more distant past when "we were oddities. . . . Both Vicky and I
understood that we were different" (11).[19] Lucy recalls her classmates
telling them they stank, teachers shaming them, and their parents,
"usually my mother and usually in the presence of my father—
[striking] us impulsively and vigorously, as I think some people may
have suspected by our splotchy skin and sullen dispositions" (12).
Lucy lets us know that "there are times now, and my life has changed
so completely, that I think back on the early years and I find myself
thinking: It was not that bad," and, as if needing to reassure herself,
"Perhaps it was not" (14). But her own fragility belies this affirmation, for she tells us "there are times, too—unexpected—when walking down a sunny sidewalk, or watching the top of a tree bend in
the wind, or seeing a November sky close down over the East River,
I am suddenly filled with the knowledge of darkness so deep that a
sound might escape from my mouth. . . . This must be the way most
of us maneuver through the world, half knowing, half not, visited
by memories that can't possibly be true" (14).[20] As if acknowledging

her own limitations, Lucy realizes, "When I see others walking with confidence down the sidewalk, as though they are free completely from terror, I realize I don't know how others are. So much of life seems speculation" (14). She wears her tenderness and vulnerability openly. She feels doom and nostalgia; her vulnerability and her tentativeness are her defining features, and in these she is so vastly different from the imposing, irascible Olive. Here we have that Jamesian moment—what is it that haunts Lucy?

Rather than narrative trajectory (or "plot," a word Strout detests), she gives us a story told in poetic images. Perhaps our life is composed of those. That's not to say the moments are all beautiful, but their vividness—not the linear direction—is how we understand our world. For example, Lucy lets us know that until she "was eleven years old, we lived in a garage. . . . Insulation nailed against the wall held a stuffing like pink cotton candy, but it was fiberglass and could cut us, we were told. I was puzzled by that, and would stare at it often, such a pretty pink thing I could not touch; and I was puzzled to think it was called 'glass'; odd to think now how much time it seemed to take up in my head, the puzzle of that pretty pink and dangerous fiberglass we lived right next to every minute" (22). Loveliness and danger are qualities of many abusive individuals, and Lucy is a skilled enough writer for this image to serve as a symbol.

Lucy in some ways is saved, unlike her brother and sister, perhaps because of sheer luck or natural propensity or a combination of both. She tells us she stays "late at school, where it was warm, just to *be* warm," and Tommy Guptill, the janitor who appears in the first story of Strout's next book, *Anything Is Possible*, Lucy tells us, "always let me into a classroom where the radiators were still hissing and so I did my homework there" (23). Tommy is kind to her, as are her teachers, who give her books, which, she explains, "brought me things. This is my point. They made me feel less alone. This is my point. And I thought: I will write and people will not feel so alone! (But it was my secret. Even when I met my husband I didn't tell him right away. I couldn't take myself seriously. Except that I did. I took myself—secretly, secretly—very seriously! I knew I *was* a writer . . .)"

(24–25).[21] If she takes herself seriously secretly, though, she also relies on others' generosity, and she achieves her dreams because people are kind to her, nurturing her abilities.

Lucy focuses not only on her own suffering but on that of her family as well. On meeting Lucy's first husband, her father becomes distressed: "When they shook hands I saw in my father's face great contortions, the kind that frequently preceded what as a child I had called—to myself—the *Thing*, meaning an incident of my father becoming very anxious and not in control of himself" (31). Just what that thing is, how it manifests itself, is unclear, but later Pete tells her that William reminded their father of two men who startled him in the war and whom he shot in the back, not knowing how young they were: "My father had murdered two German boys, and as my father lay dying he told my brother that not a day had gone by when he did not think of them, and feel that he should have taken his own life in exchange. What else happened to my father in the war I do not know, but he was in the Battle of the Bulge and he was at the Hürtgen Forest, and these were two of the worst places to be in the war" (32). As we've seen in Strout's other works, children live with the effects of their parents' trauma even if they are unaware of the originary event or how much they—or their parents—are suffering.[22] Van der Kolk explains in his analysis of work with veterans that "trauma, whether it is the result of something done to you or something you yourself have done, almost always makes it difficult to engage in intimate relationships. After you have experienced something so unspeakable, how do you learn to trust yourself or anyone else again?" (13). Lucy's story is not about her father, and yet his inability to heal from the war has influenced her life. Until we know something different, something that puts our perspective into relief, we assume our experiences are shared by many.

Lucy, like Chris Kitteridge and Bob and Jim Burgess, chooses to leave home, to find herself in New York. And Lucy, like these men, is never quite at home in the city. When Lucy tells Jeremy she can't believe she lives in New York, rather than his being kind to her, "a look went across his face—so fast, so involuntary—that was a look of real distaste. I had not yet learned the depth of disgust city people feel for the truly provincial" (39). Lucy sees again and again how people treat others with disgust, cruelty, or indifference. But Jeremy is also an astute observer of human nature, a psychoanalyst, and when Lucy's daughter tells him excitedly that her mother has had a story published, he says, "So—you're a writer. You're an artist. . . . I guess I've always known that about you" (40), and though she is sheepish, he tells her he trusts her abilities: "I can't imagine reading anything by you that I wouldn't like" (41). The other thing he says to her that she remembers is that "artists are different from other people. . . . You must be ruthless, Lucy" (40). Having been thought of as different her whole life and not wanting to be perceived as ruthless, Lucy rejects these labels. In some ways she hardly seems ruthless; she is gentle and tender to her girls, victimized by her parents, possessing a sensitivity often culturally coded as feminine. But gentleness, in and of itself, doesn't lead to artistry—to produce work, Jeremy implies, one must privilege the work. If that appears selfish to others, then so be it.

Jeremy is gay, though Lucy isn't always aware of this. When she is with him and two young men, "bony and gaunt . . . sick with this sudden, almost biblical-seeming plague," walk by, she says, "I'm almost jealous of them. Because they have each other, they're tied together in real community" (41). After she speaks, Jeremy looks at her "with real kindness in his face," and she now believes he saw what she did not, that in spite of her "plentitude," she was lonely: "Lonely was the first flavor I had tasted in my life, and it was always there, hidden inside the crevices of my mouth, reminding me. . . . He understood that loneliness about me. This is what I want to think. This is what I think" (41–42). If Jeremy appears judgmental about provincialism, he also encourages Lucy, offers her kindness. We might wonder whether withholding from speaking is an act of kindness, or whether it signifies something else. Lucy allows for multiple interpretations with her words, "This is what I want to think. This is what I think" (42).

Lucy then relates how years later she saw a beautiful woman in a boutique and asked for her advice on clothing. The woman was shy about saying her name, "Sarah Payne," and when Lucy returned home she found she owned books Sarah had written and remembered "being at a party with a man who knew her. He spoke of her work, saying that she was a good writer, but that she could not stop herself from a 'softness of compassion' that revolted him, that, he felt, weakened her work" (46). Such a description might apply to Strout's fiction—her characters, as we have seen, are often good, kindhearted people trying to make their way through life. Lucy herself considers, "I liked her books. I like writers who try to tell you something truthful. I also liked her work because she had grown up on a rundown apple orchard in New Hampshire, and she wrote about the rural parts of that state, she wrote about people who worked hard and suffered and also had good things happen to them" (46). The description sounds like Strout's stories of the Caskeys, the Burgesses, and the Kitteridges. But then Lucy continues, "I realized that even in her books, she was not telling *exactly* the truth, she was always staying away from something. Why, she could barely say her name! And I felt I understood that too" (46). This revelation is important. Sarah becomes an inspiration and a mentor to Lucy, yet Lucy's ultimate articulation and owning of her name distinguishes her from Sarah. She, as the title tells us, will tell her story confidently. She can say her name.

Even as Lydia disparages Lucy, she also comforts her daughter, who "dozed on and off listening to my mother's voice. . . . I thought: All I want is this" (55). Lucy soon realizes, however, that she "wanted something [more than comfort]. I wanted my mother to ask about my life. I wanted to tell her about the life I was living now" (55). She longs for her mother's approval, unable to see that her mother is too emotionally bereft to help her. In a poignant act, wrenching in its recalling, "stupidly—it was just stupidity—I blurted out, 'Mom, I got two stories published'" (55). Lucy's mother doesn't respond. In Lucy's angst-ridden recollection, "it was just stupidity," we see how damaged she is. Neither her accomplishment nor her wanting affirmation from her mother is stupid. The accomplishment is impressive; the desire to be seen is profoundly human. The child in Lucy longs for her mother to recognize her—as Jeremy did.

Unlike Sarah, Lucy tries to speak her history even if it is clearly discomforting to others. For example, she remembers being locked in her father's truck when she was a child, "the dirt-streaked windows, the tilt of the windshield, the grime on the dashboard, the smell of diesel gas and rotting apples, and dogs. I don't know, in numbers how many times I was locked in the truck. I don't know the first time, I don't know the last time. But I was very young, no more than five years old" (58). Lucy believes she must have been either being punished or waiting for her parents, and she felt abandoned, alone, and scared: "I did not think I would die, I don't think I thought anything, it was just terror, realizing that no one was going to come, and watching the sky get darker, and feeling the cold start in. Always I screamed and screamed. I cried until I could hardly breathe" (59). Lydia would find Lucy's fear silly; mother and daughter are unable to see the same world, yet Strout captures the child's embodied fear with agonizing clarity. Lucy's own experience may allow her to be empathic toward others, for "once in a while I see a child crying with the deepest of desperation, and I think it is one of the truest sounds a child can make. I feel almost, then, that I can hear within me the sound of my own heart breaking," but then, with brutal honesty, she admits, "I have left the subway car I was riding so I did not have to hear a child crying that way" (59). Perhaps that is the ruthlessness Jeremy says she must own, and in telling us of the incident, Lucy is honest with herself and the reader in the way Sarah Payne tells her she must be. Leaving the subway, Lucy privileges her self-preservation; she protects herself rather than comforting the child. Lucy's act of self-preservation may exemplify one of those moments when Strout unsettles the reader, jarring her out of identifying with Lucy and into realizing the distance between them. That is, though Lucy doesn't stop the child's suffering, the reader may become aware that if she has been identifying with Lucy, there is a cost to doing so. To be fair to Lucy, perhaps she wasn't so much fleeing the responsibility to stop someone's suffering so much as simply having to be aware of it. Lucy acts in a way that may be understandable and even warranted, but that allows the child's pain to continue—that is, in other words, selfish. With such a moment, Strout's reader becomes more aware of her own position of reading a narrative—she's at a remove from the story and so may marvel at Strout's powers and become more aware of her own place in the world, of how, if she chooses self-preservation (or losing herself in a book), she is not looking outward, not helping someone else.

Lydia tries to be compassionate to Lucy, going so far as to tell her, "I'm sorry we had so little money when you kids were growing up. I know it was humiliating" (65). This is the closest she can come to an apology. In good daughter fashion, Lucy tries to soothe her mother. "I don't think it mattered. . . . We're all fine now." But her mother, in one of her rare admissions, says, "I'm not so sure. . . . Your brother is almost a middle-aged man who sleeps with pigs and reads children's books. And Vicky—she's still mad about it. The kids made fun of you at school. Your father and I didn't know that, I suppose we should have" (65). Lucy wants to tell her mother about being locked in the truck, but she doesn't. She worries that what she remembers of the experience may not be true: "My mind went very strange places during these episodes of being in the truck. I thought I saw a man coming toward me, I thought I saw a monster" (59). The monster Lucy thinks she remembers may have been another figure too terrifying for her to recall accurately.

What is it that Lucy cannot see? We don't know. Tommy Guptill and her teachers are kind to her, but she is not used to tenderness from adults. Her current doctor's solicitude reminds her how "in my youth there were times that I wanted desperately to run to a stranger when we went into town and say, 'You need to help me, please, please, can you please get me out of there, bad things are going on—' And yet I never did, of course; instinctively I knew that no stranger would help, no stranger would dare to, and that in the end such a betrayal would make things far worse" (81–82). The adult Lucy leaves the child crying in the subway car; Strout thus captures the child's despair from both points of view. Fearing and adoring their parents, children don't have the words to describe their experiences, but their bodies show their anxieties: Pete Barton throws

up every morning, afraid to leave home; Lucy cries in the school
bathroom every day because she misses her mother. The children
desperately love the parents who hurt them, and even as adults, they
try to please their mother and father.

We see the child in Lucy when in the hospital she can't fall asleep
because she feels she had been unkind to her mother:

> I was agitated; I wanted to cry. When my own children cried
> I fell to pieces, I would kiss them and see what was wrong.
> Maybe I did it too much. . . . But with my mother I didn't
> dare cry. Both my parents loathed the act of crying, and it's
> difficult for a child who is crying to have to stop, knowing if
> she doesn't stop everything will be made worse. This is not an
> easy position for any child. And my mother—that night in
> the hospital room—was the mother I had had all my life, no
> matter how different she seemed with her urgent quiet voice,
> her softer face. What I mean is, I tried not to cry. (100–101)

Lucy is still afraid, and so she qualifies her statements: "what I mean
is." Such qualifications emphasize the depth of her insecurity. But I
wonder if, even as these self-effacing phrases often signify fear, they
could also signal Lucy's owning of her own voice and of the way she
speaks. Though Lydia cannot see it, we might recognize a strength in
quavering, the acquiring of her own voice.

Lucy later sees Sarah Payne at a writing workshop. Lucy gives
Sarah sketches of the hospital scene, and Sarah tells her,

> This is very good and it will be published. Now listen. People
> will go after you for combining poverty and abuse. *Such* a
> stupid word, "abuse," such a conventional and stupid word,
> but people will say there's poverty without abuse, and you will
> never say anything. Never ever defend your work. This is a story
> about love, you know that. This is a story of a man who has
> been tortured every day of his life for things he did in the war.
> This is the story of a wife who stayed with him, because most
> wives did in that generation, and she comes to her daughter's
> hospital room and talks compulsively about everyone's marriage

going bad, she doesn't even know it, doesn't even know what she's doing. This is a story about a mother who loves her daughter. Imperfectly. Because we *all* love imperfectly. But if you find yourself protecting anyone as you write this piece, remember this: You're not doing it right. (107)

Is Sarah a gimmick? Does she tell the reader how to appreciate Lucy's story and Strout's work? Is she Strout's response to how her work may have been perceived? In some ways, Sarah's words distill the novel, and they also distill a message that runs throughout Strout's work. She tells Lucy to be brave in the face of those who would diminish her, and she tells Lucy that her story is a love story. If "write what is true" sounds trite, unique to Strout is the emphasis on love; though others might see the story as one of abuse and trauma (buzzwords that reduce the suffering people face), Sarah tells Lucy her love story in reckoning with caring for others, vulnerability, and complications, in its very rich complexity—profound in its very imperfections—matters, resonates, and connects. Here we might recall Strout's other protagonists—Isabelle, Tyler, Olive, and Bob—all of whom struggle with beautiful, imperfect loving.

When Lucy is in the hospital, she is in the process of recovering from her childhood (though that phrase oversimplifies her experience). At moments she is still childlike, at others, she appears to be growing into a healthy adult. For example, when her mother calls her out on using the word "screw," Lucy asks herself,

and this is when—recording this—I think once more. . . . Why did I not just say, Mom, I learned all the words I needed to right in that *fucking* garage we called home? I suspect I said nothing because I was doing what I have done most of my life, which is to cover for the mistakes of others when they don't know they have embarrassed themselves. I do this, I think, because it could be me a great deal of the time. I know faintly, even now, that I have embarrassed myself, and it always comes back to the feeling of childhood, that huge pieces of knowledge about the world were missing that can never be replaced. (111–12).

I want to emphasize here that Lucy is kind to her mother—she doesn't call her out on her behavior. Even as an adult, Lucy puts her mother's dignity and feelings first; what's unusual, though—what indicates she has taken Sarah's lesson to heart years later—is that she recounts the scene for the book (her parents have died in the interim). If, as a young mother, Lucy protected her own mother by not confronting her in the hospital, in writing her memoirs, Lucy will not protect Lydia's legacy any longer. Since both of her parents are dead, Lucy can both protect their feelings and tell her story; telling her story may harm their reputation, but it will not harm them. At this point in her life, Lucy has the ability to be both kind and honest.

Even so, while she is in the hospital, Lucy worries that her mother will talk about their family life. She is paralyzed with fear in the hospital bed, afraid that Lydia will address her husband's mental illness. Here, Strout describes vividly the emotional state both of a young woman looking back on her childhood and the child herself, repulsed by and afraid of her parents: "I waited quite a while, quite a while I waited, lying there with my heart thumping, I can remember even now the thumping, the banging of my heart, and I thought of what I had—to myself—always called the *Thing*, the most horrifying part of my childhood. I was very frightened lying there, I was frightened that my mother would mention it after all these years, after never mentioning it ever" (114). But she doesn't. What "the Thing" is remains unspoken between them.

In the next scene, Lucy remembers attending her first Gay Pride parade after "the history of Stonewall, and then the awful business of AIDS, and many people came to line the streets and be supportive and also to celebrate and mourn those who died." This occurs after Lucy's stay in the hospital as "men walked by in purple high heels and wigs and some in dresses, then there were mothers who marched by, and all the kinds of things you see at such an event in New York" (117). Her husband sees that Lucy is stricken and he takes her home. He is the only person she ever told of how, when she was ten,

Vicky came shrieking toward the schoolyard to find me. . . .
I only remember her shriek and the gathering of people and
the laughter. My father was driving our truck along the main
street in town and he was screaming at my brother, who was
walking down the street in a pair of high heels I recognized
from the basket, and a bra over his T-shirt, and a string of
fake pearls, and his face was streaming with tears. My father
drove alongside him in our truck screaming that he was
a fucking faggot and the world should know. I could not
believe what I saw, and I took Vicky's hand, though I was the
youngest, and I walked her all the way home. My mother was
there and said that our brother had been found wearing her
clothes, and it was disgusting and my father was teaching him
a lesson and Vicky should stop her noise, and so I took Vicky
away in the fields until it was dark and we became more
afraid of the dark than of our home. I still am not sure it's
true memory, except I do know it, I think. I mean: It is true.
Ask anyone who knew us. (118–19)

After recalling the moment and then her husband's response to her
own distress and his reasonable—rather than compassionate—sense
of how the parade emblematizes pride, Lucy remembers how Sarah
Payne "told us to go to the page without judgment, reminded us
that we never knew, and never would know, what it would be like to
understand another person fully." The phrase is a mantra of Strout's,
but Lucy continues, "It seems a simple thought, but as I get older I
see more and more that she had to tell us that. We think, always we
think, What is it about someone that makes us despise that person,
that makes us feel superior? I will say that that night—I remember
this part more than what I just described—my father lay next to my
brother in the dark and held him as though he was a baby, he rocked
him on his lap and I could not tell one's tears and murmurs from the
other's" (120). Once again Strout shows the profound ambivalence
and complexity of family love. Ken Barton has publicly humiliated
his child, but also holds him with inexpressible tenderness.[23] Pete,
Vicky, and Lucy survive these horrible experiences. If the children

are not to blame for what they suffered, we might say that Mr. Barton isn't to blame either, that he has a mental illness, and in some ways perhaps blame or understanding isn't even the point; the point perhaps is to bear witness, to realize that others have suffered and that we can choose to be compassionate to them or not. Lydia Barton, it seems, does not choose compassion, and thus, like Helen Burgess, she is condemned by her indifference. Her world is smaller because she is not kind.

When Lucy is in the workshop, one of the other students talks about how a friend's father "started walking around the house just masturbating compulsively," and Lucy becomes "freezing cold in the Arizona heat. . . . I had never before heard, nor have I heard since of this *Thing*—as I had called it to myself—happening as it had happened in our home" (160). If Lucy can allow herself to see this part of her past, there may well be other parts that she cannot allow herself to see. Mr. Barton's humiliation of her brother and his compulsive masturbating may not be the worst things Lucy witnessed, but only the worst things she can remember. Later, Lucy tells us, she goes to a doctor and "wrote down things that had happened in my childhood home. I wrote down things I'd found out in my marriage. I wrote down things I could not say. She read them all and said, Thank you, Lucy. It will be okay" (161). We don't learn what Lucy writes down, but the implication is that there are incidents she both reveals and occludes within her public memoir. It is interesting, though, that Lucy does offer us so many moments of people being kind to her, whether it's her teachers, the janitor, the nurses, the therapist, Sarah Payne, or the doctor in the hospital. These moments of kindness are sprinkled throughout the narrative, offering us hope in a world haunted by death, starvation, cold, prejudice, poverty, cruelty, and suffering.

Jeremy dies of AIDS while Lucy is in the hospital; when she comes home, she is so thin, she looks as if she is starving, and strangers assume she too has AIDS:

> I wore sleeveless dresses, and I didn't realize I was so skinny.
> But I saw people look at me with fear when I went down

the street to get food for the children. I was furious that
they looked at me with fear. It was not unlike how children
on our school bus would look at me if they thought I might
sit next to them.

The gaunt and bony men continued to walk by. (154)

The connection between poverty, starvation, AIDS, and the concentration camps is important here. People fear those who are starving instead of looking at others with compassion.[24] It's that failure
to treat with compassion that Lucy finds so reprehensible. And it's
why she and Strout argue that literature matters—reading books
can teach us to be less afraid, particularly of those who need our
sympathy but who look and act otherworldly in their suffering. It's
not just Pete Barton who deserves our compassion, it's his father and
mother as well. Suffering within this novel is physical and mental.
The bodies of Lucy, Jeremy, Mr. Barton, and Pete bear the marks of
trauma, but these scars are compounded by the ostracism of others.
Indifference exacerbates suffering.

It's no accident, then, that AIDS runs throughout this narrative.
When Lucy is in the hospital and waiting to be X-rayed, she sees a
man who may or may not be Jeremy, marked as an AIDS patient,
staring at her from across the hall: "I felt in this man's gaze that he
was begging me for something. I tried to look away, to give him
privacy, but each time I glanced at him again he was still staring at
me. . . . I've come to recognize the eyes that burn, the very last light
of the body's light to go out. In a way that man helped me that day.
His eyes said: I will not look away. And I was afraid of him, of death,
of my mother leaving me. But his eyes never looked away" (140). One
question this scene raises is whether Lucy does look away from her
childhood. Can she not see what happened to her because she looks
away? Or can she not see for some other reason? That ambiguity is
important.

There are other moments Lucy does not include. She explains,

I cannot tell [the story of my marriage]: I cannot take hold
of, or lay out for anyone, the many swamps and grasses and

> pockets of fresh air and dank air that have gone over us. But
> I can tell you this: My mother was right; I had trouble in my
> marriage. And when my girls were nineteen and twenty years
> old, I left their father, and we have both remarried. There
> are days when I feel I love him more than I did when I was
> married to him, but that is an easy thing to think—we are
> free of each other, and yet not, and never will be. And there
> are days when I have such a clear image of him sitting at his
> desk in his study while the girls played in their room that I
> almost cry out: *We were a family!* (148)

Lucy has been damaged. And she loves as imperfectly as anyone
does. This reflection captures her tenderness for her earlier life—we
might ask whether it happened in the way she remembers—and in
some ways, if we follow Strout's other work, even if we know Lucy
is being sentimental, there's still a tenderness for what may have
been lost or may have never been. Lucy's protectiveness about her
marriage, her refusal to disclose what happened that led her to leave,
may speak to her kindness for her first husband. She tells the stories
of those who will not be harmed by their telling; she protects—to a
certain extent—the living. And so she expresses the complications
of that full existence, of wanting to speak and also wanting to be
kind to those she loves.

Lucy goes home to Amgash when her father is dying. When she
returns to New York, she relays,

> the world began to look different to me. My husband seemed
> a stranger, my children in their adolescence seemed indiffer-
> ent to much of my world. I was really lost. I could not stop
> feeling panic, as if the Barton family, the five of us—off-kilter
> as we had been—was a structure over me I had not even
> known about until it ended. I kept thinking of my brother
> and my sister and the bewilderment in their faces when my
> father died. I kept thinking how the five of us had had a re-
> ally unhealthy family, but I saw then too how our roots were
> twisted so tenaciously around one another's hearts. (167–68)

Lucy needs to leave home to be healthy, and yet she realizes she will never be free from the suffering of her early life.

When Lucy's younger daughter goes to college shortly thereafter, Lucy writes, "I did think I would die. Nothing had prepared me for such a thing. And I have found this to be true: Certain women feel like this, that their hearts have been ripped from their chests" (170). This intense feeling for her children connects Lucy to Helen Burgess. Her daughters leaving for college reminds her of her own original leaving, and she observes, looking back on the time, "I knew if I stayed in my marriage I would not write another book, not the kind I wanted to, and there is that as well. But really, the ruthlessness, I think, comes in grabbing onto myself, in saying. This is me, and I will not go where I can't bear to go—to Amgash, Illinois—and I will not stay in a marriage when I don't want to, and I will grab myself and hurl onward through life, blind as a bat, but on I go!" (177–78). When she believes her daughters no longer need her, Lucy puts herself first; she has decided, as her daughters forge their own path in life, so will she. She is finally as ruthless in her pursuit of her storytelling as Jeremy told her she needed to be.

But there are events over which she has no control, both personal and global. At the novel's end, Lucy remembers hearing her daughter Becka cry out, "Mommy!" when the second plane hit the World Trade Center; "when I ran to answer her cry, her look was so stricken: I think always of that moment. I think: That was the end of her childhood. The deaths, the smoke, the fear throughout the city and the country, the horrendous things that have happened in the world since then: Privately I think only of my daughter on that day. Never have I heard before or since that particular cry of her voice. *Mommy*" (187–88). She continues, "When I am alone in the apartment these days, not often, but sometimes, I will say softly out loud, 'Mommy!' And I don't know what it is—if I am calling for my own mother, or I am hearing Becka's cry to me that day when she saw the second plane go into the second tower. Both, I think" (189). Lucy is inextricably linked to her mother and to her daughter. Children yearn for their mothers to comfort them, but their suffering—whether personal or global—is too vast; the grief of children cannot be assuaged. Lucy realizes she may not understand her daughters' suffering, but she believes she "knows so well the pain we children clutch to in our chests, how it lasts our whole lifetime, with longings so large you can't even weep. We hold it tight, we do, with each seizure of the beating heart: *This is mine, this is mine, this is mine*" (190). Our suffering is that which gives our life meaning and structure. We know ourselves through our love, our longing, our disappointments. And our realizations of global tragedies are firmly rooted in our bodies and our formative relationships. Becka needs her mother at a moment of crisis, and Lucy realizes she needs her mother as well. The story Lucy tells is about her wounding, how her scars have shaped her.

The novel ends with another meditation on time, recalling the beginning, and again temporality collapses. Lucy tells us, "At times these days I think of the way the sun would set on the farmland around our small house in the autumn" (191).[25] This reverie begins in a vague present, before focusing on both a general feeling and a specific moment that may or may not have occurred, a liminal or transitional moment, a moment of change. This reverie links the present and past, the natural and philosophical, the metaphysical and empirical. Lucy moves from the first person to the second to the third as she describes "the sky lingering, lingering, then finally dark." Time is condensed, synthesized, leading Lucy to the conditional, pregnant, and enigmatic observation "as though the soul can be quiet for those moments" (191). The very phrasing underscores the unlikelihood of such a phenomenon—the soul is not quiet, but it might have the chance to be so. "All life amazes me," Lucy concludes, with a kind of receptiveness, hope, and wonder in spite of the world's pain and suffering.[26]

6
Anything Is Possible
with Everyday Grace

STROUT'S CENTER OF GRAVITY SHIFTS FROM THE East Coast to the Midwest in her next book, the short story cycle *Anything Is Possible* (2017). Strout wrote the stories while she was writing *My Name Is Lucy Barton,* and most of them take place in Lucy's hometown of Amgash, Illinois. The small town exerts a pull on the characters born there who now make their homes elsewhere, and this pull—metaphorically the effects of the past on our present—is a major theme of the book. As in *Olive Kitteridge,* although the nine stories can be read individually, next to each other they are more complex, once again showcasing Strout's compassionate vision and attention to detail across time and space.[1] Some of the characters travel—to Maine, Italy, and Chicago—yet they are connected through history, shared experience, a generosity of spirit, and a compassion for others who suffer. As we've seen in Strout's other works, the stories explore the lingering effects of child abuse, wartime atrocities, poverty, and the remarkable human ability to endure. According to Susan Scarf Merrell, "these stories return Strout to the core of what she does more magnanimously than anyone else, which is to render quiet portraits of the indignities and disappointments of normal life, and the moments of grace and kindness we are gifted in response."

In *Anything Is Possible* Strout creates once again a collective history of personal accounts where secrets and violence are revealed but not melodramatically indulged, and captures the distance and dissociation of the present from the past, even as it profoundly affects the individuals. The stories allow Strout to show how individual events have shaped us, how they are perceived by others, and how they fit together to create a shared history that can only be partially known by any one person. Like the citizens of Crosby, Maine, the people connected to Amgash, Illinois, have seen their share of suffering, but taken together, the stories suggest that through sharing—by either telling or listening to—our stories, we can move forward,[2] even if, as Ariel Levy observes, "the tone of Strout's fiction is both cozy and eerie, as comforting and unsettling as a fairy tale."

Once again Strout does not describe acts of violence salaciously; instead she presents the effects of earlier events on survivors, showing her readers how the world is full of the walking wounded and suggesting that to be ethical, we must be compassionate to those with whom we share this earth. From a psychoanalytic perspective, Strout is conducting a kind of partial cognitive therapy for her characters (who struggle with the effects of their traumatic pasts and in connecting with others). Across her entire oeuvre, through her creation of an expansive empathy in her readers, she offers a similar proposition—by reading of these individuals, their private battles, losses, and resolutions, we, too, can move forward with the awareness that if we feel alone in this seemingly impersonal, often brutal world, we still share space and time, our very planet, with others. That connectedness that acknowledges our limitations, our woundedness, our capability to do harm, our remorse, and our recognition of beauty and humor distinguishes Strout's vision, and in this book she is in full command of her powers.

Anything Is Possible, like Strout's other works, focuses on families—married couples, mothers and daughters, brothers and sisters, a father and his children. Most of the characters are older; it's rare that a young person (under the age of thirty) plays a prominent role, so it's fair to say this collection is also about aging, and the relationships that are important to people as they age.[3] Each relationship is faced with a crisis, which, if muted, is still shattering in its effects. If, in some ways, Strout's first book addressed the fairly common trope of domestic fiction, a young girl coming of age, in her later works she is showing us that it's not just young people who lead interesting lives; older people do as well—and though they have aged, they are still wrestling with their relationships. Barbara Waxman's work on the *Reifungsromane* is particularly useful here. If, in the novel that bears her name, Lucy Barton reflected on her relationship with her mother and daughters when they were all considerably younger, *Anything Is Possible* shows the poignancy and tenderness of the relationships of our older years. Those relationships might have lasted decades or be as fleeting as conversations. But again Strout emphasizes the epiphanies our interactions with each other offer us—our encounters teach us not only about others, but about ourselves as well. In this way, *Anything Is Possible* recalls *Olive Kitteridge*—when characters realize, for example, that the past is not what they thought, that their relationships are not what they thought, and that they are not who they thought they were. Notwithstanding these revelations, they still have tenderness for the people with whom they share a space—even if their relationships cannot survive in the way they had previously imagined. In *Anything Is Possible* there is an acknowledgment of the vulnerabilities of aging—it's not just the young who are open to physical and psychic wounds, the elderly are as well. But if the young can learn, Strout suggests, so can older people, a theme she continues to explore in *Olive, Again.* Perhaps the wisdom that ideally comes with age is the awareness of the necessity of compassion, the presence of grace in our own lives, and the recognition that humans hurt others in horrible ways.

The moments that shift our worldviews may be dramatic or subtle, and they're doubly poignant when they are catalyzed by the most pedestrian and therefore unlikely of sources. For example, in the book's opening story, "The Sign," Tommy Guptill, in his eighties, has believed for more than five decades that his home and barn burning down was God's sign to him to wake up and to appreciate his family.[4] Although the fire plunged the Guptills into near-poverty, in the act and aftereffects of humbling them, Tommy saw a force for good in God's call to him and was grateful for it. Now an elderly man, Tommy visits Pete Barton, who in the course of the story confesses to him that his father started the fire. What Tommy had seen as an act of grace was actually a case of arson caused by a pathetic, unstable man. However, when Tommy sees how broken the younger man is, he doesn't react in anger but instead tells Pete, "in detail, how he had felt God come to him, and how God had let Tommy know that it was all okay" (25).

Sharing this private story with Pete is an act of kindness. And if the conversation that follows gives Pete a kind of hope that his father was actually a good man, the exchange undoes Tommy, who asks himself, "Why had he told? Because he wanted to give something to that poor boy. . . . Why did it matter that he had told the boy? Tommy wasn't sure. But Tommy felt he had pulled the plug on himself, that by telling the thing he would never tell he had diminished himself past forgiveness. It really frightened him. *So you believe that?*, Pete Barton had said. He no longer felt himself" (29). Tommy, like Bob Burgess, has built his life around a belief; once Pete tells him what he thought was true isn't, he is as unmoored as any younger person wrestling with the loss of faith.

When he arrives home, Tommy tells his ancient wife Shirley for the first time how "he had felt God come to him the night of the fire" (30), but that he thinks now (sounding like Lucy Barton), "I must have imagined it. . . . It couldn't have happened, I made it up" (30). The conversation with Pete has shaken Tommy's faith to its very core. After listening to her husband, Shirley tells him that God may have come to him that night, but he realizes that "what he would keep from her now—his doubt (his sudden belief that God had never come to him)—was a new secret replacing the first. 'You might be right,' he said. A paltry thing he added, but it was true. He said, 'I love you, Shirley.' And then he looked at the ceiling; he could not look at her for a moment or two" (31). Perhaps Tommy needs to feel burdened or alone; he needs to keep a secret, something of his own, separate from his wife.[5] Pete's confession has shattered his worldview, and Tommy's response is not to share his new perception of the world with his wife, but to hold himself apart, isolated—only now it's not faith that keeps him separate but despair. Even though he is in some ways distant from Shirley (her name a pun on her certainty), he is still compassionate toward her, he still loves her—and in this way the book recalls the end of *Olive Kitteridge*, when it's the holes that make up Olive and Jack that shape their connection. The holes don't serve to separate them but to amplify their tenderness and their need for each other.

In some ways, what Tommy comes to realize is how far away he is from Shirley. It's not until he tells her how he had previously thought of the fire, and she accepts it so completely, that he realizes both how distant he had been in keeping that from her and the space between them now. The distance between people may be exacerbated by their having different worldviews, but it doesn't preclude a concomitant tenderness for the other person. Strout explores this theme in "Cracked," when Linda Peterson-Cornell realizes how far from her husband she is, that he has done things she doesn't understand; in "The Hit-Thumb Theory," when Charlie Macauley finds closeness not with his wife of decades who loves him or with the prostitute whom he loves but in the quiet sympathy of the proprietor of Dottie's Bed and Breakfast; in "Sister," when Lucy Barton returns to Amgash and has a panic attack at her childhood home with her brother and sister; and in "Snow-Blind," when Annie Appleby learns that her father was in love with another man for years. Linda, Charlie, Lucy, and Annie feel alone in some ways but also aware that others are physically if not emotionally close to them.

As "Amgash" suggests, its inhabitants suffer—often at the hands of those they love. Yet the stories also address their survival; it's fitting that the characters are older, for if they appear broken, many of them have endured extraordinary hardships. This endurance is part of the everyday miracles that this book explores: humans survive against incredible odds, and the very act of survival is a kind of victory. For example, Tommy and his family endure the burning of their home and the destruction of their way of life, and that experience leads Tommy to a profound humility. Damaged, quiet Pete Barton survives abuse and public shaming at the hands of his parents and schoolmates to say pithily to his sister, "We didn't turn out so bad, you know" (179).

Traumatic experiences can make people more sympathetic to others, which is the case with Tommy and Lucy—or they can make them callous, as if to self-preserve, they must, if not lash out at others, at least protect themselves from them. Lucy and Pete's sister, Vicky, and Linda Peterson-Cornell are not kind. Strout alludes to the suffering they faced when they were young—Vicky forced to eat out of a toilet and Linda feeling the shame of her mother leaving home. Their humiliation has hardened them. Vicky appears unhappy and embittered—she complains to Lucy, asking for and taking money from her wealthy, successful sister, without gratitude or grace, and Linda spies on her houseguests with her husband. While Lucy and Patty have developed compassion because of their early suffering, Vicky and Linda have not. Strout does not offer any explanation for why people turn out the way they do. Some people learn from their suffering, while others act cruelly, as if they have studied how to abuse rather than how to soothe.

But Strout's characters are nothing if not complex. For example, if Tommy has learned appreciation, gratitude, and compassion from his brush with death, we learn that when he saw the Bartons as children and suspected the parents of abuse, he did nothing to help them. So the suffering of the Barton children continued, and the

Guptills' silence—their removing of themselves—makes them complicit in the children's suffering. As an older man, Tommy shows Pete compassion, not only in the conversation they have in "The Sign" but in "Sister," where we learn that he and Shirley have begun taking Pete to the soup kitchen with them when they volunteer. Perhaps they take care of Pete now because they feel guilty for not stopping his suffering years earlier. If Tommy failed Pete, Lucy, and Vicky years ago, he doesn't do so now, but looks after Pete, offering him not only a friend but also a new look at and appreciation for his father.

Families, and particularly mothers, loom large in *Anything Is Possible*, even for the older characters. While Linda has run away to an abusive and possibly murderous husband, and another sister has moved to California, Patty Nicely has stayed close to her mother, who left her husband when her daughters were in high school. The girls feel betrayed by their mother having left not only their father but them as well in leaving home.[6] Angelina, who works at the local high school with Patty Nicely, also feels abandoned by her mother, who left her father when she was in her eighties. Although a grown woman with a family of her own, Angelina was shaken by her mother's carving out of a new space and a new life for her—as if in moving to Italy and marrying someone else, Mary forsook her family.

These perspectives highlight the theme that people of any age become profoundly shaken when their worldviews are challenged, when they learn that people they thought they knew have markedly different interior lives than they realized. When their partners or mothers or children do something unexpected, they feel the ground shift under them, and they are at least temporarily bowled over by how uncertain the world can be. For example, Mary stayed with her husband for years—after the girls had left home, his affairs, her heart attack and stroke, and his bout with brain cancer—before she eventually left. Angelina, however, does not see her mother as having patiently endured for decades but as spontaneously acting on a selfish whim when she leaves their home to move halfway across the world. Children, then—even adult children—seem to cling to their own conceptions of their parents, unable to reconcile new events with their version of the people they know. The way they see their parents becomes a metaphor for how individuals in general struggle to realize the limitations of perspectives. In *Anything Is Possible*, Strout is emphasizing how people continue to grow throughout their lives, how relationships with each other or with themselves are evolving. A human is not a single static being but in some ways allowed to change, ideally always learning in relation to others. One can grow by moving, as Mary Mumford does, or by staying home, as Tommy Guptill does; in both cases, it's relationships with others that allow individuals' compassion and consciousnesses to expand.

If we stay stuck, glued to our own preconceptions and so unable to see ourselves and others around us with any degree of accuracy, we neglect them and we neglect ourselves. Wisdom or perspicacity comes from seeing with the just and loving gaze that Toril Moi describes in *Revolution of the Ordinary*. If we don't see clearly, if we avert our eyes, we allow suffering to continue. But if we remove our blinders, we might see the abuse just outside our frame of vision. Many individuals, Strout shows, simply do not see abuse or suffering, stuck in their own point of view or positionality.

As in Strout's other works, the neglect and abuse take place at one remove—we don't see parents hurt their children, but we see the effects of formative experiences on them years later. We don't witness the dissolution of the Nicely or Mumford marriage (though they're alluded to in conversations and in interior monologues). Instead we see how the daughters perceive their mothers, hardly charitably. Feeling betrayed by their mothers, Angelina, Patty, and Linda don't realize—because they can't see—the suffering of their mothers. Neither does the book narrate abuse, though it shows the effects of abuse on survivors. As in her previous fiction, Strout offers a continuum of familial tragedies. She also suggests that if we allow parents to hurt their children, then we are complicit in that abuse, implying that it's a small step from ignoring the suffering of children to ignoring large-scale social abuses (as the allusion to German women averting their eyes from the concentration camps attests). Strout doesn't condemn her readers outright, but she shows us in the lived experience of survivors how our failure to protect the vulnerable makes us complicit in their suffering. If she keeps the predators at a distance, she shows us victims and how the act of bystanding leads to the suffering of others.

We see this, as I've already pointed out, when Tommy comes to the realization that he did not help the Barton children. In the story that follows, "Windmills," we see Patty Nicely interacting with Lucy's niece, a high school student. Lila Lane lashes out at Patty; in this way, one effect of the intergenerational legacy of trauma is revealed. Lila's cruelty is inherited. If her mother, Vicky, has learned to dissociate from her abuse through overeating and indifference to others (though the clinical term pains me, I think Strout is getting at the potential of fiction to plumb the suffering of the human condition in ways that psychiatric labeling cannot), Lila, too, is apathetic to others, unaware of how her callous cruelty hurts her college counselor. It simply doesn't occur to her that she could hurt the adult woman's feelings. Patty suffers, too; like her friend Angelina, she feels abandoned by her mother. But Patty also finds connection in the wounded Sibby, her first husband, and in Charlie Macauley, in whom she senses both a kindness and a kinship.[7] We learn in "Windmills" that Sibby was molested by his stepfather; we meet him in Patty's memories as an older, troubled man. Charlie Macauley, like Charlie Austin in *Abide with Me*, is a veteran traumatized by the experience of war. Patty is attracted to men who are injured. And in reaching out to them, in attempting to assuage their suffering and her own, Patty offers an alternative way to exist in the world, one based in compassion. She learns in the course of the story to offer it to Lila as well.

If abuse can be found in the most unlikely of places—at the hands of those we love and trust—grace can as well. When Tommy learns his farm did not burn down because of an act of God but rather because a disturbed man set fire to it, he doesn't turn to despair or meanness but to forgiveness of Pete's father and compassion for Pete himself. After Lila Lane is cruel to Patty, Patty is kind to her (eventually)—Tommy and Patty do not return ire with spite but rather with a sympathy that seems almost spiritual (though Strout is reluctant to call herself a spiritual writer). That sympathy, that kind of openheartedness, I think, is one aspect of life Strout is try-ing to show her readers. We can shut others down or we can reach out and open ourselves up; if that reaching out and opening up can lead to pain, it's still a way to live compassionately and ethically in the world. Strout is showing her readers how to embrace their own vulnerability. In "Snow-Blind," the adult Annie Appleby re-alizes her father (now suffering from dementia and grabbing at male nurses) loved a man desperately when he was younger, and his current behavior shows the longevity and the earnestness of love. While Elgin Appleby's treatment of the orderlies could be seen as harassment, another way to view those actions is as those of a man hungry for love and affection, reaching out in the only way his body remembers. In "Cracked," Linda Peterson-Cornell thinks she is in a hopeless situation, that her husband may have tried to rape their houseguest, but she is so emotionally inert that she doesn't see her ethical responsibility to speak against Jay. She folds more deeply into her own shell, unwilling to admit her own guilt. When she sees Yvonne's friend Karen-Lucie at a gas station, Strout offers Linda another way of being in the world—to do that which is just and honorable. Karen-Lucie doesn't judge Linda; instead she sees in the woman's face the injury of a hurt and long-suffering person, and in that act of mercy, Strout again shows us where grace can occur. In the final story of the collection, "Gift," Abel Blaine talks with the possibly deranged and certainly narcissistic half-rate actor who played Scrooge in the local production of *A Christmas Carol,* and the man who has been monomaniacally complaining finally turns to Abel as if he sees him for the first time and calls an ambulance, fearing Abel has suffered a heart attack.[8] In "Sister," when Pete is with Vicky, who has been cruel to Lucy, he recognizes her better angels—that in spite of appearing petty, she is also a strong person whose endurance speaks to the miraculousness of the human spirit. She has survived. If abuse is possible, so is grace.

We see the awareness of grace in "The Sign," when Tommy Guptill nearly loses his wife and children,

> When he saw that the barn was on fire—as he watched the
> enormous flames flying into the nighttime sky, then heard
> the terrible screaming sounds of the cows as they died,
> he had felt many things, but it was just as the roof of his
> house crashed in, fell into the house itself, right into their
> bedrooms and the living room below with all the photos of
> the children and his parents, as he saw this happen he had
> felt—undeniably—what he could only think was the presence
> of God, and he understood why angels had always been
> portrayed as having wings, because there had been a sensation
> of that—of a rushing sound, or not even a sound, and then it
> was as though God, who had no face, but was God, pressed up
> against him and conveyed to him without words—so briefly, so
> fleetingly—some message that Tommy understood to be: *It's all
> right, Tommy.* And then Tommy had understood that it was all
> right. It was beyond his understanding, but it was all right. . . .
> He had felt the presence of God since, at times, as though
> a golden color was very near to him, but he never again felt
> visited by God as he had felt that night, and he knew too well
> what people would make of it, and this is why he would keep
> it to himself until his dying day—the sign from God. (6–7)

Here, I think it's important to underscore that Strout is not a magical realist; the small miracles that occur in her books are not grand
spectacles but rather quiet kindnesses, unexpected acts of grace between people, individuals showing compassion to others at the most
surprising of times. Tommy thinks he's witnessed an act of God, but
in the course of the story he learns the miracle was an act of arson.
Nevertheless, the kindness he shows Pete and Shirley—his convey-
ing to them that he has faith—is the kind of everyday grace or miracle I've been attempting to draw our attention to.

Patty in some ways is like Tommy in that she sees God, or the
presence of hope, in signs that may not point to a divine presence

to any other people. As she drives home from visiting her senile mother, "the full moon was starting to rise," reminding her of how the moon looked the night her father died (48). Patty conflates the moon's natural splendor with the presence of God (here we might also recall Isabelle sweeping her porch); the natural and the supernatural coalesce for her: "every time the moon became full she felt that her father was watching her. She wiggled her fingers from the steering wheel as a hello to him. Love you, Daddy, she whispered" (48). It's not just the moon and her father who are synthesized, it's also her deceased husband, Sibby, who

> merged [with her father], in way, in her mind. They were up there watching her, and she knew that the moon was just a rock—a rock!—but the sight of its fullness always made her feel that her men were out there, up there, too. Wait for me, she whispered. Because she knew—she almost knew—that when she died she would be with her father and Sibby again. Thank you, she whispered, because her father had just told her it was good of her to take care of her mother. He was generous now in this way; death had given that to him. (48–49)

Unable to recognize her own generosity, Patty conflates it with her father. She's so self-effacing she doesn't see her own goodness. Because her father is dead, Patty can imagine him any way that she likes—and she makes him like her, kind, thoughtful, and grateful. Though Patty doesn't perceive her own virtues, others see her kindness. Strout does not proffer miraculous wonders, but natural events that lead us to an appreciation of the sacred, not outside of humanity but that which connects us to others. The events are not divine intervention, but they lead (some) people to acts of kindness that become a lifeline for others. Not everyone acts kindly; Strout is no Pollyanna, but she does show us some people, like Patty, who do—these people model for Strout's readers how we too can learn and grow. She models ordinary people who make mistakes, but who still, in Strout's oft-repeated words, "love imperfectly," reaching out (awkwardly!) again and again to comfort others.

In this book, it's Patty who echoes the refrain that runs throughout Strout's fiction, imagining comforting her friend who misses her
mother desperately: "We're all just a mess, Angelina, trying as hard
as we can, we love *imperfectly*, Angelina, but it's okay" (54). After
Patty reads Lucy's memoir, she realizes that Lila is rude and unkind
because she suffers from shame. Reading Lucy's book allows Patty to
realize she can help the struggling, unlikable Lila, and so the story
underscores the healing power of reading—how literature offers insights that can help us and help us to help others. Patty believes
"Lucy Barton's book had understood her. That was it—the book had
understood her. There remained that sweetness of a yellow-colored
candy in her mouth. Lucy Barton had her own shame; oh boy did
she have her own shame. And she had risen right straight out of it"
(57). If reading in some ways saved Lucy, the act might also save Lila
through Patty. Lucy's memoir underscores how college gave her a
lifeline out of Amgash, and Patty promises the same thing for Lila.[9]
Reading Lucy's book encourages Patty to not only help Lila and Angelina, but also help herself—she reaches out to Charlie Macauley
after reading it, allowing the possibility of love in her own life.

"Cracked" is different from the other stories in *Anything Is Possible* not only in its impending doom and brush with sexual violence, but also in its setting. Linda and Jay Peterson-Cornell live a
world away from Amgash: their garden houses "two sculptures by
Alexander Calder, both on one side of the large and bright blue
swimming pool; inside the house on the walls of the living room
were two Picassos and an Edward Hopper. There was an early Philip
Guston at the end of the sloping hallway that led to the guest area"
(64). But Linda is driven by shame; like her sister Patty, she hasn't
recovered from her mother's public indignities—how her family was
ostracized when her mother was caught in flagrante having an affair.
Linda's shame has not led her to compassion, but to selfishness and
self-preservation. Her demons are not only distant; in the course
of the story, she spies on a houseguest with her husband in a chill-
ing act of voyeurism.[10] Here again Strout portrays the guilt of the
bystander. Linda chooses to stay with Jay, and in so doing, she is

complicit in his crimes. She does not stop him, and that hesitation damns her (as does her daughter who calls her out on staying married to her father).

Linda Peterson-Cornell, her name aurally evoking the Pedersons, the owners of the barn where Pete sleeps before the pigs are slaughtered, lives an uneasy existence; her children have left home, and she knows her husband has had extramarital affairs and spies on women. Hovering at the margins of the story is a young woman who was killed several years earlier. The killing of this woman in the backdrop of the story evokes *Amy and Isabelle*, when a young girl's disappearance sets the predatory tone for the novel. Homes harbor criminals, and domestic spaces are not necessarily safe. But unlike the domestic gothic trope that much contemporary fiction draws on (here I'm thinking of garden variety *Girl on the Train* fare—my wife is a killer, my husband is a killer, etc.), Strout does not portray violence in exhaustive detail—instead, the murders of women haunt the main action of the story, hinting to the reader at the ubiquity of the phenomenon.

The presence of "Cracked" in *Anything Is Possible* is a bit jarring. Perhaps that is the point. If we recall Strout's nineteenth-century predecessors, we might remember that real horror lurks at home—it's not just the anonymous stranger who is frightening but the people who love you and who have the potential to hurt you. This book, like her others, is a study in relationships, and the inclusion of "Cracked" illuminates the other stories—if we live in a world where acts of kindness are possible, we also live in a world where people hurt each other in acts that can be as brutal as Jay's attempted rape of Yvonne, or Sibby's rape, or Pete's beating, or as subtle as the indifference of adults to children's suffering. One world is not distinct or separate from the other. I'd also like to take a cue from David Miall, who notes that, "in considering the 'literariness' of literary texts, it seems probable that readers will experience more fresh emotions than in subliterary texts (such as romances or thrillers)" (335). That is, perhaps in its very unpredictability, in the voyeurism and violence it addresses, "Cracked" elicits "novel rather than familiar feelings. . . .

complexes of non-standard emotions that are likely to interweave and to modify one another" (335). Strout wants to unsettle us. By surprising her readers, she keeps us engaged, on our toes, alert, and also aware of her literary powers.

Linda eventually finds out that her husband did not murder the young girl, and her relief at this revelation, she thinks, in some ways absolves him—and her—of the other acts of violence and violation that he commits. In other words, Linda is guilty of bystander syndrome. Perhaps again Strout is pointing to the tendency we have to think in terms of degree, and how, by doing so, we contribute to the suffering of others. Linda's body reveals her deep distress, underscoring Strout's connection to the literature of sensibility, when bodies—usually women's—manifest their emotional state:

> Linda Peterson-Cornell existed with a confusing disk of darkness deep insider her chest, and . . . she often broke out in a sweat. She thought she had to be crazy. She could not imagine why her body was reacting this way, why her mind itself could not stay calm. And then when it was over, finally, finally over, she forgot that she had felt this way. Only occasionally would she remember, but never with the visceral aspect of what she had actually gone through. And each time she remembered she thought: I'm a silly woman. I have *nothing* to complain about, not really, not like that, Jesus God. (71)

If Linda's night sweats are a parody of the hot flashes of menopause (and with Strout's humor, this is a possibility), they could point to a more sinister cause. As the expletive suggests, her emotional and physical reactions are warranted. Linda is complicit in crimes, and in portraying her guilt, Strout may imply that the reader is also responsible for allowing such crimes to happen, or for getting vicarious pleasure out of reading about such events. At the least she encourages us to be more attentive to people around us.

Linda acts out of self-preservation, momentarily leaving her husband when she is afraid that she will be interrogated about the cameras in their house. In the gas station restroom, Linda runs into

Karen-Lucie, who at first tells her it is Linda's duty to testify because she has "to know *somethin'* about [her] husband" (89). Just as she did in leaving the house, once again Linda steps away from doing the right thing, saying, "I don't know anything about my husband" (89). Karen-Lucie then becomes compassionate, trusting what Linda has told her, showing her a kind of grace, and Linda returns to Jay, realizing she will have the upper hand in their relationship, both of them knowing "that his exemption from trouble was possibly or partly the result of his wife's discretion" (90).[11]

Linda is terrified of becoming like her mother, ostracized and alone. Her sister Patty recovers from this trauma to a certain extent, but it seems Linda never does. So in spite of appearing more successful, Linda is stunted, so afraid of being abandoned that she hurts people, not realizing her complicity in harboring a criminal. Like Helen Burgess, Linda chooses material comfort over helping another person. Allusions to crimes and the suffering they cause surface in the other stories as well. Sibby was molested. The Barton kids were abused by their parents. The detail Strout presents in "Snow-Blind" in one sentence recalls Lauren's childhood in *Abide with Me*: "Mr. Daigle did not really yell at his kids; in fact, when Annie and Charlene took a bath he often came in to wash them with a washcloth" (214).

Such abuse occurs in a world as lovely as it is in any of Strout's works. If *Abide with Me* and *The Burgess Boys* stake out new territory for Strout, this book again expands her geographical scope. She traveled to the Midwest while she was writing the stories, observing the landscape and the people, so she could portray both landmarks and residents accurately.

Strout's lyrical observations of the natural world, its beauty and transience, situate her within the American literary tradition. In "The Gift," as Tommy drives, "all around him were open fields, the corn newly planted, and the soybeans too. A number of fields were still brown, as they'd been plowed under for their planting, but mostly there was the high blue sky, with a few white clouds scattered near the horizon" (5). The landscape is agrarian, the vista the wide fields of the Midwest. The tree that Lucy remembers as her only friend in the prior book, which "had been in the middle of the cornfield[,] had been struck by lightning a few years back, and it lay now on its side, the long branches bare and broken and poking up toward the sky" (14). If beautiful, the natural world is not idyllic. The inhabitants of Amgash don't work in the fields but pass through them, not fully living in the land, the way, say, children with their fully embodied existence do. For example, Patty "drove by a field where the corn was just inches high, and by a field of soybeans bright green and close to the ground" (34). These characters do not live in a quixotic universe. Later, when Patty drives to visit her mother past the fields,

> some with the little plants of corn, some brown, one field was being plowed under as she drove by. Then she came to the place where there were wind turbines, over a hundred of them along the horizon, these huge white windmills that had been put up across the land almost ten years earlier. They fascinated Patty, they always had, their long white arms twirling the air all at the same speed but otherwise without synchronicity. There was a lawsuit now, she remembered, there were often lawsuits, about the destruction of the birds and deer and farmland, but Patty favored the large white things whose skinny arms moved against the sky in that slightly wacky way to make energy—and then they were behind her, and once again were only the fields with the little corn plants and the fresh bright soybeans. These were the very cornfields—in their summer fullness—where, by the age of fifteen, she had allowed boys to thrust themselves against her, their lips huge-seeming, rubbery, their things bulging through their pants, and she would gasp and offer her neck to be kissed and grind herself against them, but—really?—she couldn't stand it she couldn't stand it she couldn't stand it. (41–42)

The natural landscape is fertile, fecund, but also corrupted, not a prelapsarian Eden but a gritty, dangerous place.

Strout renders the details, especially those tied to the natural world, poetically. One of my favorite moments occurs in "The Hit-Thumb Theory," when Strout draws our attention to "the top of a maple tree, the branches holding forth two pinky yellow leaves with apologetic gentleness, and how they had held on until November" (92–93). Strout homes in on the specific rather than the grand landscape; here the detail is delicately portrayed with emotional weight and sharp observation.[12] This story addresses growing older and Charlie's regrets, the leaf not only lovely in itself but also emblematic of the fragility, beauty, and preciousness of the metaphorical and literal season.

Strout also allows the beauty of a Maine winter in a snowy landscape almost painful in its loveliness: "The physical world with its dappled light was her earliest friend, and it waited with its open-armed beauty to accept her sense of excitement that nothing else could bring. She learned the rhythms of those around her, where they would be and when, and she slipped into the woods closer to town, or behind the school, and there she would sing with gentleness and exuberance a song she'd made up years earlier, 'I'm so glad that I'm living, just so glaaad that I'm living—'" (237). We see snowy Maine through the eyes of a child. If previous works portrayed the desolation, the sleet and slush that adults have to navigate, by seeing the Appleby home and woods through young Annie's eyes, Strout shows the landscape as a magical place. In doing so, she taps into one of her—and the book's—larger themes: how what we see is mediated.

When Annie returns home as an adult, she remembers, in a Lucy Barton–esque way, "walking up the dirt road holding her father's hand, the snow-covered fields spread around them, the woods in the distance, joy spilling through her—how she had used this scene to have tears immediately come to her eyes, for the happiness of it, and the loss of it. And now she wondered if it had even happened, if the road had ever been narrow and dirt, if her father had ever held her hand and said that his family was the most important thing to him" (223). That loss of something that may have been imagined is also one of Charlie Macauley's experiences. In "The Hit-Thumb Theory," he is in despair, emotionally and physically wrecked, and things are about to get worse. Charlie, like so many of Strout's characters, suffers, but to diagnose his symptoms as those of "post-traumatic stress syndrome" seems oversimplified. While Charlie is waiting to meet the woman he knows as Tracy, a prostitute who may or may not love him, he panics and experiences an overwhelming sense of being lost and longing for a home that may never have existed, missing the safety and comfort of an idealized childhood:

> He was suddenly as homesick as a child sent to stay with
> relatives: when the furniture seemed large and dark and
> strange, and the smell peculiar, each detail assaultive with a
> *differentness* that was almost unbearable. I want to go home,
> he thought. And the desire seemed to squeeze the breath
> from him, because it was not his home in Carlisle, Illinois,
> where he lived with Marilyn that he wanted to go home to,
> his grandchildren right down the street. And it was not his
> childhood home either. . . . He did not know what home
> it was he longed for, but it seemed to him as he aged that
> his homesickness would increase, and because he could not
> tolerate the Marilyn he now lived with—a woman who nev-
> ertheless filled his estranged, expatriated heart with pity—he
> did not know what he would do. (94)

He no longer loves his wife. This realization fills him with dread, guilt, and profound sadness, and the story ends at a moment of ambiguity. The essayist Leslie Jamison offers us a way to understand Charlie's desperation through her exploration of the Portuguese word *saudade*, which, she tells us, is "infamously untranslatable" and "more mysterious than sheer nostalgia. It's a longing not for what you've lost, but for what you never had. It's something like homesickness, but it could mean homesick for a place you've never been. . . . It usually takes a grammatical construction that suggests possession or company: you have *saudades*, or you can be with them. As if longing could become a kind of company. As if it could compensate for absence itself" (163). So many of Strout's characters ache existentially—Bev, Henry Kitteridge, Olive Kitteridge, Angie O'Meara, Charlie Austin, Lucy Barton, Charlie Macauley—for something they can't identify. Their mental and physical limitations trap them, but their longing is transcendent, jumping off the page, and unresolvable in the stories. That conflict between how we desire and what we can achieve or express may be at the crux of Strout's fiction and the condition of being human, perpetually reaching for something unattainable.

Strout returns to Charlie in "Dottie's Bed and Breakfast," when the innkeeper recalls his visit to her home and how when they were watching television wordlessly together,

> she became aware that he was in serious distress. He began to make a noise that she had never heard before; it was not entirely unsexual in its sound, but it was a sound of terrible pain. Unspeakable pain, she often thought later . . . Tears began slipping sloppily down the man's deeply creased face. . . . She said, "I'm not frightened by this, just so you know." And that caused a sudden extra burst of effluvia from his eyes, and he squeezed her hand hard enough to almost break it. (202)

Strout portrays emotional pain, angst, in detail so vivid it's almost tangible, Charlie's intense suffering manifesting itself physically. We know through our bodies as well as through our brains. And Charlie is relieved that he is feeling pain, that he is not apathetic as some of his fellow veterans are. Psychiatrist Bessel van der Kolk agrees that blankness is "more alarming" (16) than extreme emotion. If we learn in "The Hit-Thumb Theory" and "Dottie's Bed and Breakfast" that Charlie suffers, in "Mississippi Mary" we learn that Patty reaches out to him. Again, distress and connection are signified physically. We don't know what happens in the interstices between the short stories. Strout offers the suggestion that some moments have not been expressed, and yet she implies that Charlie and Patty have a chance at happiness together.

Strout's humor also punctuates the book, making the horribly sad moments bearable. The short story cycle is alternately lyrical,

poignant, tragic, and, then, surprisingly, very funny. Nowhere is this
more apparent than in "Mississippi Mary," when a middle-aged Angelina finds herself in Italy visiting her recently remarried mother.[13]
Octogenarian Mary finds it funny when people think she is her husband's mother, but her daughter is appalled. "You're *my* mother!"
Angelina cries out, which "caused Mary to almost weep again, because she had a searing glimpse then of all the damage she must
have done, and she, Mary Mumford, had never in her life planned
on doing, or wanted to do, any damage to anyone" (118). Strout does
not blame Mary for following her own life and dreams, but she does
portray the pain left in her wake. The children Strout's mothers leave
behind, whether they are young or old, are in a place of disillusionment, sadness—a similar place to where Strout's other characters
are when they realize the world they thought they knew, the women
they thought they knew, are different from what they thought.
Strout's revelations destabilize. Angelina is as confused as any: If I
don't know my mother, what do I know? Mary leaves her first husband after they have been married for fifty-one years. In leaving him
and their conjugal home, Mary has the chance to find happiness,
and within the story her daughter comes to realize that—and if Angelina feels bereft, she can also be happy for her mother, who finally has a chance to live the life she wants with the man she loves.[14]
Strout again explores the complications of maternal feelings—how
overwhelming and intense they can be. Mary attempts to comfort
her depressed daughter, but "she did not say, and only fleetingly did
she think: And you have always taken up so much space in my heart
that it has sometimes felt to be a burden" (138). Later in the same
story, Mary apologizes for yelling at Angelina when she was a child:
"I yelled at you, I really *yelled* at you, I have no idea what about, but
I yelled and you were frightened, and I was yelling because I had
found out about your father and Aileen, but I never told you about
that—until, well, you know, a million years later, but the point is,
honey, I frightened you, I *yelled* at you, and you were frightened. . . .
And I am so, so sorry" (140). We might remember in *Amy and Isabelle*
how Strout portrayed Isabelle's snapping at her daughter. Years later

she offers an older woman's perspective on such a moment, demonstrating its power and poignancy. Mary's regret speaks, I think, to Strout's desire to portray the whole of the human condition. It is what makes her such a rich, complex, and rewarding writer—humor laced through with the tragic, banal, and sacred.

The proximity of death seems very important and integral to the vision of this book. When Angelina tries to express to her mother that she is saddened by her moving to Italy, away from her, and that she won't be with her when she dies, Strout lets us into Mary's consciousness:

> She had to be careful because this girl-woman was her daughter. She could not tell her—this child she loved as much as she had loved anything—that she did not dread her death, that she was almost ready for it, not really but getting there, and it was horrifying to realize that—that life had worn her out, worn her down, she was almost ready to die, and she would die, probably not too long from now. Always, there was that grasping for a few more years, Mary had seen this with many people, and she did not feel it—or she did, but she did not. No. She felt tired out, she felt *almost* ready, and she could not tell her child this. And she also felt terror at the thought. She pictured it—lying here in this very room while Paolo rushed about—and she was terrified, because she would not see her girls again, she would not see her husband again, and she meant their father, that husband, she would not see all of them again and it terrified her. And she could not tell her daughter that had she known what she was doing to her, to her dearest little Angel, she might not have done it. (141)

That love for children, Strout shows, can paralyze women. Mothers desire so much to keep their children safe and to prepare them for the world that they cut themselves off from other paths. They put their children's desires and needs first. But in this story, as in *My Name Is Lucy Barton*, Strout offers us portraits of women who choose differently. Here she shows us the effects the women have left in their wake. Barbara Waxman explains that in the *Reifungsromane*, or novels of ripening, there is "an opening up of life for many of these aging heroines as they literally take to the open road in search of themselves and new roles in life" (16). Mary is no exception. If the middle-aged see themselves as tired, disillusioned, beaten down by their experiences to date, Mary sees herself as still learning, anticipating Olive's growth in the next book.

Mary's quiet revelation—that she might have chosen otherwise had she known—is like others we've seen throughout Strout's work. Those epiphanies tie her to Flannery O'Connor. But unlike O'Connor's stories, which appear to wrestle more explicitly with faith, in *Anything Is Possible*, the revelations do not lead one to an appreciation of the divine, but rather to an appreciation of the power and vulnerabilities of human beings. The revelations are just as surprising as O'Connor's are—but the characters are left very much in this world trying to make sense of their position within it when they no longer have their earlier faith.

The last story of the collection, "Gift," seems particularly reminiscent of O'Connor. The elderly Abel Blaine (cousin to Lucy, Pete, and Vicky Barton) returns to a theater to retrieve his granddaughter's small toy after a catastrophic performance of *A Christmas Carol*. While there, he meets Linck McKenzie, the actor who disastrously played Scrooge and sabotaged the production. The two participate in an honest conversation that recalls the one between the grandmother and the convict in "A Good Man Is Hard to Find," but here it's not the elderly person who reaches out to the younger, it's Linck who tells Abel (perhaps after he suffers a heart attack), "You're a good man" (252). Strout doesn't give us anything as dramatic as a multiple murder—the excitement of the story occurs when the lights go out in the theater—but the audience and the actors survive, and the show goes on.

Linck appears cranky, self-serving, obnoxious, and mean-spirited, and yet when he sees Abel suffering, he jumps out of his own misery and calls an ambulance. The kindness that Linck shows Abel is out of character with his earlier posturing, yet it's that

moment that Abel remembers while he is in the ambulance heading
to the hospital:

> Abel felt not fear but a strange exquisite joy, the bliss of
> things finally and irretrievably out of his control, unpeeled,
> unpeeling now. Yet there was a streak of something else, as
> though just outside his reach was the twinkle of a light, as
> though a Christmas window was there; this puzzled him and
> pleased him, and in his state of tired ecstasy it seemed almost
> to come to him. Linck McKenzie's voice: "You're a good man."
> This made Abel smile even as his chest felt as if rocks were
> piled upon it. . . . He had a friend. (253)

This revelation, simple and quotidian, but couched in the language
of transcendence, of *saudades,* stuns Abel. In "Mississippi Mary,"
when Angelina and her mother see an older woman riding a bicycle,
Mary says to her daughter that the spectacle "just amazed me when
I came here. Then I figured it out—the women are just versions of
people pulling up to Walmart in their cars" (123), and Angelina replies, "Everything's always amazed you, Mom" (124) recalling the last
sentence of *My Name Is Lucy Barton,* "All life amazes me." Yes. Strout
draws our attention to that awe, suggesting that if we look with that
just and loving—that attentive—gaze, the way that Mary and Abel
and Dottie do, then we, too, will be amazed, attuned to the world's
wonder. Thus, it's not just reading one book but across her work
that we get a more complex appreciation for Strout's vision. What is
wondrous are the daily lives, the quotidian sights that may be ugly
or beautiful in their revelation of multiple truths that are apparent
if we only keep our eyes open to see them. Strout call us to welcome
the awe, the wonder she sees and creates.

7 *Olive, Again*

APPEARING TWO YEARS AFTER *ANYTHING IS POSSIBLE,* *Olive, Again* (2019) reintroduces Strout's beloved crotchety heroine and Crosby, Maine. Like the book that preceded it, *Olive, Again* is a short story cycle, yet after the heaviness of subject and sacral tones of *My Name Is Lucy Barton* and *Anything Is Possible, Olive, Again* begins irreverently with a jocularity that runs throughout nearly all of the stories.[1] The characters, as in Strout's previous work, wrestle with serious and challenging issues, including the deaths of spouses, the realization of infidelity, disappointment in one's parents or adult children, physical and psychic abuse, and impending mortality. Yet there is also a lightness that in spite of the heavy subject material makes the book joyful and even laugh-out-loud funny.

For example, being pulled over by the police is no laughing matter in the United States, particularly if one is a Black American, but in the first story, "Arrested," wealthy, retired, White Jack Kennison has it happen to him. He's privileged for all kinds of reasons, and the scene doesn't lead to violence or despair; rather, Jack is puzzled by the officer's apparent erection at their encounter. Jack is an old man, troubled by his incontinence following prostate surgery and the loss of his wife, hardly thinking of himself as an object of erotic attention, and his befuddled reaction to the officer's arousal is amusing. That irreverence—and particularly its connection to our bodies—runs through the stories. Olive, for example, is surprised when she wakes up after having pooped in her sleep. The event is not disastrous, just humbling. The collection puts into relief some of the unpredictable effects of aging, what many are not forced to face until they find themselves in these situations.

In many ways, *Olive, Again* recalls *Olive Kitteridge*. As in the earlier book, Strout begins the short story cycle with a tale about a man who loves Olive (who herself appears in the background). In "Arrested," Jack is recently widowed, wondering why Olive has not returned his calls and reflecting on his marriage and his deceased wife. As he mourns Betsy, he decides to email an old boyfriend of hers to let him know of her death. The man responds, telling Jack he and Betsy had an affair some thirty years earlier. Jack is "arrested" by this news—like so many of Strout's characters, he's stunned to see that his marriage was not what he thought it was, and that the woman he had loved (and also betrayed) had a life of her own of which he was not aware. But unlike in her earlier work (say "Winter Concert" and "Basket of Trips" in *Olive Kitteridge*), in this story Strout lends a comedic tone to the revelation. Jack, unlike Janie Houlton and Marlene Bonney, is not devastated by the news but thinks, "Betsy, you son of a gun" and then "who uses the word 'dalliance'? What are you, Groger, some faggot?" (18). Jack, of course, reveals his homophobia, which we had seen earlier, but the slur also points to his own trepidation not just about aging but about his marriage and masculinity as well. If earlier similar revelations are sad and poignant, here Strout treats the epiphany with a light hand. Jack has also had an affair—leading to his leaving Harvard in disgrace and consequently known to his wife—so perhaps he is better equipped to see this revelation with resilience rather than devastation. "Resilience" indeed might be the word that best describes *Olive, Again*. The themes and acts that Strout covers have not changed dramatically, but the characters seem to bounce back from troubling revelations and to treat the world around them with a kind of levity that we don't see in Strout's earlier works.

Characters—Isabelle Goodrow, the extended families of Crosby, even the Burgesses—reappear as well. But the Bartons are absent, perhaps as if they are too heavy to be part of *Olive, Again*. We might remember that Olive originally appeared after *Amy and Isabelle* and *Abide with Me*, two relatively heavy books. Though *Olive Kitteridge* takes place in the Maine of the earlier works, it too has a humor and a lightness to it that Strout's first two books lacked. Crosby does not seem as beleaguered or depressed as Shirley Falls or as unwelcoming as West Annett.[2] In addition to being a short story cycle, *Olive Kitteridge* itself, although addressing suicide, anorexia, drug addiction, and murder, also had a lightness, in no small part due to the titular character's acerbic, understated, earthy sense of humor, as if Ora Kendall or Bev were given the chance to have a book of their own (Ora may be Olive's aunt). Perhaps after the darkness of *My Name Is Lucy Barton* and *Anything Is Possible*, a reprieve or a break in the clouds was called for.

But, as in *Anything Is Possible*, most of the characters in *Olive, Again* are older adults. The book begins with Jack Kennison, in his mid-seventies, having lost his wife, and ends with Olive, in her eighties in an old folks' home writing her memoirs on the typewriter Chris brought her. In between we meet the elderly Ringroses; Bernie Green, an ancient attorney; Danny Pelletier, a retired millworker; the Burgesses, now grandparents; and the quibbling MacPhersons. Death is always close. To write about the end of life evokes Tyler Caskey's realization that facing the prison of domestic drudgery and living to face the horrors of aging "requires a great deal of courage" (281). It's not just acts of celebrated heroism that deserve our respect, Strout tells us; the lives of quiet, loving endurance do as well. In this book, in some ways Strout comes full circle, her characters from different works returning to show they have survived in spite of the physical, mental, and emotional challenges they've faced.[3]

It is a relief to learn that Amy Goodrow has thrived, at least professionally. Isabelle and Olive meet in the home where they're both residents, and they show a kindness, a solicitude to each other that indicates a softening of their spirits—they are no longer the frustrated women they were in the books in which they initially appeared. And in that women's friendship, we see a return to the ending of *Amy and Isabelle*, when Isabelle is accepted by Bev and Dottie, welcomed to a women's community she had unwittingly excluded herself from. Here the women's friendship is more intimate, more vulnerable—their bodies are faltering, their minds may be failing, and yet they show a tenderness, a friendship to each other that also recalls the end of *Olive Kitteridge*, when Olive and Jack reach for each other in a moment of intimacy. In "Friend," the final story, we learn the women are becoming incontinent, they regret how they have treated their children, their children have grown distant, and yet Olive's and Isabelle's minds are working well enough for them to recognize the importance of a friend, of a kindred spirit (even though Olive would be skeptical of such a sentimental label).

Amy is a doctor now, and doctors who are not gastroenterologists are usually loved in Strout's world. Amy is in a helping profession, she has married, she has a child now grown; with this trajectory, Strout offers her readers the possibility that people can recover from trauma. Unlike the recent *My Dark Vanessa*, Strout presents a woman who survives her abuse and goes on to live an apparently successful adult life. If *Anything Is Possible* offers a quiet prayer of solace, grace in everyday acts of kindness, *Olive, Again* proffers a more lighthearted look at resilience—a sense that if our lives may be punctuated by moments of seemingly unbearable grief and trauma, they are also marked by laughter and hope.

Knowing what Amy faced when she was young and learning in "Friend" that she appears to be thriving, Strout offers us a context for the disturbing portrayal of a similarly predatory relationship in "Cleaning," which focuses on twelve-year-old Kayley, who sees taking her shirt off and holding her breasts as empowering, as Amy conceives of her sexual experience with Mr. Robertson in *Amy and Isabelle*. Both girls see themselves as outsiders among their peers; both are fatherless. Both their mothers are stretched thin and, if not unobservant, are on some level not attentive to their daughters' suffering. And Kayley's name sonically recalls Amy's. But if Mr. Robertson leaves Shirley Falls with his power and authority intact, Mr. Ringrose is shunted off to a nursing home at the end of "Cleaning." Amy's resilience offers the hope that Kayley too may prove strong. Kayley does not appear to be devastated by the experience—she wasn't in love with the elderly man who paid her to take off her shirt, so she seems to have more agency, more power than Amy did. In spite of the death of her father, Kayley does not seem as emotionally dependent on the older man as Amy was; she chose to return to the Ringrose home, to disrobe, and to accept payment.

Other characters within *Olive, Again* also take risks. Mr. MacPherson learns his middle-aged daughter is a dominatrix and the subject of a documentary on her profession. He comes home surprised to see his wife and daughters watching the film, which he starts to watch with them before he suffers what might be a heart attack. Perhaps, then, this is the risk, that one's heart may break faced with something it cannot handle (though Fergus, at least for the moment, survives). Olive begins writing her memoirs after she has met a famous poet, whom she taught many years ago. She comes out of her house one day to find a magazine with poems in it circled and clearly left for her. The poems speak to Olive's loneliness, and she's stunned and saddened by the cruel if accurate appearance of herself within them. That she begins to compose her memoir after this experience is an act of faith, as she bravely writes her life.

The risks people take can be dangerous, emotional, or comic. Mr. MacPherson starting to watch the film of his daughter is funny until it's not. When his daughter decides to show the documentary of her work to her sister and parents, she is more emotionally invested in the showing than her father would appear to be. When

Olive invites Chris and his family home at Jack's suggestion, the risk is emotional—and it turns out her concern was well-founded. Chris rejects her, unhappy that she has chosen in her seventies to marry a man he never met. When Jack calls Olive, he risks rejection (though he hypothesizes, correctly, that she didn't know how to use her answering machine), and his taking that risk leads to a second marriage, a new hope and home late in life for both of them. The risks, then, are acts of faith, trusts in venturing forth into the unknown. Sometimes the risks lead to tragedy (here we might think of Mr. MacPherson's heart attack, which does lead to a kindness from his wife) or to happiness.

And damage, disease, addiction, violence—shadows we've seen in Strout's other books—also haunt the pages of *Olive, Again,* but do not take center stage as they do in *Anything Is Possible.* Here we might think of "Light," "The Walk," and "Helped." What do we make of the same themes, characters, and setting running through Strout's work? Does she, as Sarah Payne says in *My Name Is Lucy Barton,* only have one story to tell? Or does the return to similar themes and settings suggest there is something to be known from returning to a place, a person, or event multiple times? I think it's the latter. The past, including the people we knew and the history we claimed, is different from what we thought, and yet the themes of predatory behavior, violence against women, the triumph of love, the sting of regret, and the perennial loneliness so many of us face through much of our lives continue to resonate. Perhaps in returning to similar themes, to the same characters and landscape, Strout offers us a way to understand the greater complexity of living in the world—to realize that that which we thought we knew in fact we didn't.

This theme is poignantly rendered in "The Walk," when the elderly Denny Pelletier sees someone he thinks is a young man on a park bench. When Denny realizes he recognizes the stranger, it occurs to him how little he understands—the man is no longer the handsome youth he once was but has fallen into addiction. Their encounter speaks to Strout's theme that people always remain mysteries even to themselves as they face, remember, or turn away from

their unknown struggles. "Helped" echoes this theme when Suzanne
Larkin learns her mother may have abused her brother. Older adults
are not necessarily beacons of wisdom or nobility. Mr. Ringrose
spies on young Kayley; Olive suffers the indignity of incontinence;
Isabelle suffers from lack of bladder control. This doesn't mean that
their lives are hopeless, but rather that we ought to be compassionate, to be respectful of the unknown struggles others may be facing.
If we're open to love, as George Atwood tells Tyler Caskey we must
be, we could find ourselves tended by, as Olive is, a Somali refugee
or an ardent Trump supporter.

With these seemingly glancing details, references to contemporary figures and events, Strout once again shows the effects of the
greater world on a very small group of people. The book's concerns
remain primarily domestic, but as Strout has underscored before,
time and place crucially affect her characters. Economic uncertainty, the opioid crisis, Trump's election, Somali immigration to
Maine, and the #MeToo movement are among the larger cultural
forces that affect the lives of the people of Crosby. Even if her work
does not appear overtly political (and in that way Strout may reach
a wider audience than if it did), domestic fiction has political ends.
Yet the book shows that that which connects us is greater—even if it
appears trivial or is trivialized by others—than that which separates
us. In that call for community, for acceptance and inclusion, Strout
engages in a political act. Olive, we might remember, in the first
book in which she appears is initially dismissive of Jack Kennison
because he's a Republican, and in this book Jack calls her out on her
prejudice and her assumption of moral superiority (if as lightly as
ever). So although the larger acts of the national or international
stage are not the subject of Strout's work, she shows us that they
resound in the most intimate or domestic of settings.

What, then, is Strout's political statement? Here we might remember that although Olive is a vocal and self-righteous Democrat,
in this book she marries a kind and thoughtful Republican, and she
learns to accept help from a Trump supporter. Through Olive, and
particularly through Olive's relationship with Betty, her certified

nursing assistant, Strout shows her readers how we can choose to shut others out, to ignore the suffering of people we don't know, or we can choose to listen, to open ourselves up to the wide panoply of human experience. Fiction, in particular, can model that empathy. Storytelling can serve as a bridge, a way for us to enlarge our hearts. Olive shows us it's never too late to learn, as she comes to understand the limitations of how she judged Jack and Betty. Just because someone supports a candidate who spews hate doesn't mean that person is also hate-filled. But Olive takes Betty to task for her racism and xenophobia. If in our current time we meet fewer strangers who challenge our beliefs than we ever have, fiction allows us a place to learn from those not like us.

It's interesting, then, that the Burgesses also return in this collection. *The Burgess Boys* ended with a moment of uncertainty, Jim on his way home to ask Helen for forgiveness and Zach in Sweden with his father. We learn in "Exiles" that Helen has welcomed Jim back to their marriage, and Bob has married Margaret Estaver and returned to Maine. *The Burgess Boys* focused primarily on the men, but here it's Margaret and Helen who occupy Strout's attention. Helen appeared petty in *The Burgess Boys*; Margaret was presented more kindly—if not a saint, on the side of the good, she is working with all of the people of Shirley Falls (including Susan and Abdikarim). Here the portrayal of Margaret is more complex. If Helen is something of a straw (wo-) man—materialistic, judging, and superficial—and Margaret appeared as her foil in *The Burgess Boys*, in *Olive, Again* we see another side to Margaret, ill at ease in New York and judgmental of Helen.

Sometime beautiful Helen, after drinking too much at Bob and Margaret's, falls, winding up in the hospital. It's an undignified act, a sign of how she has literally lost her balance and broken two ribs. Helen is off her game, no longer the ideal, perfect woman she imagined she was. In aging, all of the Burgesses seem somewhat uncomfortable. Their bodies, which may have once been powerful in their strength or in their beauty, now are failing them.

Perhaps this is one way to approach the unsettling "Cleaning." As mentioned earlier, this story recalls *Amy and Isabelle* in that a young girl becomes aware of her sexuality in a way that may trouble readers. In this story in particular, Strout is showing the problems with identification. That is, she encourages a kind of distancing that is still sympathetic but not empathetic, acknowledging one's own reading position rather than losing oneself in a character. Eighth-grader Kayley is profoundly lonely—her father recently died, her older sisters no longer live at home, and her mother is lost in her own grief. When the elderly Mr. Ringrose sees her touching her breast, she's ashamed, but he asks her to continue, and later, after watching her, he pays her for the show she puts on. At first discomfited by these encounters, Kayley grows to like them—Mr. Ringrose's watching her makes her feel appreciated and loved, in ways that she wasn't before. At the story's end, we learn that Mrs. Ringrose has put her husband in a nursing home, which suggests that his senses were failing him when he asked a young girl to perform a striptease, and that his doing so might have been more connected to his own corporeal corruption than to a moral one.

In "Cleaning," as in *Amy and Isabelle*, we see that interactions between people are more subtle and complex than only exploitive. Kayley and Amy do get something out of their relationships with Mr. Robertson and Mr. Ringrose; they are not without agency in their interactions. Kayley is paid, but she also gets an emotional satisfaction from their interactions; she is sad when Mr. Ringrose is institutionalized; lonely, she misses him. We know Kayley is particularly vulnerable because she misses her dad, but I think she would reject the label of victim. The stories thus offer us a more expansive, nuanced expression of the human condition than bumper sticker slogans do. "Cleaning" allows the readers to ask, If Mr. Ringrose is losing his mind, are his actions still predatory? Does the predator's motivation matter? How would a difference in his motivation affect Kayley anyway? The short story cycle allows Strout, particularly if we see the book in conversation with her earlier work, to show how she has grown as a writer: more subtle, less easy to categorize or to rely on easy generalizations. She works to unnerve her readers—she no longer needs to reel them in but can make them uncomfortable, sure as she is in her literary powers. This book, like the one that preceded it, in its return to Strout's inventions—characters and towns—attests to the writer's own confidence in her abilities; she can refer to other writers as she has before, but she no longer needs to, to own her authority.

If in *Anything Is Possible* there was a certain nobility to the older characters (here I'm thinking primarily of "The Sign"), this book offers a more complicated portrayal of aging. The early hint of this portrayal came in "Snow-Blind" in *Anything Is Possible*, when the senile Elgin Appleby was making passes at the nurses, but within *Olive, Again* the unseemlier side of aging is front and center. In "Helped," Suzanne Larkin visits her addled mother in the nursing home. Louise does not recognize her daughter and says that when her son was young, "he always wanted me to play with his willie. Oh my, he was a bad, bad boy" (119). Mr. Ringrose and Louise Larkin may voice urges that people at every age feel. But culturally, sexual relations with children is forbidden, frowned upon, and considered immoral. If we see Mr. Ringrose watching (and paying) Kayley, we don't know if the confessions Mrs. Larkin utters are true or not. It's unclear if she molested her son, who later killed his girlfriend. And Suzanne has to live with the consequences of not knowing, living only with the effects of her mother's utterance. Here, the elderly cannot protect themselves either, their senility offering not a gentle fading away into night but a damning look at how they and we fail our most vulnerable. Strout is giving us a frank and disturbing look at aging. If there are moments that are funny, there are also moments that are profoundly distressing. Strout calls us to be alert, watchful.

Suzanne Larkin has returned to Crosby after the family house has burned down with her father in it to discuss arrangements with his lawyer, Bernie Green. "Helped" offers Strout the chance to explore faith explicitly. Most of the story is a conversation between Suzanne and Bernie. Both wrestle with their own tragedies—Suzanne with the effects of the revelation she's just heard, finally understanding that her father may have abused her mother, her brother's violence, and her own marital infidelities. Bernie, who worked for

Suzanne's father, is now an older man, but he bears the legacy of his parents' surviving the Holocaust. Again, then, Strout shows how the personal and the small cannot be separated from the international or the profound. In their conversation, which recalls "The Sign" in *Anything Is Possible*, Suzanne and Bernie discuss faith, Bernie saying, "I don't have words to describe it. It's more an understanding—I've had it most of my life—that there is something much larger than we are" (114–15). Suzanne responds, "I used to feel that. For *years* I would have sensations of just what you described. . . . When I was a kid, and alone—I spent a lot of time alone, you know, when I wasn't at school—I would take these walks and I would get this feeling, this very deep sensation, and I understood—only the way a kid could understand these things—that it had something to do with God" (115). She explains that her therapist, who seduced her, told her that she didn't feel God but was just "mystified by life" (116). Strout offers different perspectives on what this experience could have been. It might have been mystical—as Suzanne, Bernie, Lucy Barton, and Tommy Guptill feel—or maybe not. But Suzanne concludes that "our job—maybe even our *duty*—is to . . . bear the burden of the mystery with as much grace as we can" (116). The mysteries of her home are heavy. Whatever the mysteries are—violence, murder, grace, compassion, forgiveness—she can bear witness to them and try to keep on living, including, perhaps, not burdening others with her private suffering. And she and Bernie must live with the consequences of their own and others' actions as best they can.

"Light" follows a new character, Cindy Coombs, in treatment for cancer, a middle-aged woman who, like Amy Goodrow and Olive, is drawn to poetry, observing that if she wrote, she would write about "the light in February. How it changed the way the world looked" (123). We learn that "for Cindy the light of the month had always been like a secret, and it remained a secret even now. Because in February the days were really getting longer and you could see it, if you really looked. You could see how at the end of each day the world seemed cracked open and the extra light made its way across the stark trees, and promised. It *promised*, that light, and what a thing that was. As Cindy lay on her bed she could see this even now, the gold of the last light opening the world" (124). These moments of luminous beauty, this recognition of the wonder and ephemerality of light, are key to Strout's vision. If she shows us the humor and the poignancy, the drama of the human condition on the one hand, on the other she offers us glimpses of the natural world, encourages us to turn our eyes to see these staggering details, to leave the mire of suffering wittingly and unwittingly caused by humans and look at the natural glory that abounds. If we think of February—even as it's represented in Strout's earlier works, as a month of sludge and slush—we might realize that Strout here shows us that even in that season of sleet and muck, there is grace and light if we only look. Olive, in the winter of her life, has mellowed, and after seeing her former student Cindy suffering in the grocery store, she visits her to see how she is doing. They talk, and Olive speaks of her regrets to Cindy. In the years since Henry died and she married Jack, she has had time to cultivate self-awareness, time to grow. Of her first husband, she says, "I wasn't especially good to him, and it hurts me now. It *really* does. At times these days—rarely, very rarely, but at times—I feel like I've become, oh, just a tiny—tiny—bit better as a person, and it makes me sick that Henry didn't get any of that from me" (127). In Olive's growth, Strout offers her readers hope. Perhaps we too can continue to grow. We see that possibility of love and for-giveness later in the book, too, when Chris comes to visit his mother in the hospital. Though both mother and son are stubborn, quick to anger and to lash out (even within this short story cycle), they also possess a deep well of love for each other. Strout doesn't leave the Kitteridges wallowing in the angst of depression and regret.

The proximity to mortality offers the characters a chance at redemption. After Olive tells Cindy she's afraid of dying, she con-tinues, "You know, Cindy, if you *should* be dying, if you do die, the truth is—we're all just a few steps behind you. Twenty minutes be-hind you, and that's the truth" (128). There is a matter-of-factness, an acceptance of inevitability. We are all linked by the way we leave the earth. Perhaps, then, it's appropriate that Olive shares Cindy's

appreciation for the beauty of the sky. The two women marvel at the
world around them:

> "Would you look at that," Olive said.
>
> Cindy turned to look. The sunlight was magnificent, it
> shone a glorious yellow from the pale blue sky, and through
> the bare branches of the trees, with the open-throated look
> that came toward the end of the day's light.
>
> But here is what happened next—
>
> Here is the thing that Cindy, for the rest of her life,
> would never forget: Olive Kitteridge said, "My God, but I
> have always loved the light in February." Olive shook her
> head slowly. "My God," she repeated, with awe in her voice.
> "Just look at that February light." (138–39)

The women share a moment of almost prayerful reverence, of wonder in the glory of nature. We don't know when Cindy dies, whether
the chemotherapy she's had will cure her for weeks or months or
years, but we do know that she and Olive share a moment of beauty,
friendship, and understanding.[4] These moments of grace in Strout's
work occur at moments of community—here we might think of the
end of *Amy and Isabelle* or the last story in *Olive Kitteridge* or "Mississippi Mary" and "Gift" in *Anything Is Possible*—when individuals
realize they are in communion with each other. They might attri-
bute the love they see in other people or the wonder of nature to a
higher power, but it's the action of interacting with people, of being
vulnerable to someone else, that gives a person a new appreciation
for the life ahead.

In "The Walk," we meet sixty-nine-year-old Denny out for a
stroll. "Christmas was coming soon, yet no snow had fallen for three
weeks. This struck Denny as strange—as it did many people—because
he could remember his childhood in this very town in Maine, and
by Christmastime there would be snow so high he and his friends
would build forts inside the snow banks" (143). Again, Strout draws
our attention to the different ways we understand time. Here, the
natural landscape shows the effects of climate change; the world

Denny knew no longer operates—the cyclical nature of the seasons has been disrupted by pollution and greenhouse gases. Circular and chronological understandings of time come together in this passage. If the season once offered a nostalgic comfort, it no longer does. The world and time are off-kilter, as is Denny, concerned about his children, thinking that "something was wrong" (140). As he walks, he remembers Dorothy Paige, a beautiful girl who attended high school with him and his eventual wife. Dorothy was lovely, smart, surrounded by admirers, the daughter of a doctor, and always kind to Denny. After they graduated, while Denny went to work in the mill, Dorie attended Vassar before she killed herself; and Denny finds out her father had sexually abused her for years. As a young man, he was stunned on learning this; again, Strout proffers the moment of revelation when someone learns that a person he thought he knew is not who he thought. In the present, as he walks, "a sense of uneasiness came over him, as though he was not safe; in fact, the town had changed so much over these last few years that people no longer strolled around at night, as he was doing. But he had not thought of Dorie for quite a while; he used to think of her a great deal" (145). He is lost in his troubled reverie, reflecting that his home is quiet now, when he sees a "large body . . . just draped over the back of the bench . . . not moving" (145). Denny calls the police, who inject the man with naloxone, and Denny recognizes him as the "Woodcock boy," "a kid in his daughter's class years ago. How had he turned into this person? Large—fat—with his longish hair and all doped up?" (147).

The police officer tells Denny that he "saved a life tonight, for now," but Denny doesn't feel relief at this assessment or that his "children had been safe in their childhood home, not like poor Dorie. His children were not on drugs. It was himself about which something was wrong. He had been saddened by the waning of his life, and yet it was not over" (147). He returns home, where his wife "brightened when she saw him" and says, echoing the words he said to Dorie years earlier, "Hi there" (147). Denny doesn't know what private tragedies Marie has suffered, but there's a sense of

connection, of possibility even in the dark of this early evening
and the imminence of winter.

In the story "Pedicure," Olive and Jack have been married for
five years. Again, we see the juxtaposition of chronological time
with seasonal time in the first two sentences when we learn that "it
was November [and] no snow had fallen yet in Crosby, Maine, and
because the sun was out on this particular Wednesday there was a
kind of horrifying beauty to the world" (148). As we saw in "Walk,"
climate change has affected the landscape and the weather; the days
are different from what they used to be. Strout offers the wonderful
mix of poignant and ridiculous, this time from Jack's perspective as
he reflects on his time with Olive in an illimitable juxtaposition of
desperation and annoyance: "She would put her head on his chest,
and during the night they would shift, but always they were holding
each other, and Jack thought of their large old bodies, shipwrecked,
thrown up upon the shore—and how they held on for dear life. . . .
Never in his life would he have imagined that he would spend his
final years with such a woman in such a way. . . . She irritated him"
(149). Jack, in his disposition and glibness, is much like Olive; we can
understand their affection for and knowledge of one another. Svetlana Boym tells us that "love at last sight is the spasm of loss after the
revelation; the tenderness of exiles is about a revelation of possibility after the loss. Only when the loss has been taken for granted can
one be surprised that not everything has been lost. . . . The illusion of
complete belonging has been shattered. Yet, one discovers that there
is still a lot to share" (254–55). Even now, after five years, when they
no longer cling to each other at night, Jack realizes that Olive "had
grown increasingly less anxious; quietly this made Jack feel wonderful" (149). He realizes that he has been good for Olive, and this gift to
her makes him happy—he has brought this woman some semblance
of peace. Bessel van der Kolk explains that "trauma victims cannot
recover until they become familiar with and befriend the sensations
in their bodies. Being frightened means that you live in a body that
is always on guard. Angry people live in angry bodies. The bodies of
child-abuse victims are tense and defensive, until they find a way to

relax and feel safe" (100–101). The hurts that shaped Olive to become the woman she is aren't always clear, but her time with Jack allows her to soften, to trust, to walk more gently in the world.

But their life together is not simply sweet, for he recently came upon Olive trying to cut her toenails, silently crying because "she was too big and too old to get her feet close enough to her, and she hated, she said, she just *hated* having her toenails so awful-looking" (151). Her situation is pedestrian and sad, but then we see Jack's tenderness for her; he takes her to a salon, and she is overwhelmed by the wonders of the new experience of a pedicure. Strout reminds us in this story that Henry grew up in Shirley Falls and Olive in West Annett, and Olive tells Jack stories of both places, long-ago suicides, Henry's youth, and the Somali immigrants who now live there. Jack isn't interested in hearing about Henry, and so the past then comes uneasily into the present. It intrudes more obviously when they are at a restaurant and Elaine Croft, who years earlier had an affair with Jack and then sued him and Harvard for sexual harassment, ending his career, walks in. Jack, recalling Charlie Macauley in "The Hit-Thumb Theory," feels, "not unlike falling off his bicycle so many years ago when he was a child, the slow sense of something terrible happening, and the knowledge that there was nothing he could do about it" (157–58). Seeing his former lover, Jack is ashamed of his belly, his aging, and his new wife, even as he sizes up Elaine's dinner companion: "The guy looked like an imbecile, with his round glasses and his one earring (an earring, for Christ's sake, a tiny gold hoop!) and his hair down almost to his shoulders" (159). Their conversation is brief and awkward, and Jack recalls to himself how he loved Elaine, though "her stomach had been dimpled, and her backside was not small" (162—always the humor with Strout!), and his dawning realization that Elaine was "a careerist" (162).

When the story returns to the present, Olive tells Jack, she recognizes Elaine and faults him for his "taste in women. I think she is a dreadful, dreadful woman" (165). Her assessment of Elaine bothers Olive because, she tells Jack, "it says something about *you*. When you're attracted to crap, it says something about you" (166). As in

"Cleaning" and "Helped," then, we have these moments of dissociation. Here a moment of clarity does not offer comfort but rather an
unsettling, a shifting in the world. Olive realizes she doesn't know
Jack completely, and Jack realizes

> how much of his life he had lived without knowing who he
> was or what he was doing. It caused him to feel an inner
> trembling, and he could not quite find the words—for
> himself—to even put it exactly as he sensed it. But he sensed
> that he had lived his life in a way that he had not known. This
> meant there had been a large blindspot directly in front of
> his eyes. It meant that he did not understand, not really at all,
> how others had perceived him. And it meant that he did not
> know how to perceive himself. (166–67)

Seeing Elaine, he does not recognize himself. He sees that Elaine's
face "had a coldness to it that had surprised him. Her makeup was
too perfect, there was something cold about that. And then he realized: I was cold. So he probably had been attracted to, without recognizing it, this coldness in her" (167). It's in seeing Elaine that Jack
begins to see himself, for as Helena Kadmos tells us, "the intricacy of
human relationships can be understood as the *means* through which
we come to a greater understanding of ourselves in relation to others" (41; emphasis Kadmos's). Jack's dawning self-awareness—his recognition that he does not know himself, or did not know himself at
a particular time—makes him feel profoundly sad and profoundly
lonely. He misses Betsy and regrets "they had still squandered what
they had, because they had not known" (168).[5] Later that night Olive
attempts to comfort him, but he feels "alone with his nighttime
dream" (169). The story concludes that the older man and woman are
alone, "as people always are, with these things," wrenching but perhaps pointing to a glimmer of hope, for the community of sufferers
is large and vast and one can be sympathetic to another even when
isolated in a private grief.[6] This attempt to sympathize with—not
to appropriate someone else's suffering but to tacitly acknowledge
to another person, yes, you are suffering, and I am so sorry you

are—seems to be the project of this short story cycle. We don't get an attempt to celebrate wordless ideal empathizing, but instead an acknowledgment of the limitations of our abilities to commune with and understand each other.

That isolation—from our loved ones and from ourselves—leads to the destabilizing of security, which runs through "Exiles." In this story, Jim and Helen visit Bob and Margaret in Maine, and Bob is thrilled to have his brother back home; he "felt a happiness rise in him—it overtook the apprehension he had been feeling earlier—and now he was just happy" (175), but Helen is ill at ease with her sister-in-law. In particular, Margaret's breasts "seemed positively huge to Helen, and Margaret wore a long loose dress of dark blue and they still poured forth beneath it. And her hair! Why would anyone wear her hair in such a way? Just chopped off like that. Oh dear, Helen, thought, glancing at Margaret through her sunglasses. Oh, Bobby, what a change you made! Pam had been very stylish—if not a little overdone, in Helen's view—but Bob had now lived with this other wife for almost a decade" (177). To Helen's chagrin, she finds out gray-haired, busty Margaret is beloved in Crosby, and as the two women stroll through a local art fair, Margaret is greeted by neighbors repeatedly, discomfiting Helen, who is made aware of how little she knows her brother- and sister-in-law. Jim reveals he's on antidepressants, and Bob realizes "now what was different about Jim. His edge was gone. It's not that he had mellowed, it's that he was medicated. Bob felt a slight tightening of his chest" (180). Meanwhile the women try to chat with each other, but when Helen says, "I'm talking about my grandchildren too much," Margaret does not nod soothingly, instead brusquely replying, "Yes. You are" (186). After Helen falls down a flight of stairs and is taken to the hospital, Margaret confesses to her husband, "I couldn't *stand* her. And she knew it. And it was terrible of me, I didn't even really try with her. Oh, Bob. And she knew!" (191). Margaret thinks that Helen drove her crazy because she was "rich" and "self-centered," and Bob "could think of nothing to say. But a quiet sense of almost-unreality seemed to come to him, and he thought the word 'prejudice,' and he understood that he needed to drive carefully, and so he did, and then they reached the hospital" (192). His wife's small-town provincialism surprises Bob. Unlike Jack, he doesn't call out Margaret on her reverse snobbery, the elitism of the virtuous who assume superiority over others.

Bob is tender to his wife and sister-in-law. When he returns home, he finds Margaret asleep, and she seems "almost a stranger to him at this moment. He recognized now the smallness of her response to a world she did not know or understand; it was not unlike the response his sister had had to Helen. And he knew that had he not lived in New York for so many years—if his brother, whom he had loved as God, had not lived there as well, rich and famous for all those years—then he might have felt as Margaret did. But he did not feel as she did" (193). There is an expansiveness to Bob and to Jim that comes from being outsiders, living in places where they get to know the world differently than they would have if they had never left home. Margaret and Helen, unlike the men they have married, do not trouble themselves to know another perspective, another world. They do not recognize the grace of being unsettled. Boym offers some insights here: "To feel at home is to know that things are in their places and so are you; it is a state of mind that doesn't depend on an actual location. The object of longing, then, is not really a place called home but this sense of intimacy with the world; it is not the past in general, but that imaginary moment when we had time and didn't know the temptation of nostalgia" (251). Bob no longer has that sense of intimacy with the world, and this realization moves him to "a sadness he had not felt in years. He had missed his brother—his brother!—and his brother had missed Maine. . . . Jim would live the rest of his life as an exile in New York City. And Bob would live the rest of his life as an exile in Maine. . . . He was exiled here. And the weirdness of this—how life had turned out, for himself, and Jim, and even Pam—made him feel an ocean of sadness sway through him" (193–94). Bob's body becomes a conduit for his sadness, intensifying as he later watches Helen sleep. "He ached, as though he had walked far longer than his body could walk, his whole entire body ached, and he thought: My soul is aching" (194). He realizes then that "the essential loneliness of people [should never be taken lightly], that the choices they made to keep themselves from the gaping darkness were choices that required respect" (195). As Olive does for Jack, he watches his sister-in-law, giving her some comfort in the vast unknowing and loneliness they face.

"The Poet" also addresses existential loneliness. Olive returns to center stage, this time in a diner where she encounters a former student who has become poet laureate of the United States. Though Olive thinks she sees in Andrea "a wish not to be disturbed," at eighty-two, after having "buried two husbands," Olive ignores her better judgment and approaches her (197). The women begin to talk, and Olive remembers seeing her as "a girl out walking alone, and so sad-looking. Such a sad-looking face that girl had" (200). Today, however, Andrea L'Rieux is a celebrity in her hometown. "Everyone in town seemed to have read Andrea's poetry. Her books were always center on display in the bookstore. People said they loved her work. Andrea L'Rieux had been hailed as all sorts of things: feminist, postmodernist, political mixing with the natural. She was a 'confessional poet,' and Olive thought there were some things a person need not confess. (There were '*angry vaginas*' in one poem, Olive remembered now)" (201). Olive's comment brings us back to earth again in a very funny way.

Their conversation spans both women's presents and pasts; Andrea explains she's in town because her father has dementia, and Olive relays how her own father killed himself years ago. Olive reveals to Andrea that she has read her poetry and knows she doesn't have children, before brusquely saying, "Never mind. Kids are just a needle in your heart" (203). The comment, though Olive doesn't realize it at the time, is brutal and brutally honest, revealing her own sadness at her relationship with Chris. When Andrea lights a cigarette, Olive feels "a deep tremor of disappointment, and she thought: Well, she's just a L'Rieux. That's all she is. Famous or not" (205). Recalling Patty Nicely in "Windmills," "all the way home she told Jack about what had happened; it was Jack, her second husband, whom she seemed to want to tell this to" (205), though he is dead.

Months later, Olive finds a copy of *American Poetry* in her mailbox with a poem by Andrea L'Rieux marked with a Post-it.

> Seated now at the breakfast nook, she opened it to the page that had the Post-it and read: *Accosted.* Olive did not understand why that had been marked, until slowly, as she read the poem, it came to her, like she was moving—very, very slowly under water. *Who taught me math thirty-four years ago / terrified me and is now terrified herself / sat before me at the breakfast counter / white whiskered / told me I had always been lonely / no idea she was speaking of herself.* Olive read on. It was all there, her father's suicide, her son being a needle in her heart; the poem's theme, pounded home again and again, was that she—Olive—was the lonely, terrified one. It finished, *Use it for a poem, she said / All yours.* (213–14)

The meanness of someone leaving this poem for an elderly woman whom the poem is about is pretty shocking. In most of Strout's work, we see the redemptive power of kindness; small acts of grace and forgiveness temper the petty cruelties we inflict on each other. But here someone has been cruel to Olive, and doubly so, it seems, in the anonymity of it. Perhaps it was Andrea who was cruel in telling Olive's story and describing her as "whiskered," but it seems particularly heartless to anonymously leave the poem in Olive's mailbox, to ensure that she will see how she is represented. Who did it? The poet? The waitress? The hairdresser? One of Olive's "friends"? It's not clear, and perhaps it doesn't matter. On reading the poem, Olive remembers how "years and years ago her mother had opened the door one morning and a basket of cow flaps had sat there on the step, with a note that said, For Olive. She never knew who had brought the cow flaps, and she could not think who would have brought this magazine" (214). Some people are cruel and petty and traffic in bullshit.

But Olive reflects later that she had approached Andrea because she was famous. "If she had just been what Olive would have expected of her—another woman with children and sort of happy and mostly unhappy (her sad-faced walks)—then Olive would never have approached her" (216). The story concludes in a way similar to "Exiles" and "Pedicure," when Olive considers "she had never before completely understood how far apart human experience was. She had no idea who Andrea L'Rieux was, and Andrea had no idea who Olive was, either. And yet. And yet. Andrea had gotten it better than she had, the experience of being another." She remembers her husbands and thinks, "Who were they, who had they been? And who—who in the world—was she?" (216–17). We might remember that Jack asked similar questions of himself at the end of "Pedicure."

This sense of not knowing who you have been and who you are runs throughout *Olive, Again.* If we think of young people as those who pose existential questions, Strout turns this convention on its head. Her older characters look at the world around them, and then in the mirror, as bemused by themselves as they are by their surroundings. In "The End of the Civil War Days," we meet the MacPhersons, who have appeared peripherally in other stories, "married for forty-two years, [and] for the last thirty-five they had barely spoken to each other" (218). Even so, they live in the same house, too parsimonious or unimaginative to divorce, with "duct tape separating the living room in half; it ran over the wooden floor and right up against the rug that Ethel MacPherson had put on her side of the room; and in the dining room . . . running over the dining room table, dividing it in half exactly, running down into the air and then onto the floor" (218). Their living arrangements are both funny and sad. Fergus occasionally wears a kilt and dresses up for Civil War reenactments, but he and his wife are stunned when their elder daughter, also sartorially unconventional, tells them she's a professional dominatrix. In spite of Fergus's uncommon clothing choices, he's shocked by Lisa; she attempts to explain that she always "liked to dress up, and [she likes] to tell people what to do, I *like* people, Dad, and these people have certain needs and I get to fulfill them, and that's a pretty great thing" (232). When her mother says she doesn't understand sadomasochism as a practice, Lisa says, "This is exactly why we're doing the documentary. Because people don't have to feel so—so, so, you know, marginalized anymore if they are into this stuff. It's all just human behavior, and that's what we're trying to say" (233). Her parents are not ready for Lisa's explanation, and Fergus responds, "If putting needles into some man's penis is acceptable human behavior, then something's very, very wrong. . . . *God*, Lisa. . . . Human behavior? For Christ's sake, the concentration camps run by the Nazis were human behavior" (232–33). Before she recognizes her father is reacting out of ignorance, the equally shocked Lisa weeps buckets. Like so many of Strout's characters, she has needed her parents' approval after all.

Rattled, Fergus throws away his Civil War uniform and returns home to find Lisa, her sister, and Ethel watching the documentary and hearing that Lisa "took a *dump* on" one of her clients. This utterance catapults him into what may be a panic attack, a stroke, or a heart attack, and his family bundles him up to the hospital. This moment recalls Henry Kitteridge's and Abel Blaine's apparent strokes; this old man is unable to understand the world in which he now lives, and his body gives out. He wakes up in the hospital to see his wife sitting by him affectionately. He looks at her in confusion. Simply and generously, she "began to stroke his arm." The world is incomprehensible and they have made mistakes; their lives and their children have been and are mysteries to them; but now they are together, apparently willing to weather it through with each other, their bodies talking when words fail them.

After Olive has had a heart attack in the next story, "Heart," Strout gives her readers some small consolation by allowing Chris to come to the hospital to see her. When Olive wakes up, she finds her son by her bedside, and he says to her, "Oh, Mommy . . . you scared me to death" (242). Unsure whether she is imagining him, Olive asks if she's hallucinating. He responds, "Oh *please* don't have lost your mind," and Olive replies, "Hello, Chris. I haven't lost my mind at all. I've—apparently—had a heart attack, and you have—apparently—come to see me" (242). Her quip is wry, funny, and understated—in spite of the danger she's in, Olive is as acerbic as ever. After facing death, she hasn't become morbid or drawn to the sacrosanct, but remains resolutely down-to-earth. During her recovery, she experiences time differently than she previously had: "She stayed in the hospital room for a few days, later she found out it had been seven days, and when she thought of it she thought it had seemed longer than that, and also shorter. In other words, time had become something different. She was moved to a room where her bed looked out a window onto the trees—and it was autumn and she watched the maple leaves fall off one by one, sometimes two or three of them would flutter downward—and she liked that" (245). But never one to get lost in poignancy (unlike Charlie Macauley or Isabelle Goodrow), Olive immediately recognizes that "she didn't like the woman she shared the room with, and she asked that the curtain be drawn between the two beds, and someone did that for her, and Olive said, 'Now let it *stay* that way'" (245). In one brief paragraph, Strout offers poetic rendering of natural detail, play with time, and a direct humor that breaks the reverie of any moment. Even after her near-death experience, Olive is still in the human comedy after all.

In "Heart," Olive, at eighty-three, is mellowed and humbled. She learns she cannot be discharged from the hospital until she passes gas. "And then that afternoon—oh ye gods! Olive broke wind, and broke it some more, and then she began to leak from her back end. She didn't understand at first what was happening, but as she raised herself from the bed, she stared at the mess that was there" (246–47). Once again Strout does not shy away from such indignities. And just as new parents are forced to realize how much of life is pooping, so do the aged. Somewhat ashamed, Olive tells her doctor, "My bowels moved with a frightful ferocity," and when he is unfazed, telling her it's the effects of the antibiotics, Olive "felt something close to bliss, but it was more as though time had stopped—just for these few moments time had stopped—and there was only the doctor and life, and it sat with her in the morning sunshine that fell over the bed" (247).

After Olive returns home, the first CNA who comes to care for her is a former student whom she does not recognize, a woman of fifty who drives a truck with "a bumper sticker for that horrible orange-haired man who was president" (248). Olive is appalled, more so when she sees an encounter between Betty and Halima, the Somali CNA who switches shifts with Betty. Halima is impressed that Olive knows about the refugee camps in Kenya, and the older woman is impressed by the younger woman's kindness. The next day Olive tells Betty, "I saw how you treated that woman yesterday, and we'll have none of that in this house," echoing Tommy Guptill (251). When Betty responds, "I don't like the way she looks, that stuff she wears, it gives me the creeps. And it *is* politics," frustrated but pragmatic Olive states, "Well, in my house you are to be nice to her, do you understand?" (251). Very simply, Olive is showing Betty how to treat others with dignity—and that everyone deserves respect. Again, I think this is part of Strout's greater message, that fiction can show people how fellow sufferers are trying to make their way on earth and we can choose to shut others out or we can see—and literature can help us perceive—that others have their battles and struggles and need our kindness. Building on the work of Richard Rorty and Martha Nussbaum, Rita Felski tells us that empathy with fictional persons can "expand the limits of experience, engender a sense of solidarity with distant others, and do valuable civic and political work . . . encouraging altruism and binding readers into a community—working against strong social and economic pressures toward egoism and self-interest" (105). That said, as Olive points out crisply, some behaviors are simply wrong and not tolerable. We share the world with people we do not understand.

As if recognizing the importance of kindness and of being seen, when the doctor checks in on Olive again, he tells her, "You must have been a very good mother, Olive" (255). She is shocked by his conclusion, and when she asks him, "Why in the world do you think that?" he tells her, "Because your son was so often in attendance at the hospital, and he's called me twice to make sure you're all right" (255). Whether the doctor really thinks Olive was a good mother or not is unclear, but in letting Olive know that Chris has been looking after her, the doctor gives her comfort, peace. If some are cruel, others are kind. Olive has learned to appreciate the latter.

Weeks later, Betty visits Olive and tells her how sad she was when she learned her former principal had died. As Olive watches Betty cry, she thinks about "the way people can love those they barely know, and how abiding that love can be, and also how deep that love can be, even when—as in her own case [for her doctor]—it was temporary" (263). It's a moment of gentleness for Olive. She realizes Betty is suffering and shows her compassion, asking Betty about her life, "and so Betty told her then about her two marriages that had both gone wrong, three children who desperately needed money, . . . how she eventually got herself to school to become a nurse's aide. Olive listened, sinking into this woman's life, and she thought that her own life had been remarkably easy compared to things this girl had gone through" (264). Olive is stunned that for thirty years Betty has had a crush on her high school principal, and Olive wonders, "For Betty to have carried in her heart this love for Jerry Skyler, what did that mean? It was to be taken seriously, Olive saw this. For love was to be taken seriously, including her own brief love for her doctor. But Betty had kept this love close to her heart for years and years; she had needed it that much. . . . What a thing love was. Olive felt it for Betty, even with that bumper sticker on her truck" (264). Here, then, is that crucial sympathy, that sitting with partial understanding that Strout suggests is a way to endure the bleakness of our existence: relating to others with clear-sightedness, grace, and compassion (and perhaps a dose of humor). Surprisingly, Betty becomes a friend to Olive, setting the stage for the last story of the book, when Olive allows herself to reach out yet again.

In the last story of the collection, "Friend," Olive has joined the Maple Tree Apartments retiree living community. She is lonely, bored, bitter at the folks who have managed to find some degree of happiness or community in the center and at her (dead) husband Jack: "She felt enormously angry at him for dying. And then she thought: He wasn't so much, that Jack" (267). Strout shows us here once again the vicissitudes of love. What makes Olive so charming, refreshing, and (perhaps) irritating to readers is her irascibility.

Olive tries to connect to the other residents; she "stood near the group of people in the lounge, holding a glass of white wine, but these people—she thought—made it clear that she was not one of them. They were wealthy, Olive had come to understand, and they were snobs" (268). She feels alone, left out, excluded. Later, however, she meets the gentle Bernie Green, who had appeared in "Helped," here as a resident who visits his wife in the Alzheimer's unit every day. Ethel MacPherson has also moved to the center after her husband Fergus died. And so Strout gently assembles her characters into a tableau, allowing them to meet and offer comfort or conversation to each other late in life. Olive and Chris have reconciled, and she has also been able to connect with Chris's son, Theodore, with whom she had struggled earlier. Such encounters are not romanticized or sentimentalized. Although Strout values affectionate relationships, she doesn't do so at the expense of honesty. Olive is moved by Bernie's solicitude for his wife, but she's troubled by Isabelle's apparent dementia. She remembers her husbands fondly, but she doesn't think of them as saints. In this way, again, Strout is privileging a just and loving look at the world, one that is sincere without being mawkish. But the character who has the most connection with Olive in this story is Isabelle Daignault; "Olive thought she looked mousy, and Olive had never cared for that mousy look" (272). This recalls her initial impression of Henry's assistant, young Denise. The woman was once Isabelle Goodrow.

Olive and Isabelle discuss their children, their husbands, and their mothers. Olive fears Isabelle is suffering from dementia when she hears her talking to herself, but Isabelle reassures her that speaking as her mom "comforts me. And it gets mixed up with my being a mother to Amy, because I don't think I was such a good mother to her" (286). Isabelle and Olive live with their regrets, but they also listen to and learn from each other, modeling perhaps what Strout refers to in the appendix, companionship: "Someone who sits with you through your life, [so that] while we are always separate—because people are always separate—there is also a sense of not being alone" (247).

At her request, Chris brings his mother a typewriter, and she begins to record her memories. The typewriter allows Olive to create her own curated life in the last story, and this seems to me a profound kindness that Strout gives her creation. Olive realizes she is different from the woman she once was, recalling "how in college she had thought one day, looking at the inside of a frog: There must be a God who made all these things. Now she considered this, and then typed, 'I was young then'" (275), showing us the distance between the young and older Olive. Waxman tells us that in *Reifungsromane*, protagonists often make "an internal journey to their past through dreams" (17). Who she was is a mystery to Olive, but she knows she no longer has the faith she once did. Some of her memories confuse and trouble her, leaving her grasping the way Jack did when he reflected on his affair with Elaine. Svetlana Boym explains, "To confront the unknown, particular and unpredictable, one has to risk embarrassment, the loss of mastery and composure. On the other side of ironic estrangement might be emotion and longing. . . . The border zone between longing and reflection . . . opens up spaces of freedom. Freedom in this case is not a freedom from memory but a freedom to remember, to choose the narratives of the past and remake them" (354). Olive, too, realizes she can record her story in whichever way she wants.

Echoing *My Name Is Lucy Barton* and *Anything Is Possible*, at the story's end, Olive realizes that "*she* was going to die. It seemed extraordinary to her, amazing. She had never really believed it before" (288). Once again the mysteries of the most quotidian facts of life are front and center. For all their ubiquity, those moments fill Olive with wonder—while they do not inspire quite the sense of the sacred that she saw once in the frog, they are still marvelous in their very incarnation. At the same moment, she realizes, "It was herself . . . that did not please her" (289); revelations are not always encouraging. But never one to be maudlin ("it was too late to be thinking that"), Olive looks at the rosebush planted earlier by Chris and reflects, "*I do not have a clue who I have been. Truthfully, I do not understand a thing*" (289), sounding like Henry or Jack or Bob

or Lucy.[7] Strout ends the cycle then with the same sense of destabilizing wonder. Olive, in her old age, has learned that she doesn't
know. Her losses have softened her; now she is less like Lydia Barton
and more like Lucy. Olive's wisdom is shown not in self-assured certainty but in a receptiveness to new lessons, people, and love. She
is less positional, entrenched, and self-righteous, more aware of her
dependency on others.[8] If this revelation is awe-inspiring, it can still
lead to pragmatism, for Olive decides to retrieve Isabelle for dinner,
emblematizing how Strout's fiction focuses on what Kadmos calls
"the shared experiences that shape characters' identities" (42). It's
the sacred bond of friendship, one that acknowledges the wonders
and challenges of connecting, that Strout's work celebrates, an intimacy that is honest, loving, direct, and provocative. The women,
so often alone in their early days, have found a companion, a friend,
and an understanding in each other.

8 Oh William!
The Art of Losing

OH WILLIAM! APPEARED IN OCTOBER 2021, AT WHAT some optimistically thought was the turning point of the COVID-19 pandemic, when vaccines had been distributed and much of the world was opening up again. The rise of Omicron one month later dashed the hopes of many, yet Strout's eighth book served as a kind of quiet gift to her readers in the midst of global and individual suffering. *Oh William!*, the third work in the Lucy Barton series, is a novel about loss and grief, and allowing oneself to open up to—not shy away from—these experiences. Lucy, now sixty-four, begins *Oh William!* telling us that her second husband, David, has recently died, and I read the novel, in spite of its title, as an indirect elegy to him. Within *Oh William!*, which like *My Name Is Lucy Barton* appears as a memoir, Lucy does not dwell on her relationship with David or his death, but through her telling of her first husband's and his mother's losses, she allows herself to mourn the various griefs she's endured and to recognize the gift and grace of being broken. Critics were quick to praise and readers to buy Strout's most recent book, which, as Jennifer Egan in her review in the *New York Times* explains, "is a brief swirling account of present-day events that rouse memories of past events and prompt a reckoning."

I read *Oh William!* as a widow's cry of mourning for her late husband and the collective losses of our world. That cry, which "beautifully showcases [Lucy's] tremulous heart and limpid voice" (McAlpin), is one of love, and even while the novel painfully portrays the sadness that accompanies loss, it also contains comfort for the bereaved. In the aftermath of death, divorce, and disillusionment, and the legacy of genocide, Lucy creates a beautiful story whose very existence is predicated on loss. Though I read Lucy's grief for David as the mostly unspoken subject of the book, the surface story she tells is primarily about her first husband, William, as he comes to terms with aging, the dissolution of his third marriage, and his realization that his mother is not who he thought she was. And herein lies the paradox of the book and perhaps of grief in general, which Lucy encapsulates by saying, "My second husband, David, died last year. . . . In my grief for him I have felt grief for William as well," and then, "Grief is such a—oh, it is such a solitary thing; this is the terror of it, I think. It is like sliding down the outside of a really long glass building while nobody sees you" (3). Lucy understands grief as a profoundly lonely and private experience, and yet we are all marked by it collectively as well as individually, for if "William has lately been through some very sad events—many of us have" (3). Lucy's deeply personal suffering connects her to William and, of course, to others as well. If Strout's earlier works fleetingly explore how revelations can wreak havoc on prior understandings of the world, here she unspools such moments over the course of a novel. After facing the common but nonetheless wrenching experiences of death and divorce, of being in some ways left behind, William and Lucy turn to each other and take a literal and metaphorical trip together to visit his roots while they come to terms with their family histories, their past foibles, and their current failings. That journey is one of healing for both William and Lucy; telling William's story of loss, suffering, and recovery allows Lucy to recuperate as well. Though some might see Lucy's move of telling William's story as vicarious self-indulgence, wallowing in a kind of trauma porn, I see her reflections on her first husband as a way to model for her readers how to listen to others and to become more empathetic. After all, Lucy, like William, is also broken at the book's beginning, but she shows her readers that one can endure what one perceives as catastrophic events. At moments of grave individual and general trauma, Strout, through Lucy, points the way not just toward survival but toward surviving with the faith that, although we may feel irrevocably damaged and hurt, we can still find glimpses of joy and wonder in the world. In this chapter, I draw particularly on the work of Pauline Boss and Oliver Burkeman to illuminate how Strout (1) encourages us to recognize that, even in moments of darkness, "the world is bursting with wonder" and (2) allows us, through witnessing Lucy and William's journey, "to experience more of that wonder" not only in reading about their lives but in pointing to how we can live our own as well (Burkeman, 5).

The appearance of *Oh William!* could not have been more serendipitous. As COVID continues to ravage our homes and the world, we are all, collectively and personally, mourning, "grappling" in Meg Bernhard's words, as a global community "with questions of atmospheric grief." If conventional therapy—at least as it has been generally accepted, albeit reductively à la Elisabeth Kübler-Ross—has traditionally encouraged patients to move through their grief, Boss and Strout instead posit that our own reliance on such an outcome "does not equip us to cope" with the losses we will face throughout our lifetime (Bernhard). The plague of COVID has left survivors mourning not only that which we left behind and that won't return but also that which could have been. In March 2020, before events started getting canceled and stay-at-home orders were issued in the States, most people had no idea what the world would look like one month, two months, or two years hence. We didn't know what we would lose or how we would live once the world started to embrace "a new normal." Whether it's isolating in our apartments, missing trips, avoiding friends and family, resigning from our jobs, sending our kids to school wearing masks, seeing groups of kids playing while socially distancing, the pandemic has left us alone, losing connections we would have had had COVID not nailed our country to the floor and stolen so many experiences from us, both those we knew and those we hadn't yet imagined.

In *Oh William!*, Strout shows readers how to endure disappointment and loss with grace, gratitude, and forgiveness. We might not be able to conquer grief, but what we can do is learn to live with loss, sadness, and regrets, not try to bury or hide from these experiences but instead to, like Lucy, be still and open to "pause . . . long enough to enter the coherent, harmonious, somehow thicker experience of time that comes with being 'on the receiving end' of life rather than ceaselessly trying to master it" (Burkeman, 153). That pause is what Lucy returns to throughout her life and what reading Strout offers us if we are receptive enough to heed this call.

Lucy shows us through the course of *Oh William!* that we can survive what we thought would be unendurable, that we can love and mourn those who hurt us even as we don't understand them or our feelings, and that we can still come to realize life is "amazing" (*My Name Is Lucy Barton*, 191) or "remarkable" (*Abide with Me*, 294). Neither Strout nor Lucy is pedestrian enough to claim that everything—particularly suffering—happens for a reason; rather they show us the still, small miracles of people continuing to reach out, to love, to forgive, and to forge on as much to their own surprise as to anyone else's. Strout and Lucy urge us to turn our "attention, however briefly or occasionally, [to] the sheer astonishingness of *being*" (Burkeman, 65). Loss, suffering, and grief are part of the wondrous continuum of human experience, and we can hold that grief with us, realize that debilitating sadness can be a remnant of a well-lived life. Though William and Lucy learn these lessons in the course of the book, other characters are not so fortunate.

Strout, Boss, and Burkeman all suggest that if we look at our own experiences, including our suffering, with the openness to learn from them, then we will approach others and ourselves with more compassion, kindness, and generosity. Loss, in and of itself, is not a teacher, but if we cultivate the disposition within ourselves to be receptive to loss, then it can be. It is when we wall ourselves off from possibilities, including the possibilities of grief, that we live a more stunted and compromised existence. Such a lesson, of course, is particularly relevant at our current moment.[1] Strout is never prescriptive—for her characters or for her readers—but in showing us Lucy's capacity for awe, particularly awe at the kindnesses of others and at William's learning to open up through the course of his journeys, she offers her readers a model for a fuller existence and a hope that we, too, can traverse the darkness of our private suffering and reach out to others, or see the light that others may be holding out to us.

We can read *Oh William!* as an entertaining novel that allows readers to escape from their own lives, to be absorbed in the details of Lucy's reflections on William's movement. But we can also read the book as a study in learning to be openhearted, in learning to accept that others are suffering and that though we cannot know their private griefs (indeed, they themselves may not know them), we can still approach them with a loving sensibility, recognizing that their mysterious and sometimes irritable (and irritating) facade need not prevent us from showing them kindness. Though we may not discern our own or others' hands in the darkness, we can reach out in the faith that someone else may also be extending her fingers. In a brutal world where actions both personal and global may encourage cynicism or despair, Lucy—and Strout—posit that we can cultivate our own capacity for awe at small gestures of human kindness. Even if someone isn't reaching out to us, we are still better for trying, for making the effort to believe in someone.

But make no mistake. This timely novel is primarily about grief and loss. Loss permeates the novel—the death of spouses, miscarriages, divorces, leave-takings—all these events leave their marks on the characters, sometimes physically and always psychologically. And the Holocaust, the greatest human tragedy in living memory, literally and figuratively casts a shadow over Lucy and William, warning the reader of what humans can become if we ignore our collective responsibility to care for each other. We've seen communities of the walking wounded before in Strout's work, in Amgash, Shirley Falls, and Crosby. Here the portrayal is more intimate, as she explores the complex and nuanced effects of cumulative losses on a family. That's appropriate of course since Lucy's voice is so conversational, whispering to the reader as if she were a dear friend, for Strout, in the words of Jennifer Egan, "works in the realm of everyday speech, conjuring repetitions, gaps and awkwardness with plain language and forthright diction." Rather than focusing on her own losses and regrets, Lucy plumbs the lives of William and his mother (Catherine) and how they have responded to their own losses, griefs, and disappointments. Catherine lives through denial and repression; William fills his days with work and affairs; and Lucy becomes a novelist, creating stories of other people and their own losses. And even peripheral characters—like William's third wife, Estelle, and Lucy's daughters, Becka and Chrissy—also grieve.

Oh William!, the strangely punctuated title, runs like a musical refrain through the novel as Lucy reflects on her first husband and their life together. Where is the comma? Why is it missing? Why is there no pause? Through its elision, Strout draws our attention to the turn of phrase and its literary echoes, recalling that early master of the American short story, O. Henry. O. Henry, itself a nom de plume for William Sydney Porter, specialized in stories of connections lost, meetings just missed, unfortunate lapses, and here Strout covers similar territory. Many of the earlier writer's most famous stories set the stage for a period of mourning, regret, and grief, the subjects of this novel as well.[2]

But if the title looks back across the vast terrain of American letters, the dedication looks out to the present and the future, inviting the reader to, paradoxically, feel seen by Strout: "This book is dedicated to my husband, Jim Tierney. . . . And to anyone who needs it—this is for you" (vi). Because the title emphasizes the reading experience and the dedication foregrounds marriage, Strout's own life, and her relationship with her readers, we might conclude that the act of personal connection is all-important, and that reading can be as intimate an experience as any other, if the reader allows herself to be open, to be acted upon by a book. *Oh William!*, Strout tells us, is a gift—from her—to us. In an interview with the podcast *Poured Over*, Strout reflected on her relationship with her readers and emphasized the mutuality, intimacy, and trust possible between author and audience:

> I think of myself as being in a dance with the reader. You know, we're dancing. And I have to take the lead. God forbid I would ever do that in real dancing, you know what I mean. I don't even know how to dance. But the point is, in my mind, I'm thinking, okay, we're dancing, and we're doing this together. And I am doing this for the reader with the hope that the reader will come with me, you know, for this little journey and even if there are parts that don't seem that pleasant, they'll feel safe in my hands and they will go. And then when they come through the journey, they'll see things just a little bit differently, just momentarily, maybe, a little transcendence, a little popping in their lives. They really just might be a little bit higher for just a few minutes. They might recognize themselves or they might recognize other people, but they will have somehow been a little bit changed and helped, I hope. This is from one living mind to another. (Messer)

The pair together—reader and writer—creates something greater than either of them singly. It's not just the words on the page that matter, then—it's what the reader brings to them as well, "especially the Lucy books," Strout adds, because "they're more porous and there's more room for the reader to bring their own story" (Messer). When read, Strout's words perform a kind of incantation, not a hypnosis but a creation more wonderful than either the book or the reader was previously.

This awareness makes sense when we consider where and how Lucy—and Strout—see awe. That is, if Lucy finds natural landscapes awe-inspiring and poised to welcome viewers to transcendence (we might recall the end of *Lucy Barton*, for example), she also finds wonder in the grace of human interactions. With her dedication, Strout extends that wonder beyond Lucy and William or Lucy and David or William and Catherine or any of the other dyads within the novel to the person who is holding the book in her hand. "You, too," she suggests, "with me, create a new kind of perspective, a new way of seeing the world that we didn't have before we met." She invites us to see our own participation as part and parcel of a magical experience.

It's fitting, then, that the book's inspiration also comes from a moment of collaboration that Strout alludes to in the closing acknowledgments. Laura Linney was in rehearsal on the London stage considering her role as Lucy Barton and contemplated aloud, "I wonder if William had an affair." Offstage, Strout thought to herself, "Oh William!" In the *Poured Over* interview, Strout reflected in more detail: "And [Laura] put her glasses on top of her head, and I will never forget it because at that moment I thought, 'Oh, William,' and that was the moment I realized, 'Oh, let's think about William,' because of course he has a story. Everybody has their story. But she somehow—it just blossomed in the air—this 'Oh, William,' and so therefore I understood." The novel is born from an interaction between two individuals. Between them, Strout and Linney created the space for this seed to germinate. When we consider that the conversation took place in a theater, a location that would eventually include an audience, a director, and a crew, the importance of human connection becomes even more apparent. Linney reflects, Strout imagines, and an audience will bear witness and make its own meaning. *Oh William!* holds the past, present, and future, its very existence contingent on interactions between people—both those seen and unseen.

The book begins like *The Burgess Boys*. That is, the narrator speaks briefly about herself and then begins to tell a story about other people. But unlike *The Burgess Boys*, here we know who the narrator is—we've met Lucy Barton in other books—and she also more deliberately makes herself a part of the story she tells. Foregrounding Lucy's voice, vision, and experiences represents a kind of evolution of Strout's sense of interconnectedness. After all, Lucy says, "we were married for almost twenty years before I left him and we have two daughters, and we have been friendly for a long time now—how, I'm not sure exactly. There are many terrible stories of divorce, but except for the separation itself ours is not one of them. Sometimes I thought I would die from the pain of separating, and the pain it caused my girls, but I did not die, and I am here, and so is William" (4). Whereas the unnamed teller of *The Burgess Boys* all but disappears, Lucy—in her story of William and of his mother—also lets us know that the story is about herself and her families, not only the family she shares with William but also the family she left behind in Amgash, and the family she and David create years later. The presence of all these families—physical, psychological, estranged, and unconventional—underscores how we, our personal feelings and inconveniences notwithstanding, are not alone, but deeply related to each other, in ways both known and unknown. In Strout's, Boss's, and Burkeman's worlds, a story is not just about its ostensible subjects but about others as well.

The titular subject of the book is William Gerhardt,[3] Lucy's first husband, the septuagenarian who reaches out to her because he is having trouble sleeping: "It's in the dark when things come to me. . . . I've never had this sort of thing before. But they're terrifying, Lucy. They terrify me" (10). William explains to Lucy that they aren't nightmares exactly—not complex narratives but rather evocations of his mother, his father, or death. The terrors speak to William's unconscious awareness of his own incipient mortality, his professional decline, and his unarticulated concern about his third marriage failing, but they also summon, for he carries with him, the effects of his parents' unresolved trauma. Previous readers of Strout may remember that William's father, Wilhelm, was a German prisoner of war, captured by Americans, and brought to Maine. Wilhelm is an exile—like the other exiles in Strout's work, he is a man alone who rarely talked with his son before he died when the boy was four-teen. Boss explains that many immigrants suffer from ambiguous loss, never fully at home in their country of adoption, and Strout hints that Wilhelm may have been so troubled.[4] William's recollec-tion of his father when he is an old man points to his unresolved grief at losing him at a young age and guilt over his father's par-ticipation in the Holocaust: "This might have been William's worst terror, because his father had been fighting on the side of the Nazis, and this fact would visit William in the night sometimes and cause him terror—he would see very clearly the concentration camps—we had visited them on a trip to Germany—and he would see the rooms where people were gassed" (12). The Holocaust, and by association other moments, including our own instances of collective cultural guilt, hovers at the margins of this narrative. I see Strout's inclusion of these references as a sign of respect for the victims and as rais-ing the question of how in our current moment we ought to think about past tragedies and their complex legacy and not try to close the book on them. In portraying William's memories as fragments of dreams, Strout evokes the gas chambers, genocide, and legacy of collective cultural guilt without appropriating the experience. We learn later that William rarely talks to Lucy about his father, but his family's past haunts the elderly man decades later. Wilhelm remains an unknown figure, marked by his rapturous piano playing and not much else.[5]

Another terror that visits William is "not nameable, but it had something to do with his mother. His mother . . . had died many, many years earlier, but in the nighttime terror, he would feel her presence, but it was not a good presence and this surprised him because he had loved her. William had been an only child, and he had always understood his mother's (quietly) ferocious love for him" (11). Catherine's dream presence shocks Lucy as well because she had always seen her mother-in-law as exceptionally well-grounded, put-together, and stable. Lucy says of William's mother, "We loved her. Oh, we *loved* her; she seemed central to our marriage. She was vibrant; her face was often filled with light" (39). William's third terror is the fear of death: "It had to do with a sense of leaving, he could feel himself almost leaving the world and he did not believe in any afterlife and so this filled him on certain nights with a kind of terror" (12). William doesn't know what to do with these visions other than to express them to Lucy. Throughout her oeuvre, Boss explains how grief is often nonlinear, claiming that we do not get over losses or traumas but that they continue to affect us and can manifest themselves in unconscious ways, including, as here, in dreams.

The fact that William reaches out to Lucy signals a change from his previous habitual aloofness, a softening in him in his senescence. Lucy, Estelle, and their daughters have always perceived William as reserved, but here, in his moment of need, he turns to his first wife. Lucy says:

> To get over this terror while he lay awake in bed next to his
> sleeping wife—he told me this that day, and it kind of killed
> me—he would think of *me*. He would think about the fact that
> I was out there alive, right now—I was alive—and this gave
> him comfort. Because he knew if he had to . . . he knew if he
> *should* have to, that I would take a call from him. He told me
> my presence is what he found to be the greatest comfort. (11)

That he doesn't turn to his current wife speaks to fissures in their marriage that he is unaware of. Having learned repression from his parents, he has built a shield around himself to (unsuccessfully) guard against human vulnerability. That act of turning to someone, perhaps without even realizing that he is doing so, is one of invitation and of love. In asking Lucy to comfort him, he allows for a tenderness he can't find elsewhere, and one that speaks to the greater favor he will soon ask.

William will soon suffer two more blows. For Christmas, his wife gives him a subscription to a platform like Ancestry.com, which to his shock reveals that he has a half sister. Initially, he can't wrap his head around this new knowledge. But as the novel continues, he, Lucy, and the reader learn that his mother left not only her first husband for William's father but also her infant daughter. William is dumbstruck by this revelation, and his disbelief stems from how carefully and seamlessly his mother had created an alternative story and life for herself. Following this shattering revelation, when he is out of town, his third wife Estelle leaves him, seemingly without warning, taking their young daughter. Bewildered, William again turns to Lucy, asking her to accompany him on a trip to Maine to find the sister he never met and to understand his mother better. It's another expression of vulnerability for William, who had "always been a mystery" to his spouses and children (13). Unconsciously not trusting security, he has sabotaged it throughout his life by having extramarital affairs and distancing himself from his wives. The younger Lucy had intuited that William was suffering, and she responded not with patience, as she does when she's older, but a testiness.

She tells us, "At times in our marriage I loathed him. I saw, with a kind of dull disc of dread in my chest, that with his pleasant distance, his mild expressions, he was unavailable. But worse. Because beneath his height of pleasantness there lurked a juvenile crabbiness, a scowl that flickered across his soul, a pudgy little boy with his lower lip thrust forward who blamed this person and that person—he blamed me, I felt this often; he was blaming me for something that had nothing to do with our present lives" (26). The younger couple did not yet know the shadows they carried with them.

Years later when William asks Lucy, widowed and mourning, to accompany him, she agrees; it's on the road trip that the elderly William comes to realize that his parents suffered—Wilhelm from his actions in World War II and his self-imposed exile after he returned to the States when the war had ended, and Catherine from her childhood poverty and abandoning her baby daughter. His parents, he realized, reacted to that grief by unsuccessfully attempting to shut it away, as he himself has done through most of his life. But in taking the trip, in seeing (if from a distance) his sister and his mother's childhood home, William begins to heal, begins to realize that he doesn't need to be afraid to look at his past the way his parents had been. He begins to see the effects of what Boss calls their "frozen grief" (1999, 4), and his night fears do go away. At the book's end, he invites Lucy to accompany him on another trip, this time to the Cayman Islands. The two of them had gone there de- cades earlier—with Catherine—and so this trip, like the earlier one to Maine, is another kind of looking back, but it also serves another purpose, not the beginning of a fantastic reunion, but a sign of two adults who love and care about each other picking their own way through the world, giving each other tenderness.[6]

William's disbelief stems from his complete trust in his mother's heavily edited version of her history. In marrying Wilhelm, Cather- ine largely managed to erase all vestiges of her earlier life. She rarely spoke of Clyde Trask, her "unpleasant" (57) first husband, the potato farmer, and never of her baby girl or birth family. Catherine instead reinvented herself as in some way coming to life when she heard Wilhelm playing the piano in her living room. Lucy imagines their encounter years hence:

> This is when Catherine fell for him frantically, irretrievably. She said she had never heard anything as beautiful as what Wilhelm played that day; it was summer and a window was partly open, and a breeze picked up the curtain and tossed it gently, and he sat there and played that piano. It was Brahms he played, she found this out later. . . . Whenever Catherine told us this story her eyes got very far away; you could tell that she was picturing this: the man who had stepped into her house and taken his cap off and sat down at the piano and played. (58–59)

Catherine never told her son or Lucy of the families she left or the pain she carried with her. And in remembering Wilhelm as a prisoner of war and a musician, Catherine in some ways allowed herself to ignore his previous life in Germany and her first marriage. She por- trayed herself as an ingenue swept up by a romantic stranger. As an older woman, she was kind, generous to Lucy in ways that she didn't need to be, yet small cracks appeared on her surface, though Lucy didn't realize it at the time. Lucy remembers Catherine asking her to tell me about my family, and I opened my mouth and then tears came down my face, and I said, "I can't." And she stood up from where she had been sitting in a chair and she came and sat next to me on the tangerine couch and put her arms around me and said, "Oh Lucy." She kept saying that, rubbing my arms and my back and then pressing my face to her neck. "Oh Lucy."

She said to me that day "I get depressed too." And I was amazed. No one I ever knew, no grown-up, had ever said that—and she said it sort of casually—and she hugged me again. I have always remembered that. She carried within her that kindness. (44)

In the present moment, armed with the knowledge of Catherine's early poverty and first marriage, Lucy realizes that her mother-in-law was troubled, her involvement in their marriage and her sleepless nights pointing to a profound unhappiness rooted in silently grieving the lives she left behind. Usually, Catherine appeared to William and Lucy as "light itself," though occasionally, Lucy says, "she seemed more subdued, and she would say, almost laughingly, 'Oh, I have the blues'" (41). Lucy and William are shocked when they track down Catherine's home on their trip:

It had been abandoned for years, it seemed. But it was the tiniest house I think I had ever seen. I had grown up in a very small house, and this one was much smaller. It was one story and looked as though it had two rooms. And next to it was a very small garage. The roof of the house sagged—it had been a flat roof, and the center of it seemed to be almost falling in. . . . The house was so—so—small. . . . Through the windows the inside of the house was dark; nothing could be seen. Only a little bit could I imagine people moving about in there. The grass had grown very high around the place, and saplings were standing close to it. Two saplings had even grown through the house, they came out of the almost-fallen-down roof. . . . William looked so bewildered, it made me ache for him. And I understood: Never in my life would I have imagined Catherine coming from such a place. (195–97)

William realizes—as so many Strout characters do—that he has never understood his mother.

In the course of the trip, Lucy meets Lois, the half sister of William, now widowed and still living in the home of the woman who adopted her. Lois tells Lucy that Catherine once came to visit her, years earlier (the summer Lucy was hospitalized). That Catherine talked with Lois suggests that she perhaps somewhat came to terms with what she had done, but though she tried to forge a connection with her daughter, she never told William, the pain and shame too great for her to live with openly. Lois feels doubly rejected, learning that her birth mother kept her visit to herself. Catherine models a kind of deeply private grief, one that she cannot speak aloud, and in so doing, she is also profoundly tragic.

When Lucy talks with Lois—William is too chastened to leave the car—Lois explains she lives in the house of the onetime Marilyn Smith, who married Clyde Trask shortly after Catherine left. Lois tells Lucy she always thought of Marilyn as her mother but that when she was eight years old, her parents sat her down and told her how her birth mother left home when she was a baby. Lois claims the revelation didn't devastate her—and in this way, she may be like Catherine, living in some kind of denial, though Lucy sees Lois as possessing something "that seemed deeply—almost fundamentally—comfortable inside herself, the way I think a person is when they have been loved by their parents" (76). Though Lucy reads Lois as secure, raising her own family in Marilyn's house, staying after her children have moved out and her husband has died, suggests otherwise—that Lois has a desperate, unconscious fear that she may be abandoned again and a deep resentment toward Catherine and her new family. We see Lois's hostility in her description of Catherine's parents, the Coles, who, she claims, "were a troubled family from way back. They just weren't much. Apparently Catherine's mother was a drinker, and her father could never keep a job. There was talk that he was abusive as well—I mean to the kids and his wife" (178). That Lois doesn't meet William when given the opportunity—that she tells Lucy she is not ready to see him—points to an emotional stunting, a suspicion that what she has may be taken away from her, that she is not ready to open her heart.[7]

Though the older Lucy is receptive to love and to hurt, her younger self was not. At the time of this story, neither is Estelle, William's current wife. She is twenty-two years younger than William and a vivacious actress who deliberately got pregnant without telling him, a mark perhaps of the insecurity she carries and harbinger of duplicities.[8] We learn that Estelle, too, suffers from insomnia, though she doesn't sit with it as Lucy or William does, but takes tablets to sleep. Beautiful and professionally successful, Estelle still strikes Lucy as desperate, uncomfortable with silence, and looking for validation from older men. Lucy ironically remembers the younger woman appearing in a deodorant commercial, linking her to Lucy and to Catherine, who wear perfume, Lucy's therapist suggests, because they're afraid they carry the stench of their childhood poverty on them. Estelle, however, comes from money, and is comfortable in her current affluence: "I have an image of their apartment all done up for the holidays with a big Christmas tree, Becka had told me about it; she said, wryly, that it was as festive as Macy's" (35). Becka's comment is a bit snide; Estelle is kind to Lucy, inviting her to their home for Christmas. She shows solicitude to the older woman: "We know it has to be hard with David gone. . . . Oh Lucy—I feel so bad for you" (35), though Lucy rejects Estelle's overtures.

Lucy likes Estelle even less after she walks out on William (wincing since she herself left him decades earlier). But Estelle and Lucy share a surprising and important moment toward the novel's end, which the earlier invitation anticipates. The two women run into each other unexpectedly, and Estelle, guilt-ridden for hurting William, reaches out to Lucy, who "caught a glance at her face and there was tremendous pain there." "My heart unfolded," Lucy says, "and I said, 'Wait.' And she turned back, and I said, 'Estelle, you do what you need to do and don't worry about the rest of us.' Or I said something like that, I was trying to be nice to her" (215). In that moment Lucy acts magnanimously, generously extending a dose of human kindness to her. When she sees how broken Estelle is, Lucy "almost loves" her and realizes, "I think she saw in my face that I did, because she put her arms around me, and we kissed each other's cheeks, and she said, and she was starting to weep. . . . 'Oh Lucy, it was wonderful to see you'" (216). In allowing Estelle that refrain twice, Strout endows her with the words that Lucy later echoes in the novel's concluding benediction. As in *Abide with Me*, when it's crabby Charlie and Doris Austin who reach out to Tyler Caskey, or in *The Burgess Boys*, when it's Susan Burgess who reaches out to her brother, here Strout shows compassion coming from the unlikeliest of people. It's not just the easily generous, likable individuals who offer solace; disagreeable folks do so as well, and Lucy learns—unlike her mother or Lois—to accept kindness when it is offered to her, even by individuals she does not have an instinctive liking for.

This lesson in openness, in reception, is so important. If showing kindness to others is easy for some people, it is hard for nearly everyone to be on the receiving end, yet Strout shows that that willingness to receive is one of the greatest gifts we can give others as well as ourselves. We don't know what haunts Estelle, just as we don't know what haunts Pam Carlson (Bob Burgess's first wife, who makes a few appearances in this novel) or Helen Burgess. And yet, testament to Strout's deftness, the minor characters are not caricatures of other women; their performative femininity speaks to a deep-seated anxiety (which leaves them ripe for further exploration).

William's daughters—as well as his wives—are also affected by loss and grief. Although Lucy waited until her girls were considerably older than Bridget (William and Estelle's daughter) when she left their father, their subsequent troubles indicate that their mother's departure still marked them. Chrissy develops anorexia when she is at college. Her forthright therapist tells Lucy and William that their daughter is starving because she's hurting. Lucy is ashamed; she blames herself for Chrissy's trouble. Lucy had not realized the consequences of her actions, how, in some ways, in saving herself by leaving the marriage, she was wounding her daughter. Becka is furious with their mother at this time, so profoundly afraid for Chrissy and telling Lucy, "I can't stand you. . . . Look at her! You're killing my sister. . . . You are *killing your daughter*" (148). Years later, while on the trip with William, Lucy realizes, "I understood this *fully* with no mitigating in my mind, is what I am saying—that it had been my fault. Because I was the one who had walked out on the family" (149). She must live with the pain of having hurt her daughter.

Years later, Chrissy suffers yet again. She gets pregnant but miscarries and is devastated. Lucy, too, is distraught, wanting but unable, just as she was years earlier, to ease her daughter's suffering. Chrissy, Becka, and Bridget will learn to carry their loss and grief with them, as Lucy, Estelle, and Catherine have. But like their mother, Chrissy and Becka are openhearted, generous. Lucy is amazed at how healthy her daughters seem to be, how they weathered their experiences with loss, and appear resilient, generous, and strong. We see that resilience in their kindness to their younger half sister. Neither Becka nor Chrissy appears to resent William's youngest child; instead they take her under their wing, out for tea in a show of caring after her mother has left their father. Lucy marvels at how far she and her daughters have come—their lives are so vastly different from the Bartons'. Ruminating on her mother and her daughters, Lucy "thought how my mother had never said I love you to me, and I thought how Chrissy had been going to call the baby Lucy. She *loved* me, my daughter! Even knowing this, I was surprised. In truth, I was amazed" (47). This isn't to say that Chrissy and Becka are whole, or that there is a way to leave the past behind; rather it's that they appear generous and self-assured enough to help others who they think may be suffering: "It was very strange to think that the children I had were already—in just one generation—so different, so very different, from me and what I had come from. And from what Catherine had come from as well" (211).

Lucy changes in the course of the novel from the repressed young woman to the openhearted widow. While Catherine and Lois try to ignore their losses, deal with them by not dealing with them, Lucy is always writing about loss, but in this book it's usually about someone else's—not her own. Although, like her mother, she appears to prefer not to address her own personal tragedies head on, they creep into her reflections implicitly. Eventually, she addresses some of those losses explicitly, and ultimately Strout suggests Lucy's way of grieving is more salubrious than that adopted by Catherine or Lois. By portraying Lucy in all of her vulnerabilities and insecurities and still willing to love, to care about others, and to admit her mistakes and the pain she's caused other people, Strout offers her readers a healthy way to live with the kind of losses that affect all of us. Lucy periodically turns to William; she explains, "Both with the discovery of David's illness and then again with his death, it was William I called first. I think—but I don't remember—that I may have said something like 'Oh William, help me!' Because he did" (33). Attempting to ignore trouble completely or to deal with it independently—the way that Catherine and Lois do, Catherine in her complete immersion in the upper-class Connecticut lifestyle she marries into and Lois in her owning of her stepmother's house and her refusal to see her brother—keeps the women locked in what Boss would call frozen grief.

While they are on their road trip, William tells Lucy that her joy is what drew him to her decades earlier. During their trip, she is self-deprecating, focusing on her similarities to Catherine, and particularly how both women left their husbands and their daughters, but William refuses Lucy's self-assessment, focusing instead on her joy. William was so mesmerized by Lucy's zest for life, which sounds similar to Catherine's, Becka's, and Chrissy's, that he wanted to be near her, he tells her. And so he offers Lucy kindness as well. Though he is less exuberant than she is, he can still tell when his ex-wife is in need of solicitude.

But if William was drawn to Lucy, Lucy as a young and middle-aged person was not mentally equipped or stable enough to give either him or herself what each needed. The day of their wedding, she emotionally shut down; unconsciously, she was afraid to be vulnerable. While Lucy, Becka, Chrissy, and Estelle all independently assert that William holds himself back from others, the older Lucy now recognizes that trait in her younger self. Realizing that the Bartons were not coming to see her and feeling guilty about leaving them, resentful of their refusal to see her, and ambivalent toward them, Lucy began to withdraw psychologically on her wedding day. So as she left one family to begin a new one with William, she retreated:

> It felt a little bit like things were not entirely real. . . . And William looked at me with great love and kindness as though to help me through. But the feeling did not go away.
>
> . . . I did not feel quite like I was really there. Everything felt a little bit far away, is what I mean, like I was removed from it. And that night in the hotel I did not give myself as freely to my husband as I usually did, the feeling I had was still with me.
>
> The truth is this: That feeling never went away.
>
> Not entirely. I had it my whole marriage with him—it ebbed and flowed—but it was a terrible thing. And I could not describe it to him or even to myself, but it was a private quiet horror that sat beside me often, and at night in bed I could not be quite as I had once been with him. (55)

Lucy's feelings make sense: she would be suspicious of entering into a relationship built on shared vulnerabilities, coming as she did from an abusive home in which the people who were supposed to care for and protect her wound up failing at this primary purpose. Traumatized people are often self-destructive in order to exert a modicum of control: they run roughshod over situations to ruin them on their terms, not on someone else's or in a way that surprises them. Lucy unconsciously tried to destroy her marriage herself because her very foundation had been built on unsettled ground.

At the same time, she—as most people do—loved her first family tremendously. In spite of her ambivalence for the Bartons, she misses them, imperfect and harmful as they were. We don't see much of them in this book. Lucy explains that this story is William's—not her own—but we also get the sense that some recollections are too painful for Lucy to address. She briefly relays that "very bad things happened in the garage and then later in that tiny house. I have written about some of the things that happened in that house, and I don't care really to write any more about it" (17). As a child, she lived in a home that wasn't safe. When her therapist tells her she is suffering from post-traumatic stress disorder, the diagnosis relieves Lucy, and she's grateful for the understanding that a label confers. Even so, Lucy explains, "I still get very frightened. I think this must be because of what happened to me in my youth, but I get scared very easily. For example, almost every night when the sun goes down, I still get scared. Or sometimes I will just feel fear as though something terrible will happen to me" (17–18).

And yet, she married William—and later David—in acts of love and faith and trust and hope in a future that would not resemble the past. Perhaps it's that hope that young William saw and identified as joy that Lucy possesses in such abundance. We learn fairly early on in the novel that William has had multiple affairs, though Lucy suggests it's not the affairs that doomed their marriage but the way that William and she held themselves back from each other. The affairs manifested an emotional distance already there.

Lucy also lost her second family, explaining that it took her nearly a year to leave her first marriage. While she reveals William's infidelities fairly early on, it's not until midway through the book that she discloses she had been having an affair as well. In withholding that detail, she in some ways enacts the same kind of distance that William does, isolating herself. But the affairs and the distance alone did not compel William or Lucy to end the marriage. Lucy says she left William because she needed more space to become the writer she wanted to be. But she also admits that there was a cost to this—not only in losing a childhood dream of having a perfect family but also in the effects on Chrissy, who falls into an anorectic depression, and on Becka, who resents her at the time and still hopes for a reunion between her parents. Becka and William call Lucy out on her solipsism, and she admits the cost of her self-preservation. She sacrificed her family in following her literary ambitions. And Lucy misses this family, the unit they once were, or could have become, both the time they spent and the time they could have spent together.

Later, Lucy realizes she also misses her perception of William and her sense of safety when she was with him. Her losses—like William's—are connected. But in losing that marriage, those families, and that perspective on her first husband, she gains something else, a new kind of vision, a trust in herself, and a perception of the world that embraces its fallibilities. Lucy comes to terms with her losses, realizing that by losing, she is allowed a more expansive view of the world, learning, in the words of Stanley Kunitz, that "the heart breaks and breaks / and lives by breaking."

At first, like so many of Strout's aching, lonely characters, Lucy unsuccessfully attempts to assuage the void within her with lovers, work, her daughters, and her imagination. She explains how after she left William, she would lie in bed looking at a building across the street. As the Chrysler Building does in *My Name Is Lucy Barton*, the lighted window in a museum offered Lucy hope; she believed that someone else was awake and working through the night, and she rested more easily, trusting that the two of them, though separate, were not alone. And then she explains, "Only many years later did I realize I had been sustained by a myth. There was no one in the tower during those times. . . . The light in the tower had helped me though. But the light had not been what I thought it was" (234). Even so, Lucy realizes that the new knowledge, the knowledge of lack and of loss, is still a gift. To be alone does not preclude a sensibility to wonder. Instead she learns that that wonder is not external but internal to her.

Lucy's recognition of her own capacity for hope is important because she has just lost her beloved husband. She grieves not only for herself but also for the life David left behind, the lives she has previously left behind, her daughters, and her former mother-in-law. David, Lucy tells us, "had been raised a Hasidic Jew right outside of Chicago, and he had left that community when he was nineteen; they had ostracized him then, and he had had no contact with any of his family" (37). He also played the cello rapturously—it's his cello playing that Lucy first fell in love with. His musical abilities link him to Wilhelm. The former Nazi and the Jewish man both left their families to find love and transcendence through sublime music playing. What are we to make of the coincidence? Is it merely a similarity? An authorial sleight of hand? Or does Lucy give Catherine a story she wishes the woman had or a story she herself wishes she had? We can't know. Strout doesn't answer these questions, but she raises them about art, absolution, forgiveness, and trauma, and how we forge forward after devastation.

When Lucy writes about David, it's with a tenderness and none of the irritation William generates in her: "My husband's name was David Abramson and he was—oh, how can I tell you what he was? He was *him!* We were—we really were—kind of made for each other, except that seems a terrifically trite thing to say but—Oh, I cannot say anymore right now" (33). Perhaps this affection suggests she is simpleminded about her complex feelings, or, more positively, we could hope that she may have learned to love wholeheartedly—not naïvely—by the time she met him. Before they met, she watched him play in the philharmonic and tells us she "noticed the man who played the cello. . . . He always walked very slowly and very unevenly and he looked older than he was; he had gray hair around a small bald spot. And he played the cello beautifully. When I first heard him play Chopin's Étude in C sharp minor I thought: This is all I want. Except I do not know that I even had that thought. I just mean there was nothing else in the world I wanted except to listen to him play" (225). By the time she introduced herself to David, she had already lost two families, so perhaps she was no longer afraid of losing, and she held nothing back. She tells us she walked right up to him and said, "Excuse me, I'm so sorry to bother you, but my name is Lucy and I love you. . . . Oh I mean I love your music" (226). They married six weeks later. Lucy and David were both raised poor and lonely: "It is hard," Lucy explains, "to describe what it is like when one is raised in such isolation from the outside world. So we became each other's home. But we—both of us felt this way—we were perched like birds on a telephone wire in New York City. . . . David was a tremendous comfort to me. *God,* was that man a comfort to me" (78). And her feelings are returned. Lucy remembers how David would say every morning, "Lucy B, Lucy B, how did we meet? I thank God we are we" (139).

At the book's end, Lucy realizes that the life she and David created together was miraculous, recognizing that their home might not have been the ideal home she imagined when young but that in its very holes, in the damage and losses that they brought to each other, they had a home that was more meaningful than an imagined, idealized one. In loving and losing David, Lucy cultivated a kind of expansiveness that allows her to love others as well—not in the way she did when she was younger, but in accepting their imperfections and limitations and still being grateful that they are living in this world together. Such a love is only possible in the context of loss. Loss, Lucy realizes, allows that love and that wonder to grow and to thrive. In the various portrayals of loss and responses to them, Strout offers her readers a panorama of the ways suffering affects and afflicts us.

Chrissy grieves the child she never had. Catherine mourns the child she left behind. Lucy mourns the Bartons, troubled though they were. And she misses the family she once had with William. Becka mourns the family she once had with her sister and parents, asking her mother hopefully, "Are you getting back together with Dad?" William mourns his father and mother, both the people he knew and the selves they never shared with him. Lois misses the mother she never knew. Wilhelm mourns the family and country he left behind. David mourns the family and community he left. Pam misses her first husband. Estelle mourns something we do not know. And through it all Lucy mourns David. Familial ruptures are the only certainty within this community. Catherine's abandoning Lois and Chrissy's miscarriage bookend the past and the present. Such events suggest our very existence is framed by loss. The human experience begins and ends with severing.

Those ruptures also speak to the novel's lack of linear narrative. Strout tells Lucy's story in bits and pieces, as Lucy reflects on her own life, William's, and Catherine's. As we've explored throughout this study, Strout's writing process is nonlinear, and her books are not conventionally chronological. Instead, as is her writing process, Strout's representation of time is fragmented; she moves fluidly between present and different pasts, near and distant. Consistently, Strout offers a notion of time that may appear counterintuitive. *Oh William!*, in spite of being narrated by one character, is no exception. The book suggests our lives are not the summation of events, well-plotted narratives that lead to a climax followed by a downward arc, but rather are punctuated by Olive Kitteridge's "little bursts," these moments of revelation that illuminate not only our present but our past and our connections with others as well. Burkeman suggests that such moments are "expansive and fluid, suffused with something it might not be an exaggeration to call a kind of magic . . . a luminous, awe-inspiring dimension . . . a heightened awareness of the vividness of things" (21). Strout, through Lucy, offers us a way to become more open to those moments, to sharpen our susceptibility to wonder. In calling us to the present, Strout, Boss, and Burkeman also point to an alternative understanding of time, one that isn't based on how much we do—or can cram into a day—but instead on moments of awe—those moments in which we become aware of the wonder of the world around us, when we allow ourselves, in Lucy's words, to be amazed. Perhaps to be amazed is to be outside of linear time, to allow ourselves a moment of being lost, of conventional time melting.[9]

Through Lucy, Strout encourages a kind of receptivity to the world around us that will allow us to approach our lives not with a sense of closure but rather a sense of openness. In such moments, time can collapse and we can simultaneously inhabit past, present, and future. These moments are not necessarily pleasurable. Pain, too, can transcend conventional boundaries. For example, Lucy explains:

> Crying, for me, has often been difficult. What I mean is I
> will cry; but I will feel very scared by my crying. William
> was good about that; when I really cried hard he did not get
> frightened the way I think David might have; but with David
> I never cried as I had in my first marriage, not the gasping
> sobs of a child. But since David has died there are times when

> I will sit on the floor near my bed—between the bed and the window—and weep with the utter and horrifying urgency of a child. (48)

Grief, Lucy shows and Boss explains, can transport us. Ambiguous loss, Boss says, "may be frustrating to those who crave absolute parameters, but its haziness is the point" (Bernhard). We might be lost or stuck as Catherine or Wilhelm appear to be, or we might allow ourselves the full expansiveness of grief, as Lucy does, and as William learns to do. Our present—whether we are content or miserable or feeling any other emotion—contains multitudes if we allow ourselves to perceive them. And reading—like loving—can encourage a transcendent reaching across. We witness such a traversing at the end of *Oh William!* when Lucy writes,

> When I think Oh William!, don't I mean Oh Lucy! too?
>   Don't I mean Oh Everyone, Oh dear Everybody in this whole wide world, we do not know anybody, not even ourselves!
>   Except a little tiny, tiny bit we do.
>   But we are all mythologies, mysterious. We are all mysteries is what I mean.
>   This may be the only thing in the world I know to be true. (237)

In that inclusive ending, Lucy reaches out to the reader in a way that the dedication also reaches out to us. There's a kind of circularity, perhaps a reassurance that Lucy is now not looking just at William or at herself but at the reader as well. If "we are all mysteries," it's not just Lucy or William or Catherine who is, but us, the individuals reading the book as well. Strout and Lucy draw our attention to the wonder of our current moment of reading, and of understanding how reading a book, as Jane Thrailkill tells us, can transcend time (2007, 250). When a book is read, a wondrous new relationship is formed. Strout returns to the magic of those relationships again and again across her oeuvre; if people are receptive to them, they are miraculous and give our life meaning and comfort—and loss and grief.

To be in a relationship authentically and honestly is to live with the awareness of its end; in Boss's words, "the price we pay for loving others is the pain of loss and grief" (2022, 95). The relationship's transience does not make it less meaningful but more so. With the dedication and the conclusion, Strout underscores the wonder of allowing oneself to be acted upon even in the knowledge of the loss that will come. In cultivating that openness, we become more aware of the awe of our own lives.

This ending serves as a kind of benediction—though Strout shies away from spiritual language, I think she offers her readers a kind of sacred understanding of the wonder of the world, particularly as manifest in the kindness of people. What is most magical are those quiet, understated acts of kindness. To receive another person's love—as Tyler Caskey learns to do—and as William learns to do—is as miraculous a lesson as any other. Lucy models for Strout's readers a way to live in a world that is as full of despair and shadows and meanness as ours is and yet still not shut ourselves off from others but allow them to affect us. To allow ourselves to be loved, and to allow ourselves to be hurt, seems to be one of the gifts that Lucy—and Strout—suggest we ought to give ourselves, and in so doing, we can live a more shimmering, multilayered existence.

Epilogue

STROUT'S CHARACTERS MOVE FROM BEING READERS to being writers—we might remember Isabelle wrestling with Shakespeare and finding herself in Flaubert, and Amy savoring Edna St. Vincent Millay—and then recall how in *Olive, Again*, Olive Kitteridge, a mother, retired math teacher, and widow of two, finds herself writing her memoirs, wondering what she knows and how she knows herself. In between we meet Tyler Caskey, who relies on Scripture, the mystics, and early twentieth-century spiritual writers to make sense of his world, and Lucy Barton, who, in the book that bears her name, explains how reading saved her when she was a child and how she writes to offer solace to others. Subtle literary echoes permeate Strout's work—Austen, the Brontës, Dickens, Eliot, Stowe, James, Wright, Messud, and Winterson, among others, reverberate in Strout's turns of phrases and her attention to detail. This literary legacy matters to Strout's characters and to Strout herself, and her turn to writing as a subject suggests that she realizes she has earned her place within this pantheon. She has joined a company of visionaries who not only inspire and console readers, but who also illuminate the personal and collective suffering in individual and global communities.

Strout's recognition of the loneliness of much of human existence may speak to many readers, to conditions that Eliot and James

identified more than one hundred years ago and that show no sign
of evaporating even in our age of increased social connectivity. In
this moment, she offers readers a sense of companionship and belonging that is deeper and more serious than the superficialities of
Twitter and TikTok. But she's also playful; we see this irreverence
not only in the acerbic observations of Ora Kendall or Olive Kitteridge in her early work but also in the more recent *Anything Is
Possible* and *Olive, Again*. In these short story cycles, companions to
My Name Is Lucy Barton and *Olive Kitteridge*, she again shows that she
is in command of her powers—writing what she wants to write, returning to whom she wants to, and honing her own voice and vision.
If early in her career Strout paid homage to a literary tradition, her
recent forays speak to the confidence she has in her own work. She
no longer needs to refer overtly to Shakespeare, Millay, or Yeats for
authority or validation; she can refer to herself, and she can write
with both trepidation and humor, whichever she finds most appropriate. What a triumph!

Crosby, Shirley Falls, and Amgash—fictional settings that
Strout imagined and created—appear throughout her oeuvre, allowing her readers a kind of readerly self-consciousness as well: not only
an immersive experience but also an appreciation for the creator of
these worlds. By returning to the same town and characters in another book, Strout may offer her readers the comfort of returning to
that which is known, but she also emphasizes the reader's position
as outsider reading about someone rather than reading as someone.
We don't lose ourselves in the fiction but become more aware of
Strout's powers as a writer when she returns to a place we've seen
before. The reading experience itself then is front and center; and
the return emphasizes the limitations or subjectivity of perspective.
If Strout has joined a conversation of writers, echoing, reflecting,
refracting, and responding to them, she also makes her readers
aware of our own desire to return to characters, to a place, to a story
that she wrote but where we find our own meaning. In emphasizing that awareness, Strout shows her readers the liminality of our
worlds—whether that's past and present or reality and fiction. The

perviousness of such boundaries underscores our connectedness, and in some ways the inability to separate ourselves from others, whether those are fictional or real people or places. Strout's hope is that the reader finds what she needs in the work before her. Reading, like writing, then is a kind of conversational practice, one that's interactive, intersubjective, a meaning-making process rather than an experience that is individual or solipsistic.

This vision of the world, this vision of reading, becomes particularly important after months of literal distancing and decades of being driven apart socially, technologically, professionally, ideologically, and economically. We crave conversation and community. Strout offers her readers, those who might have found themselves in parks or churches or fellowship halls at other times, a kind of connection, one that respects the wisdom of others and the power of one's own individual imagination and insights. Perhaps Strout's most important leap of faith is this one, the one that, yes, lets her work stand on the shelves alongside that of others, but just as importantly engages her readers in a kind of conversation, urging us to look at and to appreciate not only the magic on the page, but also the magic around us, to sharpen our own powers of perception and to cultivate our own sense of awe in the world.

This message—to be attentive—resonates with another facet of her work and of this study. That is, if Isabelle and Tyler turn to Scripture—to another source—to understand the wonder of nature, Olive does not. She looks at the light of a February day, marveling at the glow with her new friend Cindy. The two women don't turn to God to recognize the miracle in front of them. If Strout has always been a writer's writer, in recognizing the power of her own imagination, she owns her own worth, she tells us her words are valuable. We can, I think, extend this outward. Our words, our visions are valuable as well. Strout deliberately couches these lessons in accessible language, speaking to readers across classes and continents. If we're not accessible, if we keep ourselves distinct, we don't grow, we don't learn, we stay stuck. That very accessibility allows her to reach a wider audience than many academics do, and that we can learn

from. If we want to stay in whichever cubicle, department, or appa-
ratus we choose, of course we can do so, but if we wants to venture
forth, what a world is waiting—to teach and to learn from! Aesthetic
objects, including novels, Jane Thrailkill tells us, can be "mind- and
world-expanding and [put] us in touch with our common embodiment" (2007, 250), but so, as Strout tells us, can our relationships
with other people. Her fiction, like our friends, can "[sit] with [us]
through [our] life, and while we are always separate—because people are always separate—[they can also give us] a sense of not being
alone" (247).

Appendix

An Interview with Elizabeth Strout

Questions Answered August 22, 2019

Could you please address writing as an act of faith?

I guess I see writing as an act of faith because you just don't know. I mean you just don't know if it will land on the person who needs it, or will be received in a way that I hope it will be. So it's an act of faith—you put it out there and you hope.

How has your work evolved over the years? Your perspective? Characters? Subjects?

I know that my work has evolved over the years, but in truth I can't really describe how. It has evolved, though, because I have, I think. I have had—as we all do—many more life experiences and so I continue to see things with a fresh eye. This is not helpful, but it's the best I can do with this question.

Who do you read? Who do you consider your greatest literary influences? I've seen you cite Tolstoy, Chekhov, Cheever, Roth, Munro, Woolf, and Trevor. How about James? Austen? Eliot?

I read all the people I have mentioned as influences, and yes to Eliot (love her) and James and also Austen. But I read Colm Toibin and Colum McCann and Zadie Smith and Colson Whitehead and people like that as well. I read anything that I feel has good sentences. If the sentences do not fall on my ear right, I will not keep reading it. And I read a great deal of poetry. I have scrapbooks of poems I have collected over the last many years, and every so often I go through them, and I often think: Why did that poem capture me back then? Because I won't always remember. But poetry has always been very important to me. At the moment, for the last year or so, I mean, I have been reading a lot of biographies. Of Einstein, Tolstoy, Updike, William Sloane Coffin—that sort of thing. But I am always aware how much the biographer plays a role in giving me whatever message I am reading about the person.

Do you consider yourself a spiritual writer? How do spirituality and mysticism affect your works?

You know, in this time that we are living in, I shy away from the word "spiritual"—it can mean too many different things to people. So I would not say that I was a spiritual writer. I will say that I hope for a sense of transcendence to come through to the reader, in whatever way they need that to be, that the world becomes larger to them, that everything may not be just as it seems. I think "mysticism" is a term that I am more comfortable with—but even then, I shy away from categorizing myself as anything.

What would you like your readers to know about you?

In truth, I would like my readers to know nothing about me! Hahahaha, but that is the truth. I would like only the text of my work to rise off the page to them; anything they need to know about me as a person is just not relevant, I am in all my work. When *Amy and Isabelle* was published, I asked my editor if I could not have a photo on the back flap because I did not want it interfering with what a reader might take away from the story. But of course he said no, and I had no clout, and there we are . . . or here we are . . .

To me, your books seem in some ways didactic, but not preachy. That is, they instruct readers through example about the grace of compassion or of forgiveness. Do you see your books as teaching lessons, as having an ethical subtext?

I think my books do have some ethical subtext, not because I am out to put it there, but because it is who I am and so it shows up in my work. I want to write books that—as Lucy Barton says—make people feel less alone. But I also want to write books that open up things to the reader that they might not have quite known they knew, or maybe didn't know at all until they read about someone different from themselves.

Names seem so significant to your work—Shirley Falls; Cross by(e); Am gash; O live; Wizzle (!); Lucy—would you speak about their significance?

You know, the right name is absolutely essential for a story to work. I first learned this with Amy and Isabelle—I knew Isabelle would be called Isabelle, but I could not get Amy right, I started with Stephanie and then Pam, and it wasn't until I found the name Amy that it began to really get written. So I learned the importance of names. I just love names, I just adore them. My husband and I will go to graveyards to find names, especially in the Midwest when I was writing the Lucy books, and also I remember names when I hear them, and also sometimes they just come to me. But I will look at lists of names as well, for the time period of the character's life if I feel like it. It's instinctive in the end,

though, what their name will be. Almost everything I do
I do because of instinct, is the truth of it.

The movement from Maine to New York to Illinois—do you see
yourself as an American writer? What does an American consciousness look like? How is it different from a regional or local
consciousness?

I do see myself as an American writer. This is because I am
American. I do not see myself as a regional writer because
if it cannot transcend the region, it is only, to quote
Marjorie Rawlings, "quaint," and that is not what I am
interested in. I cannot explain the American consciousness, I can only write about it through my own.

In "Strout, Again," Mary Pols writes that you "serve as a literary
historian of American culture. [Your] characters are people of
Puritan stock, the kind [you] know best, but who are fading
in relevance." Yet your characters also include midwesterners,
Somali immigrants, and Italians—could you talk about writerly
empathy? Is there a danger of appropriation, a kind of literary
colonization—or can White people ethically write about people
of color? How do we do so?

At the time I wrote *The Burgess Boys* there was no talk (that
reached my ears) about cultural appropriation. Thank
God! I might not have dared to do it. But I knew if I did
not take on a Somali point of view, they would remain
"the other," and the whole point of the book was to make
them not that. So I worked for seven years on getting to
know their culture and eventually making my way into
their homes in Lewiston, Maine, through some contacts I
had, but it took a long, long time to do that and to believe
I could get it right. I think if any writer feels they can
truly know another culture—and it is very hard to know
another culture—they can write about it. I do know about

different classes, which is why I can write about the class structure in this country.

How has being a mother affected your writing?

Being a mother has surely affected my work. I cannot say how, but it is the biggest part of my life in many ways, my daughter. I love her so much it feels almost pathological. If I had not had her I cannot imagine being able to write about the bonds of parents and children, even though I have had parents, of course. But she has opened the world to me in countless ways. I really cannot tell you in what ways exactly, but she has brought the world to me.

I love how bodily functions appear in your work. You don't steer away from them—and those observations make me laugh out loud; thank you! Would you reflect on bodily functions?

Bodily functions. Thank you! Well, we all have them. And I think because they are so much a part of being human that they need to be recorded, although not with a heavy hand. But they are part of us all, and that's why I write about them. That simple.

In the Ariel Levy piece in the *New Yorker*, Zarina is quoted as saying, "[You and your husband] have an intense relationship with Maine. . . . It's a need and an adoration and a loathing." Is this how you would describe your relationship with Maine?

Yes, Zarina had it right. Although I don't think (understandably) Mainers want to hear that I at times loathe the place, but it is true, because it is the place I know best. And throughout my life I have been very unhappy there and also very happy there, and whenever you know a place as deeply as I know Maine there is apt to be ambivalence. At least on my part. But I also love it, wearily, I do.

The tones of some of your books—*Amy and Isabelle, Abide with Me, Olive Kitteridge, The Burgess Boys, My Name Is Lucy Barton*—seem very different. Why?

> You know, the tone of the book—as you put it—is always related to the subject matter of the book. For example, *My Name Is Lucy Barton*, being written in the first person, has to have her very specific, almost breathy voice. [In] *Abide with Me* I was trying for a more conversational narrative, to tell the story of something a while back—almost like it was a folktale. So each book has to have its own narrative voice because of what the book is about. I think—I hope—my writer's voice remains there in all of them, but specifically what I learned in my college Shakespeare class I think is true: Style is substance.

In the interview with Vorwald, you reflect on the quality of "ruthlessness" for writers. "If you really want to do this, then you've got to do what it takes to do it. . . . Now I'm going to go back to the gender thing, actually, because I think it's more difficult for women to say, 'All right, this is what I'm going to do. This is what I need. I need six hours a day by myself, and I might need twenty years of nothing ever getting published.' . . . I think it's easier for a man to say, 'This is what I'm going to do. Bye.'" Could you expand on the commitment needed? And the gendering? It seems that raising children gives people insights, but also takes away time—and of course this work is gendered . . .

> I think if you're going to do this kind of work—for me it is a vocation—then you need to really do it. And by that I mean it has to come first except for kids and husband. If you have a kid, as I do, she has to come first, but the work has to be done, and the house does not get clean and you do not throw dinner parties and all sorts of other activities that more ordinary people do. At least I have found this to be true for me. I am not really interested in the gender

issue—except it is there—because it *is* there, and so you have to work with that. Yes, women generally have far more obligations domestically than men do (I think this is still true), but you have to work with that, and in my case, it was difficult. I was not good at the domestic stuff. But I loved and love my daughter. I left my first marriage when she went to college because I needed to devote myself to writing in a way that I could not in that marriage.

What advice do you have for writers?

My advice for writers is very simple. Read good sentences a lot, and then write a lot. And never stop.

It seems to me we often use monikers or labels like "woman writer" or "regional writer" to diminish writers. How does gender and/or place affect your sensibility? Do they matter? Do you see *Abide with Me* **and** *The Burgess Boys* **as doing something different than** *Amy and Isabelle, Olive Kitteridge,* **or** *My Name Is Lucy Barton?*

I ignore the labels "woman writer" and "regional writer." They are meaningless to me. Place is important in literature, but that has nothing to do with the ultimate quality of the book. My stories take place in certain places, because life takes place in a place. Being a regional writer is not interesting to me, nor is being a woman writer. I am a woman and I write.

But I am a writer. Period.

If I would like to understand your work better, what writings by Bonhoeffer and Niebuhr do you recommend I read?

Honestly? I think you could read anything by Niebuhr and Bonhoeffer. Bonhoeffer's *Letters from Prison* were especially interesting to me, but I don't know that reading either would help you understand my work better.

Are the places based on real places? Would you be willing to
share them with me on a map? (I'd love to include a map in the
book.)

> The places I write about are made up. Sorry, but they are.
> I make them up by using different towns I have known, or
> cities (Park Slope in *The Burgess Boys* is real), but for exam-
> ple Shirley Falls is a combination of Lewiston, Maine, and
> Dover, New Hampshire, and a few other mill towns that
> I have seen in Maine. West Annett is made up from West
> Minot, Maine, and other small towns around that area. But
> they are always a combination of certain aspects—Crosby,
> Maine, is totally made up. But I grew up on the coast of
> Maine, and so I can combine its coastal qualities with
> Brunswick, Maine, where I live now part time.

Would you be willing to share your uncollected short stories with me?

> No, I'm not going to share any unpublished stories with
> you. If they haven't been published it's because they're not
> good enough, is my thought. So, no—sorry!

Do your books take place in specific years? Would you be willing
to share those dates with me?

> *Amy and Isabelle* takes place in the mid-seventies, but I
> never said that because I wanted the book to be timeless
> and universal. But there are clues there, because it is about
> the time that things are changing with pregnant teenagers,
> Stacy's parents don't hide it, whereas Isabelle felt very
> embarrassed by her own pregnancy as an unmarried young
> girl. Also, it says that in ten years Fat Bev would have to
> give up smoking in the workplace. So there are clues.
>   *Abide with Me* very specifically says almost immediately
> that it takes place in the last months of 1959. I wanted to
> be specific about that and chose that year because it was
> postwar, but if I had it 1960, that would make the reader

think about the sixties and I wanted their mindset to be in the fifties.

    Olive Kitteridge ends during the presidency of George Bush, "the cross-eyed cocaine addict cowboy" she refers to.

    The Burgess Boys takes place in 2007, I think.

    My Name Is Lucy Barton looks back at a time when there was the AIDS crisis and moves through time with the towers falling.

    Anything Is Possible takes place around 2017.

Abide with Me appears to literalize or materialize some of your common themes—that is, while silence and spirituality permeate your other works, this novel is about a minister with a daughter who does not speak. Is that different for you from your other ventures?

> For years and years I had wanted to write about a minister. I saw that in old drafts from many, many, many years ago—I had obviously been wanting to write about a minister, and so I did. It was hard work. I had to give myself a course in theology in a way, since I had to know his reference points, and I talked to any Congregational minister who would talk to me, and many did, especially the older ones, and I went to the Bangor Theological Seminary and found course catalogs for the time period Tyler would have been there and tried to study what they were. So it was quite an undertaking and meaningful to me. I worry because I think the book never fully did what I needed and wanted it to do, but I have a special place in my heart for it.

Would you talk about the role of food in your work? Weight? I wonder if this is connected to women's embodiment, the way we live in our bodies.

> I'm not sure about the role of food in my work, I think I just write what I think the character would eat. But I do

have a few overweight people, women, and some readers
have written to me complaining about this (they are
overweight, the readers who write to me tell me this),
and this makes me feel terrible. Because if I am to write
about people in a real way, then I have to write about the
ones who are fat as well as the ones who are skinny. I can't
censor that, but I feel awful when I hear from a reader
who feels I have been unfair to overweight women. I don't
think I have been unfair. I think I am recording the human
experience as truthfully as I can.

Would you reflect on doughnuts?

Doughnuts. There used to be a joke that doughnuts were
Maine's state food. And they kind of were for me, growing
up in Maine. I loved doughnuts and ate a great deal of
them, as did most of the people I knew.

**Where do you think literature is going now? How do you see the
literary landscape changing?**

Truthfully—I have absolutely no idea where literature is
going. I'm not capable on commenting on the landscape of it.

**In some ways your work reminds me of Austen's—the per-
ceptiveness and quick wit; for example, we see this in your
characterization of Helen Burgess or in Olive Kitteridge. In
other ways, your work reminds me of George Eliot's or Henry
James's—with its attention to a kind of melancholy that cannot
be named. Would you talk about your style, which seems both
humorous and poignant?**

I'm glad you think I am both humorous and poignant;
that makes me glad. I can only say that my style (I happen
to think I'm very funny) is not really something that
happens on a conscious level. I am just trying to tell a
story truthfully. And humor and poignancy are part of it.

As I said, almost everything I do is instinctive. But I think pathos and humor are directly related. Sometimes I will read a writer's work and it will be funny, but will lack the connection to the real stuff of life, and then I will read a very serious book—that deals directly with the horrors of real life—and in both cases I think there is some connective tissue missing. Life is funny and tragic; they are of the same cloth.

Would you talk about the role of memory in your work? Do you think recovery from trauma is possible? It seems that what recovery would look like is forgiveness, in your words, recognizing that we—and others—love and receive love imperfectly. Is that how we endure—by realizing others are suffering also?

I don't know if recovery from trauma is possible. Probably not completely. I don't know how much of a role forgiveness plays because I think some things are just not forgivable. Look at poor Charlie Macauley and all he had to do in the Vietnam War; he is outside the realm of forgiveness—I mean he can never forgive himself. But I think if one is loved, as he is by Patty Nicely, it can do tremendous things for the pain of trauma. I don't know that we endure pain by experiencing the pain of others, as much as understanding that other people have endured terrible things can help break down the barriers of the self.

About memory: Are you asking about the role of my memory, or the role of memory in my characters? I remember an awful lot. My mother once said when someone asked her how I wrote these books, "She observes everything and she never forgets anything." I do forget certain things, of course, but I think she made a good point. About my characters' memories, I feel that they remember the way most people do—certain aspects of things that then become their own personal narrative. If that makes sense, and it may not.

Do you concur with Sarah Payne that "writers have only
one story to tell . . . [but write that] story many ways"? If so,
would you be willing to tell us your story? In the interview
with Fassler, you say, "Fiction can help people have a greater
appreciation for how big and complicated experience is. I just
want to have respect for the enormous amount of mess that
everyone is living with and living through. That would be my
goal, I think." In an interview with Lynn Neary, you say, "I
guess all my books are about imperfect love. My hope is that
people can be more empathic by reading about people who are
not like them."

> I understand Sarah's point of view. I wrote her, so I
> understand why she would say that. But in my case, I seem
> to have more than one story. Mothers play a big role in
> my work, though. I have noticed that. Is that my story?
> My mother? It's part of my many stories, I think. But it
> is not my only story. And I stand by what I said in those
> interviews; it is my hope that people can see something
> larger than themselves for even just a moment, and so they
> can feel for someone else.

Would you tell us what Lucy's illness is? Or is its lack of diagnosis
important—like Esther's in *Bleak House?* What is the significance
of not knowing? Her trauma, her illness cannot be named. That
seems vitally important.

> Truthfully I don't have a diagnosis for Lucy's illness.
> She just could not get better—until she did. I think the
> mysterious element of it is important. The working title
> of that book was—for a few months—*Idiopathic*, meaning
> no known cause. But then I realized that *My Name Is Lucy
> Barton* is the title that is the right one. The causes, under-
> stood or not, are not as important as her taking agency
> over her life.

My mom covered the labor movement for thirty years and was a union journalist, so I grew up with a keen appreciation for work. I love how labor appears in your novels. What is it about pharmacists, teachers, and janitors? And podiatrists and gastro-enterologists? (Is that you just being funny?)

I have always loved pharmacists. My father was a scientist—he was a parasitologist at the University of New Hampshire, and when I saw him at work, which I did frequently, he was always wearing a white coat. And I think there is something about the white coat of a pharmacist that is involved in that. My father was a wonderful man. I also knew a pharmacist for years in New York City who was a lovely man, and I have used that subliminally, I think. My mother was a teacher (as was my father), so I have a real respect for that. There was a janitor in my high school who was a tender and sweet fellow; I suspect these things come back to me. I don't know any podiatrists, but I had a gastroenterologist one time who was also a great—a lovely—person. Who knows? The joke about Suzanne being a gastroenterologist came to me because a woman once said to me, "Who would become that kind of doctor?" I always remembered her saying that, so it came back to me when I was writing about Suzanne. And about labor in my work in general: people work. To not write about a person's work would be to write about a shell of them.

In your interview with Sally Campbell and Martha Green-grass, you observed, "Time and place—with the injection of character—make a story what it is." Could you please elaborate?

Well. I don't know if I can elaborate. You need a time and a place for a story to take place in. Time and place—to me—are very important. So you put a character in that time and place and see what happens. Or more likely,

I start with the character, but because they live in a
time and a place, those aspects will come to me almost
immediately.

I've read in prior interviews that you write scenes rather than sit
down and write out a novel. At what point do you sketch out a
plot—or a narrative arc? At different points for different works?

I never sketch out a plot. I never even think about plot. I
hate the word. Look at it. Plot. I learned years ago when
my daughter was small and I had only a little bit of time
each day to work that if I could write a scene that was
real, that had a heartbeat to it—if I kept doing that then
eventually these scenes would connect. It was a wonderful
discovery, and I have worked that way ever since. At some
point things will come together, and many parts of the
so-called plot don't show up until the very end. It's kind
of weird, really. But I am aware at some point—in a vague
kind of way—that things have to change from the beginning of the story (or the book) to the end of it; there must
be a change of some sort, so that is always kind of going
around in my head as I arrange these scenes and think
about it.

I'm curious about the relationship between the interior and
exterior worlds that you address in the conversation with [Lynn]
Neary. You say, "I've always been interested in the internal versus
the outward world. We all live in the external world, and we all
bump into each other in that world and we all have relationships
in that world. But we all have an interior life."

Right. We all have an interior life—of some kind. And
then we live in the world. And it's just fascinating to me
to think of the difference between what's inside us, what
is us, and what the world is doing to us. One time I gave
a talk in New York City and I said, I want to be writing

about all the things nobody tells their psychiatrist. Boy, that room got quiet. And I realized probably half the room were psychiatrists and the other half was going to them. But my point is, there are always things (I think) that we never share with anyone, these things we almost can't articulate to ourselves but are there. This is what is so fascinating to me, to try and find that part of my characters.

Would you address the role of violence in your work? Is writing about violence—or the effects of it—a kind of witnessing, a way to teach compassion?

I don't really know what to say about the violence in my work. Except it is there because there is violence in the world, and I am trying to write truthfully about the world, so there would have to be violence.

[The original subtitle of this study was] *A Companion to Elizabeth Strout.* **Would you talk about the role of companions—women friends perhaps but not necessarily—in your work and in your life?**

My main companion in my life is my husband—he is my second husband, and he is a real companion. It's a wonderful thing to have a companion, it makes me think of Patty Nicely, who said about her first husband and his love for her that it was a protective skin between her and the rest of the world. I am probably misquoting her, sorry. But it is a sharing of one's life, that is what I think a companion is, someone who sits with you through your life, and while we are always separate—because people are always separate—there is also a sense of not being alone.

Women friends also play a huge role in my life. I have three or four whom I have known for many years—longer than I have known my second husband. (Or even my first.)

The role they play is very large; they are real companions, even when I can't always see them physically because of where they live. But the best women companions I have are from childhood and college—I think this is because they knew my parents and I knew their parents and because of the countless hours we have spent together. They knew me before I was a writer known to others, and for some reason this is very special to me. To the extent that we can ever know anyone, they know me as *me*, and I know them.

Notes

1. Strout's multipronged appeal anticipates the recent scholarly interest in "how ordinary readers experiencing ordinary emotions construe literary narrative" (Miall 324). For example, Strout describes her writing as both storytelling and an exercise in empathy-building (though the latter turn of phrase is mine). She hopes that by reading her fiction, her audience may begin to approach others with more compassion than they did before they encountered her work. For instance, in an email regarding *Oh, William!*, she says, "What interests me about people is the murkiness of emotions that we are working from, all the inner parts of our lives that we may not even fully know about ourselves. . . . I hope so much to hand to you—the reader—something that is true. You may not be Lucy, or William, but I hope that you can take them into your heart, and hopefully by hearing their story a ceiling may be lifted—even just a tiny bit in your own world." Strout's empathy project may speak to the relative paucity of critical responses to her work. Only recently have literary critics come to appreciate Strout and empathy. The two oversights are related, for, as David Miall tells us, "among readers who read for the pleasures and challenges that literary narratives afford, that is, 'ordinary' 'common' readers, acts of interpretation as practiced in literature classrooms or scholarly writing are rarely to be found" (324). In other words, Strout's books encourage a reading practice different than one valued by some scholars. But Strout's audience—even if they don't "murder to dissect" professionally—still reflect on reading in meaningful ways.

2. I paint "chick lit" with quick strokes, though doing so ignores subtleties within the genre. Nevertheless, I follow Jennifer Scanlon in recognizing

the genre's "winning combination of romance, heterosexual angst, and conspicuous consumption[, which] has successfully attracted female readers for over a dozen years. Negotiating ephemeral concerns like fashion alongside supposedly timeless moral questions about finance and fidelity, Chick Lit protagonists find ways to humor and instruct while they shop" (92).

3. Barbara Waxman terms the genre of "women writing about aging women" the *Reifungsroman,* or "novel of ripening, opposing its central tenet to the usual notion of deterioration in old age" (7).

4. Cathy Yardley explains that chick lit is "generally a coming-of-age or 'coming of consciousness' story where a woman's life is transformed. . . . Irreverent in tone, these novels were characterized by sharp internal observations, a fair dose of comedic venting, and sharp-as-a-razor dialogue" (4–7).

5. And in her focus on individuals struggling emotionally and financially in small towns or cities, Strout apprehends the importance of the small-town White working class and the media attention devoted to them since Trump's election.

6. Suzanne Keen posits that "novels inviting empathy do better in the marketplace (perhaps because they get better word-of-mouth recommendations) and . . . empathic reading habits make up a core element of middlebrow readers' self-image. . . . Narrative empathy may be less influential as an effect of reading and more important as a sought-after experience—tantamount to a pre-condition for success with a large segment of the book-buying and novel-reading public" (*Empathy and the Novel,* 104–5).

7. The denigration of women readers is related to the disparaging of women writers and femininity in general. Suzanne Keen reminds us that many academics "at least until the recent past [were led] by a tacit stereotyping of readers by their tastes: the sophisticated, trained reader who engages with narrative enigmas and appreciates the character who surprises in a convincing way, versus the ordinary reader who prefers that characters and plots live up to their generic contracts without disturbing deviations" ("Readers' Temperaments," 303).

8. Keen cautions that Strout and I may expect too much of reading, which might lead "most readily to other bookish activities" (118); even so, "what empathetic reading by itself may not accomplish . . . a teacher or guide may still achieve, if one considers the link between novel reading and active steps on behalf of real others desirable. Thus, while fiction reading alone may not form citizens committed

to justice, democracy, and nuanced understandings of other cultures, pedagogical practices could . . . help citizens respond to real others with greater openness and consciousness of their shared humanity" (*Empathy and the Novel*, 147).

9. See Barbara Waxman's *From the Hearth to the Open Road* (1990).

10. Suzanne Keen tells us that "for most of the twentieth century, middle brow readers' feeling responses to emotionally evocative narratives and immersion in novels occurred in a sphere set apart from the practices of literary studies" ("Introduction: Narrative and the Emotion," 30). It is that space that Strout claims. And in this project I am attempting to show the value of that space as well.

11. Keen relays that "women outnumber men among novel readers in Western countries. . . . An average of 45 percent of citizens described themselves as *book* readers, not necessarily fiction readers; but 65 percent of the book buyers are women, and they do prefer fiction" (*Empathy and the Novel*, 108–9; emphasis Keen's).

12. She's not without her critics, however. In her review of *Olive, Again*, Rhea Côté Robbins claims that Strout's portrayal of French Canadians is particularly problematic.

13. This may be unduly optimistic on my part. Janice Radway warns that so-called "middlebrow books . . . may have endowed us with an ample and refined vocabulary for articulating and achieving affective states, [but] too often the solution they ventured with respect to serious social problems involved the moral, ethical, and spiritual rehabilitation of the individual subject alone" (13).

14. I use the term "feminine" to describe a kind of socially sanctioned performance of gender, embodied in the practice and portrayal of conventional womanhood. Strout's most decent characters—those who are kind, empathic, sensitive to others, and willing to grow—may be male or female, but the humility, sensitivity, and vulnerability they exhibit is culturally coded feminine behavior.

15. Helen Taylor would suggest that Strout is successful: "I believe women have long understood what scientists and experts are now claiming: reading fiction can improve empathy, brain function, and relationships with others; reduce depression symptoms and dementia risks, and increase well-being throughout life" (226).

16. Janice Radway offers a less sanguine meditation on fiction, suggesting that readers wish "for attachment and connection beyond the self. Indulging in sentiment enabled the reading subject to conjure momentarily the vision of a mutual, equable, social relation constructed

through the magic of narrative and symbol and their capacity to promote identification and empathy in the reader" (285).

CHAPTER 1: THE WOMEN'S WORK OF LOVING IMPERFECTLY IN *AMY AND ISABELLE*

1. We might think, for example, of Gail Godwin, Lee Smith, Bobbie Ann
   Mason, Alice Munro, or Ann Beattie.
2. Amy's naïveté is underscored by his being referred to as Mr. Robertson throughout the novel, a gesture funny and telling (recalling aurally
   Simon and Garfunkel's paean to Mrs. Robinson and the 1967 Mike
   Nichols film *The Graduate,* in which it appeared).
3. Here we might think of the eighteenth-century sentimental tradition,
   notably *Clarissa* and *The Coquette.*
4. See *Embroidering the Scarlet A: Unwed Mothers and Illegitimate Children
   in American Fiction and Film* and *Following the Tambourine Man: A Birthmother's Memoir,* by Janet Mason Ellerby.
5. Janet Ellerby tells us that "the narrative of the fallen woman is in a
   state of constant transformation. It is copious, fluid, and too com-
   plexly lived to be contained. It encompasses desire, punishment, lib-
   eration, sin, alienation, allure, shame, secrecy. . . . It is as entrenched
   as patriarchy, but it is not stable. It is always open to revision, artisti-
   cally open to change, and, therefore, potentially open for escape from
   a vexed and fraught history" (*Embroidering,* 164).
6. Stacy's giving birth to and giving her baby up for adoption may be one
   of the unresolved stories within the novel. Though Stacy appears at
   peace with her decision, in her analysis of *Juno,* Janet Ellerby suggests
   that such a conclusion, "although seemingly benign, portends tragedy
   later down the road" (216). In reflecting on her own story and how teen
   mothers and their children have been represented in fiction and film,
   Ellerby writes, "Birthmothers do not move on; they do not forget; and,
   especially when they misguidedly agree to closed adoptions, there is
   no happy ending" (224).
7. Some might consider Strout's humor, focusing on bodily functions
   and bodily types, as bordering on cruel. For example, Bev is often referred to as "Fat Bev," and her weight is a preoccupation for her. But
   while Bev's lumbering to the bathroom to empty her bowels is played
   for laughs, her wrestling with her weight is treated with dignity; she
   asks herself, "Did people think she *liked* being fat? Jolly Bev. Fat Bev.
   She didn't like being fat. But that dark red ache was there, like a swirling vacuum, a terrible hole" (41). This admission of the importance of

bodies may be a particularly feminine concern, and a sign of Strout's honesty as a writer. That is, she doesn't shy away from acknowledging the human effects of struggling with weight or that heavy people are objects of contempt (self- or otherwise) for many Americans.

CHAPTER 2: ENDURING FAITH IN *ABIDE WITH ME*

1. If we treat our family members with cruelty, how can we expect to do anything but treat those whom we don't know with contempt, indifference, and inhumanity?

2. Indeed, Strout's oeuvre continues to address the relationship between the clique and the outsider, which we saw originally in *Amy and Isabelle* and will see later in *The Burgess Boys* and *Anything Is Possible*.

3. Concerned about her friend, Carol offers her daughter a child's ring, which Lauren takes (but never gives to Katherine). The symbols of femininity Lauren hoards are attached to sexuality, not to legitimacy. The ring eventually becomes fodder for gossip about Tyler and his relationship with Connie. If the minister's deceased wife is no longer fair game for the rumor mill, then the social outcast is.

4. Katie and Jeannie appear peripherally in *Olive Kitteridge*, and life seems to have been hard for them, suggesting that the legacy of trauma weighs heavily on the girls.

5. Here we might remember Bev's compulsive eating in *Amy and Isabelle*.

6. Strout's not showing us this scene recalls the moment in *Amy and Isabelle* when she does not reveal what mother and daughter say to each other, and anticipates *My Name Is Lucy Barton*, when Lucy says she will not talk about her marriage. With these moments, Strout is drawing our attention to the act of reading, I believe, making *us* aware of our positions, and doubly aware that we only have a partial perspective on the lives of the characters.

7. In this way he resembles Mr. Robertson; Amy and Connie feel seen for the first time in their lives, but Tyler is not predatory.

8. Cheryl Coleman asks, "Is his choice an act of 'taking up his cross' to help her, sacrificing his own religious convictions? Is it a compromise between his faith and his own will to leave the choice to her? Or is his decision—a type of refusal to decide—simply selfish? . . . By leaving the room . . . he allows his wife to die alone, which, some readers might reason, is a greater failure than any possible violation of his faith. By leaving the pills beside her bed while she sleeps, he enables her to end her life but without overtly making a horribly difficult decision of his own or taking any sort of responsibility for his actions, another

example of a characteristic pattern in his life that has been based on self-protection and selfishness" (9).

9. Keen advises "that scant evidence exists for narrative empathy's contribution to real-world altruism. This devalues neither narrative empathy nor the widespread trust in the socially beneficial yield of novel-reading, which I regard as an admirable hope shared by many novelists. I do question causal arguments that equate experiences of narrative empathy with real-world empathy for living others" ("Introduction," 37). Perhaps Strout and I are more optimistic about the power of literature than Keen is. Jane Thrailkill addresses the field of literary studies generally, but her insights can also be applied to Strout and particularly *Abide with Me* when she says the subject can "cultivate awareness of 1) the stories that shape our everyday experience; 2) the certainty of feeling, not just to individual belief and action but to human affairs and the search for truth, more broadly constructed; and 3) the consequent necessity for collaboration, testing, and above all *revision* in producing interpretations of individual and collective experience" (176). In other words, by recognizing the process of life, by seeing faith perhaps not as something one has but as a developing relationship, *Abide with Me* offers the reader a way to live in the world.

CHAPTER 3: FINDING HER VOICE IN *OLIVE KITTERIDGE*

1. I follow Helena Kadmos, who defines the short story cycle as "a collection of independent stories linked through one or more elements, whether common characters, focalization, setting, repeated events, motifs or themes [which] may be read as privileging notions of relationality because of the signature characteristic of simultaneous independence and interconnectedness" (40). Other possible names for the genre could include novel, collection, short story sequence, or novel in stories. Maggie Dunn and Ann Morris tell us that such a genre, which they call "composite novel," is "a literary form that combines the complexities of a miscellany with the integrative qualities of a novel. In other words, it is a grouping of autonomous pieces that together achieve whole-text coherence" (1).

2. Though Rolf Lundén prefers the term "short story composite" to "short story cycle," I find his insights useful for the genre; he suggests that the specificity "consists in the autonomy of its discrete stories and the interstices between them and in relation to the short story collection it is determined by the intratextuality between the stories. As a consequence of these distinctions, the stories of the composite exist

simultaneously as self-contained entities and as interconnected parts of a larger whole. The reader experiences a 'doubleness' present in individual stories. Ultimately, the most characteristic feature of the short story composite is this 'double' existence of the stories, and the tension that emerges from that doubleness" (46).

3. As a short story cycle, *Olive Kitteridge* is not exactly the *Reifungsroman* that Barbara Waxman identifies, though it does share many of the qualities she observes, including "great mobility, recursiveness, or rambling in narrative structure, and passion as well as candor in the disclosures of the protagonists" (16).

4. In this way, Strout's characters recall the creations of another nineteenth-century writer, Thomas Hardy.

5. If Strout's earlier works are fragmented, marked by a back-and-forth movement between the present and the past, such a stylistic quality serves this genre remarkably well.

6. To the contrary, the book, Kadmos tells us, is about relationships, and she continues, "The intricacy of human relationships can . . . be understood as the *means* through which we come to a greater understanding of ourselves in relation to others" (41).

7. Jane Thrailkill tells us, "Stories, the small ones that live in the mind as well as those formalized as novels, can be helpfully understood as tools of navigation. They situate individuals, imaginatively and corporeally, within a world of 'affairs'—of not just things and events but also relations, persons, and other, sometimes competing stories—and suggest options for action based on felt values and opportunities" ("Ian McEwan," 173).

8. We see this theme further explored in *Olive, Again*.

9. We will see similar movements and physical attempts at reconciliation in "The End of the Civil War Days" and "Pedicure" in *Olive, Again*.

10. Our bodies may not offer an idealized, wordless perfect communion, but they are tools we can use to hurt or to soothe others, if incompletely or imperfectly (we might also consider the marriages of the Guptills as portrayed in "The Sign" in *Anything Is Possible*).

11. In her interview with Cathy Schine for Book Passage, Strout says "A Little Burst" was the first story for the collection she wrote:

> At that time I thought, okay, I'm gonna write a book and I thought at the moment it was going to be called "The Olive Stories" but that doesn't matter. The point is I did realize very early on that she was a lot to take for the reader and that if I was the reader I wouldn't want to see Olive's name on every single page of that

book because she's just too much and then I realized, "Oh, well, look, but let's think about point of view." I mean point of view is so fascinating to me, so you take somebody like Olive and you think, okay, here she is, and she's sort of larger than life in some ways and yet everyone in town knows her in a completely different way and that was so interesting to me that I thought, yes, so let's get the piano player her version of Olive, which is really just a wave over the head, you know, but let's give somebody else a different version of Olive and that was when I realized, okay, this is how I'm going to handle Olive being too much. I'm not going to control her, but I'm going to control how much the reader gets to see her.

12. In "Helped" in *Olive, Again*, Strout puts this man's cruelty into relief, for the elderly Bernie Green asks Suzanne Larkin why she would tell her husband about an affair she had—for if doing so might temporarily alleviate her own suffering, it would devastate him and shake the foundation of their marriage.

13. Rebecca Cross observes, "The 'blackness' of the ink of the squid represents the desperation of Olive's yearning for Christopher to understand how much she loves him and for their relationship to be closer" (72).

14. As Maggie Dunn and Ann Morris suggest, Strout may build on the nineteenth-century village sketch tradition, in which a writer "could capture 'a sense of place' in many minute particulars, including among those particulars an ethos of community that reflects a complex network of human lives" (23).

15. If this story appears of out of place, jarringly violent, I think, as we'll see in *Anything Is Possible* and *Olive, Again*, Strout makes such a choice deliberately. She acts to unsettle the reader, making her aware, making her think. She does not want to lull us with a comfortable soporific but to engage us, keep us alert and on our toes. Crosby is not immune from violence. The act of reading a Strout story is not like listening to a lullaby that soothes but calls us to attention, makes us wake up. And such violence is not outside the realm of possibility, as psychiatrist Bessel van der Kolk tells us that "the majority of Americans experience a violent crime at some time during their lives" (21).

16. Barbara Waxman explains that "*Reifungsromane*, mirroring reality, consistently demonstrate how central sexuality is to human beings' life even in senescence. . . . Sexuality is an affirmation of one's humanness, a declaration of optimism about the potential and the desire for interactions with others" (151).

CHAPTER FOUR: *THE BURGESS BOYS,* LITERARY LEAVE-TAKINGS
AND HOMECOMINGS

1. In some ways, then, Strout's career helps to create readers who, in Janice Radway's words, are not "singularly tied to some unchanging essence but more multiple, mobile, and fluid, with more porous boundaries and therefore intensely intertwined with the object-world and distinctively receptive to the constitutive and transforming gaze of others. [She] may have nurtured a self potentially open to engagement with the social world in new ways, a subject not sealed off and autonomous but desiring and dependent, a subject therefore open to the possibility of fostering unprecedented connections and forging surprising alliances" (359–60).

2. Strout has said this incident was based on a similar event that occurred in Lewiston. She transforms that event in this novel. Michael Tager observes, "Strout scrambles the chronology of events to suit her purposes, having the pig's head incident lead to a tolerance rally in 2006, whereas the tolerance rally actually occurred four years prior. . . . She also changes the perpetrator from a 33 year old man . . . to an 18 or 19 year old. . . . No trial ever occurred because [the perpetrator] killed himself with no note or explanation before the trial date" (433).

3. But *Abide with Me* has one speaker; the interlocutor is absent. Here we have a conversation between two people, further emphasizing the constructedness of narrative.

4. The careful reader might remember when she meets Margaret Estaver later in the novel that she will marry Bob.

5. We might recall the speech cited in the introduction.

6. In this book, *Amy and Isabelle, Olive Kitteridge, Anything Is Possible,* and *Olive, Again,* acts of brutal violence occur just outside the boundaries of narrative. Characters briefly allude to the violence and how it reverberates for them emotionally; I think with these instances and echoes Strout is attempting to represent brutality ethically. She acknowledges that these events happen and that we must recognize them, but not in a way that sensationalizes them. With this particular narrative choice, she underscores the constructedness of her emotional world and the reading experience.

7. Perhaps there are some people whom Strout can't sympathize with. If so, this might speak to her upbringing. She talks about this in various interviews—how although her father was a professor and her mother a high school teacher, they identified as working class and were skeptical about the wealthy who would summer in Maine and New Hampshire.

CHAPTER FIVE: DECLARING *MY NAME IS LUCY BARTON*

1. Alexandra Schwartz counters, "How [Lucy] learns to become [ruthless] is the subject of this quiet yet surprisingly fierce book" (70).

2. As Bessel van der Kolk tells us, "one does not have to be a combat soldier, or visit a refugee camp in Syria or the Congo to encounter trauma. Trauma happens to us, our friends, our families, and our neighbors. Research by the Centers for Disease Control and Prevention has shown that one in five Americans was sexually molested as a child; one in four was beaten by a parent to the point of a mark being left on their body; and one in three couples engages in physical violence. A quarter of us grew up with alcoholic relatives, and one out of eight witnessed their mothers being beaten or hit" (1).

3. We'll see a similar perspective in Strout's recent books, *Olive, Again* and *Oh William!*

4. Brontë's Lucy Snowe is an unreliable narrator who mysteriously, inexplicably, and quickly falls sick in *Villette*. While some critics have diagnosed the diseases that afflict Lucy Snowe and Esther Summerson, their metaphorical illness, that condition that debilitates them, that makes them more sensitive and understanding to others, I would argue, is an unnamed melancholia, and also femininity.

5. Van der Kolk explains that, in the United States, "for every soldier who serves in a war zone abroad, there are ten children who are endangered in their own home. This is particularly tragic, since it is very difficult for growing children to recover when the source of terror and pain is not enemy combatants but their own caretakers" (21).

6. See also the light in *Olive, Again*.

7. Mary Barton is working-class, and within the novel that bears her name, Elizabeth Gaskell offers graphic descriptions of living conditions for the working poor.

8. Strout has reflected publicly that she made a similar decision and move.

9. Vicky and Pete Barton's suffering is explored in greater depth in *Anything Is Possible*.

10. The narrative also performs Lucy's experience with trauma. That is, as Van der Kolk explains, "even years later traumatized people often have enormous difficulty telling other people what has happened to them. Their bodies reexperience terror, rage, and helplessness, as well as the impulse to fight or flee, but these feelings are almost impossible to articulate. Trauma by nature drives us to the edge of comprehension, cutting us off from language based on common experience or an imaginable past" (43).

11. *My Name Is Lucy Barton* is also a meditation on how reading offers solace to the bookish. Lucy remembers how when she was young, she read a book "that made me want to write a book," a book about a girl who appears "strange and unattractive because she [is] dirty and poor" (24). Tilly is initially ostracized by the novel's protagonists, who learn from their "nice mother" to "be good to her." Lucy's daughters later find the book banal—and this also is interesting—but what's significant is that Lucy believes reading *The Pink Maple House* changed her life; it inspired her to write, and that desire may be what ultimately catalyzed her leaving Illinois, unlike her brother and sister (though the Little House on the Prairie books are important to the adult Pete, and Vicky reveals she has read Lucy's books). Within *The Pink Maple House*, the sad, poor, young Tilly is undone when Mrs. Trent hugs her. In an interview in the *New York Times*, Strout describes how she read *The Pink Maple House* when she was in third grade: "And I loved that book with my whole heart. I think it was about two girls with a really nice mother who move to a new house and meet a girl named Tilly who had a strange mother and the girls made fun of her until the nice mother made them stop and then they all became friends. I think maybe there was a house fire too, something dramatic. And sandwiches. And the maple tree. It's hard to express how much I loved that book, what it meant to me. Later I had an antique book finder get a copy and I gave it to my daughter when she was in third grade and she thought it was really boring" ("By the Book").

12. I think this struggle is particularly feminized, that women, whether genetically or socially, are so motivated to help others, to sacrifice themselves, that they are not as prolific as men are. Such an acknowledgment is not new. We can go as far back as *A Room of One's Own* (1929) to see it articulated.

13. And, in fact, her writing does—even in Strout's multiverse. For example, we might recall how Patty Nicely feels when she reads Lucy's memoirs in *Anything Is Possible*.

14. Strout has talked about her own abstemious childhood, how she and her brother did not go to parties, dances, or the movies, and so were unaware of many of the markers and implications of contemporary American rites of passage.

15. But most divorces are actually initiated by women.

16. Lucy tells her mother that when she was a young child at school, "I'd miss you all day. I couldn't talk when a teacher called on me, because I had a lump in my throat. I don't know how long it lasted. But I missed

you so much, sometimes I'd go into the bathroom to cry" (66). Lucy's mother has just told her she finds her resilient in ways that her brother and sister are not, but even Lucy, this apparently most resilient of her children, suffers from the terror of not being able to speak.

17. Alexandra Schwartz suggests there is also the possibility "that Lucy has fantasized her mother's visit, whether in the haze of sickness or in the more productive intentional imaginings of a fiction writer" (71).

18. Here again, then, we see the Bartons, as we saw Lucy's daughter, unable to express themselves. Lucy's fear of speaking runs throughout the book. She recalls being in the hospital and wanting "terribly to talk to my little children then, but if my mother was asleep I couldn't wake her by speaking into the phone next to the bed" (82). Strout portrays Lucy in this moment of tension, when she wants so much to converse but feels too paralyzed by her mother's presence to do so. It's also, of course, the tension between Lucy as a daughter and Lucy as a mother. She has competing desires, and at this point her desire to please her mother is ultimately more powerful. By the time she writes her memoirs, her desire to speak—to tell her story—prevails.

19. Strout recalls in an article in the *Washington Post* how she knew of "a boy in elementary school who was so poor that no one spoke to him, how in third grade, the teacher said to him one day, 'You have dirt behind your ears. No one is too poor [not] to buy a bar of soap.' I remember the kid's face turning bright red" ("How Do We Become?").

20. Lucy's involuntary vocal expressions echo her father's.

21. One of the first books that offers Lucy comfort and that she later offers her daughters is Christine Noble Govan's *The Pink Maple House* (1959). When Lucy's own daughters read it, they dismiss it, perhaps because they didn't need the same lifeline that Lucy did, as Zarina did (see note 11). But I'd also like to draw our attention not only to the kindness of Mrs. Trent and the desolation of Tilly's house, as Lucy does, but also to the description of the Trent house, surrounded by maple trees, which appear throughout Strout's fiction: "In the first place the maples had turned and were the loveliest shade of goldy pink imaginable. The morning sun shone through the leaves. They seemed made of some sort of rosy precious stone. Polly knew that she had never seen anything as beautiful as those trees in all her life" (22–23). Govan may have been one influence who taught Strout how to see, how to pay attention.

22. Van der Kolk tells us that "trauma affects not only those who are directly exposed to it, but also those around them. Soldiers returning home from combat may frighten their families with their rages and

emotional absence. The wives of men who suffer from PTSD tend to become depressed, and the children of depressed mothers are at risk of growing up insecure and anxious" (1).

23. We see the love, and consequently the ambivalence, Lucy feels for her father when she remembers as a child her father carrying her, telling her "no reason to cry," and "the feel of his warm hand spread against the back of my head" (60). This detail is important. Olive Kitteridge silently berates herself because she is not the type of person to comfort a child by placing her hands on her head. The same image also appears in *Abide with Me* and *The Burgess Boys*—so just as there are aphorisms that run throughout Strout's work, so there are images, including this physical manifestation of love and kindness.

24. Here we might remember "Starving" in *Olive Kitteridge*. When Olive sees anorectic Nina, she tries to help her rather than ostracizing her. If Strout shows how people fear that which they do not understand, she also urges us to be compassionate—to realize we can treat people with indifference or with sympathy. Within the novel, this lack of understanding ties into the fear the Germans and Poles had of Jews and White people had of Indians.

25. If she began the novel telling a springtime story ("It was May, and then June"), she ends in the fall.

26. Strout is tapping into feelings that literary critics have recently begun to attempt to tease out. Jane Thrailkill draws on the work of Théodule Ribot when she describes wonder as "the feeling that most vividly united the aesthetic, the philosophical, and the scientific in describing a particular stance of open-ended interest in the world outside the self. Wonder is exemplary, to quote Ribot, as 'not being provoked by, but on the contrary provoking [the intellectual state]'" (9). And Rita Felski describes such a state as a "feeling with: a relation that is more than the sum of its parts. . . . Attunement is about things resonating, aligning, coming together . . . the strength of a full connection" (43). Janice Radway, reflecting on the gatekeepers of the Book-of-the-Month Club, concludes that what gave the editors the greatest pleasure "was a feeling of transport and betweenness, a feeling of being suspended between the self and the world, a state where one flowed imperceptibly into the other, a place where clear boundaries and limits were obscured. Good reading, as they described it, produced an awareness of the self expanded, a sense that the self was absorbed into something larger, not dissolved exactly, but quivering in solution, both other and not" (117).

CHAPTER SIX: *ANYTHING IS POSSIBLE* WITH EVERYDAY GRACE

1. Helena Kadmos focuses on *Olive Kitteridge*, but her observation "that contemporary collections of interconnected stories open new ways of understanding women's relational autonomy and the importance of continuing relationships of interdependence and care" has implications for *Anything Is Possible* and *Olive, Again* as well.

2. Setting, Maggie Dunn and Ann Morris tell us, "is a primary element of interconnection in a large number" of what I call short story cycles and they term "composite novels" (15).

3. Here we might remember how Helena Kadmos explores *Olive Kitteridge* as a book about relationships.

4. We might also remember the barn burning in Gavan's *The Pink Maple House*, as well as the more famous conflagrations of Thrushcross Grange and Manderley.

5. Ariel Levy observes that Strout's "characters are nearly bursting with feeling. One of the central agonies of their lives tends to be an inability to communicate their internal state."

6. Here we might recall the ending chapters of *My Name Is Lucy Barton*, when Lucy reflects on how her daughters responded to her separation from their father.

7. Sibby, Patty's nickname for her husband Sebastian, aurally echoes "sibling," alluding perhaps to their chaste relationship and how Patty cares for him in some ways fraternally.

8. Here we might recall "Pharmacy" in *Olive Kitteridge*, when Denise reveals to Henry that she suffered a pulmonary embolism. Strout's metaphorical hearts are capable of infinite compassion, though the physical ones are fragile, liable to break.

9. In *Oh William!*, we learn that Lila left college to go to work with her mother at the nursing home, belying the notion of guaranteed social mobility.

10. Voyeurism is also portrayed in *Amy and Isabelle* and *Olive, Again*.

11. Karen-Lucie accepts Linda's statement at face value. She might recognize Linda's guilt or she might not, but she lets Linda leave without prolonging the confrontation. Karen-Lucie may be kind or dense; Strout leaves her rationale for letting Linda go ambiguous.

12. This line also recalls the end of "Incoming Tide" in *Olive Kitteridge*: "Look how she wanted to live, look how she wanted to hold on" (47). We might also remember Govan's *The Pink Maple House*, referred to in *My Name Is Lucy Barton*.

13. Maria DiBattista and Deborah Epstein Nord would recognize Mary's move to Italy as important, for "through a close focus on the domestic

and conjugal lives of women—the household, the family, marriage, sexuality, and the female body—[Strout meditates] on the relative value of differing cultural systems and gender ideologies. Through the narrow sphere of home, in its most literal sense, [she broaches] the broadly political. . . . [She imagines] relocation as an existential affair, the necessary quest of individuals rather than national, ethnic, or migrant groups—to find a place or a mode of belonging" (200).

14. We see within "Mississippi Mary" the kind of tenderness that formerly married spouses still have for each other (which we also see in *My Name Is Lucy Barton*, *The Burgess Boys*, and *Oh William!*). A marriage ending does not mean feelings end: "she thought of her husband, her ex-husband, more often these days. She worried about him. You could not live with someone for fifty years and not worry about him. And miss him. At times she felt gutted with her missing of him" (132).

CHAPTER SEVEN: *OLIVE, AGAIN*

1. Rolf Lundén offers a useful insight here for the genre I am calling "short story cycle" and that he calls "the short story composite": "For all their autonomy, the individual stories interlock with preceding and subsequent stories, creating bridges and enjambments, which to a degree strengthen the reader's expectations of ultimate cessation. . . . Proceeding from one story to the next, the reader experiences an expansion or modification which causes the earlier stories to gain an added dimension" (66). Strout takes the genre a step further in her multiverse—that is, not only do the stories in an individual book mean more in relation to each other, but when characters from other books reappear, we get a more multifaceted appreciation for them and for their creator as well.

2. Maggie Dunn and Ann Morris remind us that "the village *is* its people, and vice versa. . . . The trajectory of the narrative, then, is from the individual to the community, reflecting the forging of communal bonds necessary for survival and growth in a village setting" (31).

3. And yet not all of the characters, including the ones we might have been most worried about, return. Patty Howe, Christopher Coulson, Marlene Bonney, and Angie O'Meara remain elusive. Have they died? Moved on? Their absence could suggest either one. That ambiguity is perhaps important as well.

4. I think in some ways that Strout's hope with this scene is to, in Jane Thrailkill's words, "embody and stimulate our capacity for wonder" (*Affecting Fictions*, 208).

5. This recalls "Tulips" in *Olive Kitteridge*, when Olive remembers the days

"when Henry would hold her hand as they walked home, middle-aged people, in their prime. Had they known at these moments to be quietly joyful? Most likely not. People mostly did not know enough when they were living life that they were living it" (162).

6. Susan Gubar tells us that "old lovers know that love does not conquer all, that our intimacy cannot establish a safe haven somewhere, someplace for us. We are vulnerable to miseries that make us opaque to each other. Yet even if we are stuck or stumped, we are living and learning and loving" (86).

7. Rolf Lundén suggests the genre which I am calling short story cycle and he calls the short story composite often "refuses to fulfill the reader's expectation of an end. A characteristic of closure is that the reader at the end senses that nothing of importance has been left out. At the end of a [short story cycle] the reader is not certain. . . . The final story [may so disrupt] the possible preceding plot development as to function as an anti-closural unit" (87). But Olive, in writing her life, in looking at her memories and attempting to record them, allows readers to see how when we read we are, in Jane Thrailkill's words, "all like Narcissus staring into a puddle: delighting in that 'extra you' who, far from being a solipsistic illusion, is a neurologically nested affective companion keeping us from our isolation by suturing us, body and mind, firmly to ourselves and to the world in which we live" (*Affecting Fictions*, 55).

8. Susan Gubar's wonderful *Late-Life Love* meditates not only on the literary tradition of aging and romance but also on how such relationships also lead "to a range of desires: to keep on writing or reading, to go on seeing and savoring beloved places or works of art, to continue nurturing each other or progenitors or descendants, to prolong the kaleidoscope of fractured and reformed memories that accrue as a diminishing future is enhanced by a lengthening past that embellishes the present" (295).

CHAPTER EIGHT: *OH WILLIAM!*

1. In her most recent book, *The Myth of Closure*, Boss explains, "While simplistic declarations of closure are comfortable for bystanders, they are hurtful for the bereaved. . . . Research shows that we do better to live with grief than to deny or close the door on it. Our task now, after a time of so much suffering, is to acknowledge our losses, name them, find meaning in them, and let go of the quest for closure" (xv–xvi).

2. We might remember, for example, "The Gift of the Magi," "An

Unfinished Story," and "The Third Ingredient." I also read *Oh William!* as a sly reference to *Olive Kitteridge* and *Olive, Again.*

3. Ancestry.com tells us that "Gerhardt" is a Germanic name comprised of *Ger,* which means "spear," and *hard,* meaning "brave" or "strong." When she marries William, Lucy changes her name to Lucy Gerhardt, changing it back to Lucy Barton after his mother dies.

4. In *Ambiguous Loss,* Boss explains that "homesickness became a central part of [her] family's culture" after they immigrated to the US. She continues, "Losses of beloved family members were never resolved [for immigrants], and so those who lived with them also experienced the ambiguity of absence and presence" (1–2). Furthermore, "the legacy of frozen grief may affect their offspring for generations to come, compounding itself as more ordinary losses inevitably occur" (4).

5. On the trip he takes with Lucy, William remembers his father talking to him when he was twelve and saying, "'What happened in Germany is very bad. I'm not ashamed of being German, but I am ashamed of what the country did.' . . . I mean he wanted me to know that he did not support—at least at the point he was telling me about this—what Germany had done" (130).

6. It's an interesting move for Strout to make since the Cayman Islands bear the scars and legacy of slavery, imperialism, and colonialism. Perhaps Strout is suggesting that there are no innocent places left in the world—Northern and Southern Hemispheres both bear witness to terrible human tragedies.

7. Lois says to Lucy: "Do you know [Catherine Cole] had the gall to talk to me about that man, her son? She raved about him, and, Lucy—I'm telling you—you would have thought he was the most brilliant scientist who ever lived. This was not what I needed to hear!" (184).

8. William responded in kind: "He realized that she had gotten herself pregnant on purpose, and he immediately went out and had a vasectomy—without telling Estelle" (21).

9. Lucy explains such moments to William as "a bit like stepping between universes" (125).

References

PRIMARY SOURCES

Strout, Elizabeth. *Abide with Me.* New York: Random House, 2006.

———. *Amy and Isabelle.* New York: Random House, 1998.

———. *Anything Is Possible.* New York: Random House, 2017.

———. *The Burgess Boys.* New York: Random House, 2013.

———. "By the Book." *New York Times Sunday Book Review,* March 28, 2013, BR 7.

———. "How Do We Become Aware of Class in America?" *Washington Post,* August 28, 2017. https://www.washingtonpost.com/entertainment /books/one-writers-life-elizabeth-strout/2017/08/25/35130bde-7b96 -11e7-9d08-b79f191668ed_story.html.

———. "How Laura Linney Inspired My New Book." Received by Katherine Montwieler, September 16, 2021.

———. "I Have Never Written Anything from Beginning to End." *The Guardian,* March 4, 2017. https://www.theguardian.com/books/2017 /mar/04/elizabeth-strout-my-writing-day.

———. Interview by Cathy Schine. Book Passage, November 28, 2020. https://bookpassage.extendedsession.com/session/elizabeth-strout/.

———. *My Name Is Lucy Barton.* New York: Random House, 2016.

———. *Oh William!* New York: Random House, 2021.

———. *Olive, Again.* New York: Random House, 2019.

———. *Olive Kitteridge.* New York: Random House, 2008.

SECONDARY SOURCES

Abraham, Nicolas, and Maria Torok. *The Shell and the Kernel: Renewals of Psychoanalysis.* Edited and translated by Nicholas T. Rand. Chicago: University of Chicago Press, 1994.

Bernhard, Meg. "What If There's No Such Thing as Closure?" *New York Times,* December 15, 2021. https://www.nytimes.com/2021/12/15/magazine /grieving-loss-closure.html.

Boss, Pauline. *Ambiguous Loss: Learning to Live with Unresolved Grief.* Cambridge, MA: Harvard University Press, 1999.

———. *The Myth of Closure: Ambiguous Loss in a Time of Pandemic and Change.* New York: Norton, 2022.

Boym, Svetlana. *The Future of Nostalgia.* New York: Basic Books, 2001.

Burkeman, Oliver. *Four Thousand Weeks: Time Management for Mortals.* New York: Farrar, Strauss, and Giroux, 2021.

Campbell, Sally, and Martha Greengrass. "An Exclusive Waterstones Q & A with Elizabeth Strout." Waterstones.com Blog, March 3, 2017. https:// www.waterstones.com/blog/search/tag/elizabeth-strout.

Charles, Ron. "Running on Faith: Review of *Abide with Me* by Elizabeth Strout." *Washington Post,* March 19, 2006. https://www.washingtonpost .com/archive/entertainment/books/2006/03/19/running-on-faith -span-classbankheada-recently-widowed-pastor-struggles-to-keep-his -beliefs-alive-span/924810bb-9a3b-44d1-8545-dc1ab179110c/.

Coleman, Cheryl. "A Minister's Loss of Faith in Elizabeth Strout's *Abide with Me.*" *Literature and Belief* 28 (2008): 1–19.

Cross, Rebecca. "Yearning, Frustration, and Fulfilment: The Return Story in *Olive Kitteridge* and *Kissing in Manhattan.*" *Les Cahiers de la Nouvelle* 66 (2016): 67–84.

Day, Elizabeth. "Masterful Chronicler of Small-Town America." *The Guardian,* April 23, 2017. https://www.theguardian.com/books/2017/apr/23 /anything-is-possible-elizabeth-strout-review.

DiBattista, Maria, and Deborah Epstein Nord. *At Home in the World: Women Writers and Public Life from Austen to the Present.* Princeton, NJ: Princeton University Press, 2017.

Dunn, Maggie, and Ann Morris. *The Composite Novel: The Short Story Cycle in Transition.* New York: Twayne, 1995.

Egan, Jennifer. "Elizabeth Strout Gets Meta in Her New Novel about Marriage." *New York Times,* October 18, 2021. https://www.nytimes.com /2021/10/18/books/review/oh-william-elizabeth-strout.html.

"Elizabeth Strout." Accessed November 30, 2020. Elizabethstrout.com.

Ellerby, Janet Mason. *Embroidering the Scarlet A: Unwed Mothers and Illegitimate Children in American Fiction and Film.* Ann Arbor: University of Michigan Press, 2015.

———. *Following the Tambourine Man: A Birthmother's Memoir.* Syracuse: Syracuse University Press, 2007.

Farr, Cecilia Konchar. "It Was Chick Lit All Along: The Gendering of a Genre." In *You've Come a Long Way, Baby: Women, Politics, and Popular Culture*, edited by Lilly J. Goren, 201–14. Lexington: University Press of Kentucky, 2010.

———. *Reading Oprah: How Oprah's Book Club Changed the Way America Reads*. Albany: State University of New York Press, 2005.

Fassler, Joe. "When Memories Are True Even When They're Not." *The Atlantic*, May 2, 2017. https://www.theatlantic.com/entertainment/archive/2017/05/elizabeth-strout-when-memories-are-true-even-when-theyre-not/524976/.

Felski, Rita. *Hooked: Art and Attachment*. Chicago: University of Chicago Press, 2020.

Gavan, Christine Noble. *The Pink Maple House*. New York: Aladdin, 1950.

"Gerhardt." Ancestry. Accessed January 1, 2022. https://www.ancestry.com/name-origin?surname=gerhardt.

Gubar, Susan. *Late-Life Love: A Memoir*. New York: Norton, 2019.

Jamison, Leslie. *Make It Scream, Make It Burn: Essays*. New York: Little, Brown, 2019.

Kadmos, Helena. "Women's Relational Autonomy and the Short Story Cycle *Olive Kitteridge* by Elizabeth Strout." *Short Fiction in Theory and Practice* 9 (2019): 39–51.

Keen, Suzanne. "Empathetic Hardy: Bounded, Ambassadorial, and Broadcast Strategies of Narrative Empathy." *Poetics Today* 32 (2011): 349–89.

———. *Empathy and the Novel*. New York: Oxford University Press, 2007.

———. "Introduction: Narrative and the Emotions." *Poetics Today* 32 (2011): 1–54.

———. "Narrative and the Embodied Reader." In *The Edinburgh Companion to Contemporary Narrative Theories*, edited by Zara Dinnen and Robyn Warhol, 43–55. Edinburgh: Edinburgh University Press, 2018.

———. "Readers' Temperaments and Fictional Character." *New Literary History* 42 (2011): 205–314.

Kunitz, Stanley. "The Testing-Tree." Poets.org. https://poets.org/poem/testing-tree.

Levy, Ariel. "Elizabeth Strout's Long Homecoming." *New Yorker*, May 1, 2017. https://www.newyorker.com/magazine/2017/05/01/elizabeth-strouts-long-homecoming.

Lundén, Rolf. *The United Stories of America: Studies in the Short Story Composite*. Amsterdam: Rodopi, 1999.

Lyall, Sarah. "The Author Elizabeth Strout on 'Lucy Barton' and How Her Characters Come into Being." *New York Times*, January 13, 2016. https://

www.nytimes.com/2016/01/16/books/the-author-elizabeth-strout-on
-lucy-barton-and-how-her-characters-come-into-being.html.

McAlpin, Heller. "Lucy Barton Returns—and Reconnects with an Old
Love—in 'Oh William!'" NPR, October 19, 2021, https://www.npr.org
/2021/10/19/1047132621/elizabeth-strout-oh-william-review.

Merrell, Susan Scarf. "'Anything Is Possible' Demonstrates What Elizabeth Strout Does Best." *Washington Post,* April 24, 2017. https://www
.washingtonpost.com/entertainment/books/anything-is-possible
-demonstrates-what-elizabeth-strout-does-best/2017/04/24/e2ea3a36
-1df2-11e7-ad74-3a742a6e93a7_story.html.

Messer, Miwa. "Elizabeth Strout on *Oh William!*" October 19, 2021. In *Poured
Over: The Barnes & Noble Podcast,* MP3 audio, 44:34. https://www
.elizabethstrout.com/news/2021/10/19/bampns-poured-over-podcast
-elizabeth-strout-on-oh-william.

Messud, Claire. "Elizabeth Strout's 'My Name Is Lucy Barton.'" *New York
Times,* January 4, 2016. https://www.nytimes.com/2016/01/10/books
/review/elizabeth-strouts-my-name-is-lucy-barton.html.

Miall, David. "Emotions and the Structuring of Narrative Responses." *Poetics Today* 32 (2011): 323–48.

Miller, Alice. *The Drama of the Gifted Child: The Search for the True Self.* Translated by Ruth Ward. New York: Basic Books, 2007.

Moi, Toril. *Revolution of the Ordinary: Literary Studies after Wittgenstein, Austin, and Cavell.* Chicago: University of Chicago Press, 2017.

Montwieler, Katherine. "An American Haunting: The Specter of Memory
in Elizabeth Strout's *Olive Kitteridge.*" *Short Story* 20 (2012): 73–82.

Polls, Mary. "Strout Again." *Maine Women Magazine,* August 5, 2019. https://
www.elizabethstrout.com/news/2019/8/5/maine-women-magazine
-strout-again.

Probyn, Elspeth. *Outside Belongings.* London: Routledge, 1996.

Radway, Janice. *A Feeling for Books: The Book-of-the-Month Club, Literary
Taste, and Middle-Class Desire.* Chapel Hill: University of North Carolina Press, 1997.

Randolph, Ladette. "About Elizabeth Strout: A Profile." *Ploughshares* 111 (2010).
https://www.pshares.org/issues/spring-2010/about-elizabeth-strout.

Robbins, Rhea Côté. "Maine Voices: 'Olive, Again' Makes It OK to Hate
French-Canadians Again." *Portland Press Herald,* January 11, 2020.
https://www.pressherald.com/2020/01/11/maine-voices-olive-again
-makes-it-ok-to-hate-french-mainers-again/.

Scanlon, Jennifer. "What's an Acquisitive Girl to Do? Chick Lit and the
Great Recession." *Women's Studies* 42 (2013): 904–23.

Schwartz, Alexandra. "Home Truths: 'My Name Is Lucy Barton' Explores the Legacy of Family Trauma." *New Yorker,* January 27, 2020, 70–71.

Tager, Michael. "Divided America in Elizabeth Strout's *The Burgess Boys.*" *Critique: Studies in Contemporary Fiction* 60 (2019): 432–46.

Taylor, Helen. *Why Women Read Fiction: The Stories of Our Lives.* Oxford: Oxford University Press, 2019.

Teicher, Craig Morgan. "'On Both Sides': Elizabeth Strout's 'Olive Kitteridge.'" *Publishers Weekly,* February 4, 2008. https://www.publishersweekly.com/pw/by-topic/authors/interviews/article/6184-maine-idea.html.

Thrailkill, Jane F. *Affecting Fictions: Mind, Body, and Emotion in American Literary Realism.* Cambridge, MA: Harvard University Press, 2007.

———. "Ian McEwan's Neurological Novel." *Poetics Today* 32 (2011):177–201.

Van der Kolk, Bessel A. *The Body Keeps the Score: Brain, Mind, and Body in the Healing of Trauma.* New York: Viking, 2014.

Vorwald, Samantha. "A Conversation with Elizabeth Strout." *Booth: A Journal,* September 1, 2017. http://booth.butler.edu/2017/09/01/a-conversation-with-elizabeth-strout/.

Waxman, Barbara Frey. *From the Hearth to the Open Road: A Feminist Study of Aging in Contemporary Literature.* New York: Greenwood, 1990.

Yardley, Cathy. *Will Write for Shoes: How to Write a Chick Lit Novel.* New York: St. Martin's, 2006.

Index